How to access your on-line resources

Kaplan Financial students will have a MyKaplan account and these extra resources will be available to you online. You do not need to register again, as this process was completed when you enrolled. If you are having problems accessing online materials, please ask your course administrator.

If you are not studying with Kaplan and did not purchase your book via a Kaplan website, to unlock your extra online resources please go to www.en-gage.co.uk (even if you have set up an account and registered books previously). You will then need to enter the ISBN number (on the title page and back cover) and the unique pass key number contained in the scratch panel below to gain access.

You will also be required to enter additional information during this process to set up or confirm your account details.

If you purchased through the Kaplan Publishing website you will automatically receive an e-mail invitation to register your details and gain access to your content. If you do not receive the e-mail or book content, please contact Kaplan Publishing.

Your code and information

This code can only be used once for the registration of one book online. This registration and your online content will expire when the final sittings for the examinations covered by this book have taken place. Please allow one hour from the time you submit your book details for us to process your request.

Please scratch the film to access your unique code.

Please be aware that this code is case-sensitive and you will need to include the dashes within the passcode, but not when entering the ISBN.

CIMA

Case Study

Operational Level

Study Text

KAPLAN PUBLISHING'S STATEMENT OF PRINCIPLES

LINGUISTIC DIVERSITY, EQUALITY AND INCLUSION

We are committed to diversity, equality and inclusion and strive to deliver content that all users can relate to.

We are here to make a difference to the success of every learner.

Clarity, accessibility and ease of use for our learners are key to our approach.

We will use contemporary examples that are rich, engaging and representative of a diverse workplace.

We will include a representative mix of race and gender at the various levels of seniority within the businesses in our examples to support all our learners in aspiring to achieve their potential within their chosen careers.

Roles played by characters in our examples will demonstrate richness and diversity by the use of different names, backgrounds, ethnicity and gender, with a mix of sexuality, relationships and beliefs where these are relevant to the syllabus.

It must always be obvious who is being referred to in each stage of any example so that we do not detract from clarity and ease of use for each of our learners.

We will actively seek feedback from our learners on our approach and keep our policy under continuous review. If you would like to provide any feedback on our linguistic approach, please use this form (you will need to enter the link below into your browser).

https://docs.google.com/forms/d/1YNo3A16mtXGTDIFJzgJhcu377QA4Q4ihUgfYvVKclF8/edit

We will seek to devise simple measures that can be used by independent assessors to randomly check our success in the implementation of our Linguistic Equality, Diversity and Inclusion Policy.

Published by: Kaplan Publishing UK

Unit 2 The Business Centre, Molly Millars Lane, Wokingham, Berkshire RG41 2QZ

Acknowledgements

We are grateful to the CIMA for permission to reproduce past examination questions and the official CIMA answers.

Notice

The text in this material and any others made available by any Kaplan Group company does not amount to advice on a particular matter and should not be taken as such. No reliance should be placed on the content as the basis for any investment or other decision or in connection with any advice given to third parties. Please consult your appropriate professional adviser as necessary.

Kaplan Publishing Limited and all other Kaplan group companies expressly disclaim all liability to any person in respect of any losses or other claims, whether direct, indirect, incidental, consequential or otherwise arising in relation to the use of such materials.

Kaplan is not responsible for the content of external websites. The inclusion of a link to a third party website in this text should not be taken as an endorsement.

Kaplan Publishing's learning materials are designed to help students succeed in their examinations. In certain circumstances, CIMA can make post-exam adjustment to a student's mark or grade to reflect adverse circumstances which may have disadvantaged a student's ability to take an exam or demonstrate their normal level of attainment (see CIMA's Special Consideration policy). However, it should be noted that students will not be eligible for special consideration by CIMA if preparation for or performance in a CIMA exam is affected by any failure by their tuition provider to prepare them properly for the exam for any reason including, but not limited to, staff shortages, building work or a lack of facilities etc.

Similarly, CIMA will not accept applications for special consideration on any of the following grounds:

- failure by a tuition provider to cover the whole syllabus
- failure by the student to cover the whole syllabus, for instance as a result of joining a course part way through
- failure by the student to prepare adequately for the exam, or to use the correct pre-seen material
- errors in the Kaplan Official Study Text, including sample (practice) questions or any other Kaplan content or
- errors in any other study materials (from any other tuition provider or publisher).

British Library Cataloguing in Publication Data

A catalogue record for this book is available from the British Library.

ISBN: 978-1-83996-241-7

Printed and bound in Great Britain

Contents

Introduction

Acknowledgements

Every effort has been made to contact the holders of copyright material, but if any here have been inadvertently overlooked the publishers will be pleased to make the necessary arrangements at the first opportunity.

How to use the Materials

Test your understanding – Following key points and definitions are exercises which give the opportunity to assess the understanding of these core areas. Within the work book the answers to these sections are left blank, explanations to the questions can be found within the online version which can be hidden or shown on screen to enable repetition of activities.

Illustration – to help develop an understanding of topics and the test your understanding exercises the illustrative examples can be used.

Quality and accuracy are of the utmost importance to us so if you spot an error in any of our products, please send an email to mykaplanreporting@kaplan.com with full details.

Our Quality Coordinator will work with our technical team to verify the error and take action to ensure it is corrected in future editions.

Exam Introduction

To complete the CIMA qualification and be able to use the designatory letters of ACMA and CGMA, candidates for this prestigious award need to achieve three things:

- attain the entry requirements for the professional level qualification
- study for and complete the relevant professional level assessments and examinations
- complete three years of relevant practical experience.

This text concentrates on the second of these requirements, and in particular to study for and complete the Operational level case study exam.

Overview of exam

The case study exam will be available four times a year. The purpose of this exam is to consolidate learning at each level by reflecting real life work situations. The exam is human marked.

This approach allows a wide range of knowledge and skills to be tested including research and analysis, presentation of information and communication skills whilst still ensuring competence in key skills.

CIMA believe that this format will provide the commitment to delivering the competencies which employers desire thereby improving 'employability'.

For example, the Operational level case study exam will be set within a simulated business context, placing the candidate in the job role matched to the competency level. In the case of the Operational level, the job role is that of an entry level finance professional (usually a management accountant) with responsibility for some of the consequences of implementing strategy. The focus will be on the short-term.

Typical aspects of such a role could include the following:

- An understanding of costs and cost accounting, in order to start preparing budgets, and to advise about short-term changes in products, volume and prices.
- Putting budgets together for the business will require communicating aspects of the budget to non-finance staff; both in the preparation and the delivery.
- Preparation of financial reports to show how the business is performing. This will require knowledge of the regulatory environment, financial reporting, and business taxation.
- Analysing and advising on working capital, cash and short-term finance.

The exam is intended to replicate "a day in the life" of a finance professional operating at the operational level and provide a simulated environment for candidates to demonstrate the required level of proficiency in each of the competency areas. Consequently, the exam will be set and marked according to the weightings for each core activity at the level.

The case study exam is 3 hours in duration and is made up of a series of timed tests or tasks. This makes the case study exam different from most exams you will have sat to date – once you have submitted a particular task (or the time limit is reached, whichever is sooner) you will be moved on and will not be able to return to that task. This should reduce the problem of not completing the paper but does mean you will need to be very disciplined when attempting each task.

Candidates will be provided with access to pre-seen information approximately seven weeks before the real exam.

Assessment aims and strategy

The Case Study Examination tests the knowledge, skills and techniques from the three pillars within one simulated scenario and is taken at the end of each level of the CIMA Professional Qualification. Candidates are given a fictional Case Study before the examination and are expected to give solutions to the situations and challenges presented within the examination – based on the knowledge and skills acquired from the three subjects. The Case Study mimics their role in a real-work scenario, at each level of the qualification.

The case study is three hours long. The case study will include both pre-seen and unseen material, the latter being made available during the examination. They will incorporate short written answers, emails, letters and any form of appropriate communication required within the tasks set.

In terms of the CIMA hierarchy of verbs (see below), the focus for the Operational Case Study is mainly level 3 (application), with some analysis and evaluation (levels 4 and 5, respectively).

Simulated business issues in the case studies provide candidates with the opportunity to demonstrate their familiarity with the context and interrelationships of the level's technical content. This reflects the cross functional abilities required in the workplace. Skills will include research, analysis, and presentation of both financial and nonfinancial information and communication skills.

Feedback will be provided to candidates with their results. Exam sittings for the case studies will occur every three months. Candidates must have completed or be exempt from the three objective tests at a particular level before attempting the relevant case study.

Core activities and assessment outcomes

Within each Operational Case Study Examination, six "core activities" will be assessed. These core activities represent the tasks that are most frequent, critical and important to the entry level finance professional role.

The six core activities are:

A Prepare costing information for different purposes to meet the needs of management.

B Prepare budget information and assess its use for planning and control purposes.

C Analyse performance using financial and non- financial information.

D Apply relevant financial reporting standards and corporate governance, ethical and tax principles.

E Prepare information to support short-term decision-making.

F Prepare information to manage working capital.

The core activities require and draw together the knowledge, skills and techniques acquired while studying for Objective Tests and combining them with the mindset of a CIMA finance professional.

Each core activity is translated into a number of "assessment outcomes". These are a clear assertion of what a CIMA qualified finance professional should be able to do when the Examination has been completed and what the assessment will be designed to measure. Case Study assessment outcomes will be synoptic.

These are discussed in more detail in chapter 1.

Assessing skills – the CIMA verb hierarchy

CIMA has adopted a skill framework for the assessments based on the revised Bloom's Taxonomy of Education Objectives. Bloom's Taxonomy classifies a continuum of skills that learners are expected to know and demonstrate.

The case study exam will focus on Levels 3, 4 and 5.

Skill level	Verbs used	Definition
Level 5 Evaluation How you are expected to use your learning to evaluate, make decisions or recommendations	Advise	Counsel, inform or notify
	Assess	Evaluate or estimate the nature, ability or quality of
	Evaluate	Appraise or assess the value of
	Recommend	Propose a course of action
	Review	Assess and evaluate in order, to change if necessary
Level 4 Analysis How you are expected to analyse the detail of what you have learned	Align	Arrange in an orderly way
	Analyse	Examine in detail the structure of
	Communicate	Share or exchange information
	Compare and contrast	Show the similarities and/or differences between
	Develop	Grow and expand a concept
	Discuss	Examine in detail by argument
	Examine	Inspect thoroughly
	Interpret	Translate into intelligible or familiar terms
	Monitor	Observe and check the progress of
	Prioritise	Place in order of priority or sequence for action
	Produce	Create or bring into existence
Level 3 Application How you are expected to apply your knowledge	Apply	Put to practical use
	Calculate	Ascertain or reckon mathematically
	Conduct	Organise and carry out
	Demonstrate	Prove with certainty or exhibit by practical means
	Prepare	Make or get ready for use
	Reconcile	Make or prove consistent/compatible
Level 2 Comprehension What you are expected to understand	Describe	Communicate the key features of
	Distinguish	Highlight the differences between
	Explain	Make clear or intelligible/state the meaning or purpose of
	Identify	Recognise, establish or select after consideration
	Illustrate	Use an example to describe or explain something
Level 1 Knowledge What you are expected to know	List	Make a list of
	State	Express, fully or clearly, the details/facts of
	Define	Give the exact meaning of
	Outline	Give a summary of

How to use the material

These Official CIMA learning materials brought to you by CIMA and Kaplan Publishing have been carefully designed to make your learning experience as easy as possible and give you the best chances of success in your Case Study Examinations.

This Study Text has been designed with the needs of home study and distance learning candidates in mind. However, the Study Text is also ideal for fully taught courses.

The aim of this textbook is to walk you through the stages to prepare for, and to answer, the requirements of the Case Study Examination.

Practical hints and realistic tips are given throughout the book making it easy for you to apply what you've learned in this text to your actual Case Study Exam.

Where sample solutions are provided, they must be viewed as just one interpretation of the case. One key aspect, which you must appreciate early in your studies, is that there is no single 'correct' solution.

Your own answer might reach different conclusions, and give greater emphasis to some issues and less emphasis to others, but score equally as well if it demonstrates the required skills.

If you work conscientiously through the official CIMA Study Text according to the guidelines above, as well as analysing the pre-seen information in full, you will be giving yourself an excellent chance of success in your examination. Good luck with your studies!

Planning

To begin with, formal planning is essential to get the best return from the time you spend studying. Estimate how much time in total you are going to need for each subject you are studying for the Case Study Examination.

This book will provide you with proven study techniques. Chapter by chapter it covers the building blocks of successful learning and examination techniques and shows you how to earn all the marks you deserve, and explains how to avoid the most common pitfalls.

With your study material before you, decide which chapters you are going to study in each week, which weeks you will devote to practising past exams, and which weeks you will spend becoming familiar with your case study pre-seen material.

Prepare a written schedule summarising the above and stick to it! Students are advised to refer to articles published regularly in CIMA's magazine (Financial Management), the student e-newsletter (Velocity) and on the CIMA website, to ensure they are up to date with relevant issues and topics.

Tips for effective studying

1. Aim to find a quiet and undisturbed location for your study, and plan as far as possible to use the same period of time each day. Getting into a routine helps to avoid wasting time. Make sure that you have all the materials you need before you begin so as to minimise interruptions.
2. Store all your materials in one place, so that you do not waste time searching for items every time you want to begin studying. If you have to pack everything away after each study period, keep your study materials in a box, or even a suitcase, which will not be disturbed until the next time.
3. Limit distractions. To make the most effective use of your study periods you should be able to apply total concentration, so turn off all entertainment equipment, set your phones to message mode, and put up your 'do not disturb' sign.
4. Your timetable will tell you which topic to study. However, before diving in and becoming engrossed in the finer points, make sure you have an overall picture of all the areas that need to be covered by the end of that session. After an hour, allow yourself a short break and move away from your Study Text. With experience, you will learn to assess the pace you need to work at. Each study session should focus on component learning outcomes – the basis for all questions.
5. Work carefully through a chapter, making notes as you go. When you have covered a suitable amount of material, vary the pattern by attempting a practice question. When you have finished your attempt, make notes of any mistakes you made, or any areas that you failed to cover or covered more briefly. Be aware that all core activities will be tested in each examination.
6. Make notes as you study, and discover the techniques that work best for you. Your notes may be in the form of lists, bullet points, diagrams, summaries, 'mind maps', or the written word, but remember that you will need to refer back to them at a later date, so they must be intelligible. If you are on a taught course, make sure you highlight any issues you would like to follow up with your lecturer.
7. Organise your notes. Make sure that all your notes, calculations etc. can be effectively filed and easily retrieved later.

Relevant practical experience

In order to become a Chartered Global Management Accountant (ACMA, CGMA), you need a minimum of three years' verified relevant work-based practical experience.

Read the 'Applying for Membership' brochure for full details of the practical experience requirements (PER).

Information concerning formulae and tables will be provided via the CIMA website, www.cimaglobal.com.

Chapter

1

Introduction to case study exams

Chapter learning objectives

- To gain an overview of the case study exam, its purpose, structure and the process involved.

1 The structure of the CIMA Operational Level

Each level of CIMA's professional qualification consists of three objective test 'pillar' exams, followed by the Case Study Examination.

You can only attempt the Case Study Examination after all objective tests for the level have been completed or if exemptions have been given.

For the 2019 syllabus the three Operational level pillar exams are as follows:

- E1 – Managing Finance in a Digital World
- P1 – Management Accounting
- F1 – Financial Reporting

The objective tests for each of these individual subjects ensure the acquisition of the breadth of knowledge, skills and techniques that provide the foundation for approaching the Case Study Examination.

2 Why a Case Study Examination?

The CIMA Case Study Examinations are 'capstone' examinations designed to demonstrate mastery of previously acquired knowledge, skills and techniques and the drawing together of these to provide solutions to unstructured, synoptic problems.

Each synoptic assessment combines the content covered in all three pillar subjects at the level into a single assessment. Its aim is the "undoing" of the pillar and subject divisions of the syllabus and the application of knowledge, skills and techniques to the type of problems that you might encounter in the workplace in a role matched to the appropriate level of the qualification.

The examination uses a simulated Case Study to provide a rich, immersive scenario to prepare and to provide a context for the tasks in the examination. The scenarios are developed around today's modern business environment and the challenges that you will face – allowing you to demonstrate the 'core activities' that have been identified by employers as critical.

Examination tasks will be practical and applied, not theoretical or academic. To be successful, you will have to perform these core activities in the same way and to the same standards that would be valid and valued in the workplace.

The Case Study Examination is thus an attempt to simulate workplace problem solving, and allows examiners to move one step closer to the assessment of competence than is possible with objective test questions. It is a test of both professional competence and, by implication, employability.

In addition, the purpose of the Case Study Examination is to assess your proficiency in those specific skills that are less likely to be automated.

The purpose of this text is to suggest how you might prepare for the examination by developing and practising your skills. Since the examination tests a range of different skills, preparing for this examination needs to be different from studying for a 'traditional' examination.

3 Your role

Each case study exam will be set within a simulated business context, placing the candidate in the job role matched to the competency level.

In the case of the operational level your role is an entry level finance professional or a finance officer, typically a management accountant, reporting to first line managers and/or peers within the organisation.

This role can be broken down as follows:

- The role simulated is that of a finance officer working within a collaborative team in the finance department that is responsible for planning and coordinating business operations through the preparation of budgets and other reports. The role focuses on the short term; assisting with the preparation of useful and relevant financial reports, drawing upon data collected by the company's information system. The finance officer may be asked to evaluate short-term opportunities and threats, such as selecting between alternative courses of action and may also provide information to support decisions on working capital, cash and short-term finance.
- The finance officer offers insights that influence the decisions taken by colleagues and superiors. The finance officer must act in a professional manner, ensuring that reports are sufficiently complete and accurate to facilitate decisions.
- The finance officer makes full use of the technologies that are available for the collection, cleansing and analysis of data. The preparation of reports also relies heavily on understanding of how the business is structured. The finance officer is required to interact with colleagues from finance and all other functional areas of the business.
- The finance officer also assists in the preparation of financial reports to enable external stakeholders to understand how the business is performing. That requires an understanding of the regulations relating to financial reporting and business taxation.
- The fact that the finance officer's work affects the behaviour of internal and external stakeholders can raise ethical implications. The finance officer must be aware of personal responsibilities working within the role.

In summary, the Operational level focuses on the short term and the implementation of decisions. Thus you will work with others in the organisation and use appropriate data and technology to translate medium- term decisions into short-term actionable plans.

The competency level is described as "entry-level", requiring you to demonstrate the ability to analyse and advise on various aspects and consequences of the implementation of strategy.

4 The exam 'blueprints'

4.1 Overview

For the first time, CIMA has released blueprints for its Professional Qualification Examination. The intent is that blueprints will demystify the examination – giving greater clarity on examinable topics; assessment approach, design and weightings; and learner expectations.

The Case Study Examination blueprint contains the following:

- **Core activities** – Business-related tasks that are common to the role being simulated and valued by employers which, if performed satisfactorily, enables the demonstration of the assessment outcomes.
- **Assessment outcomes** – A clear assertion of what a CIMA qualified finance professional can do when the Examination has been completed and what the assessment will be designed to measure. Case Study assessment outcomes will be synoptic.

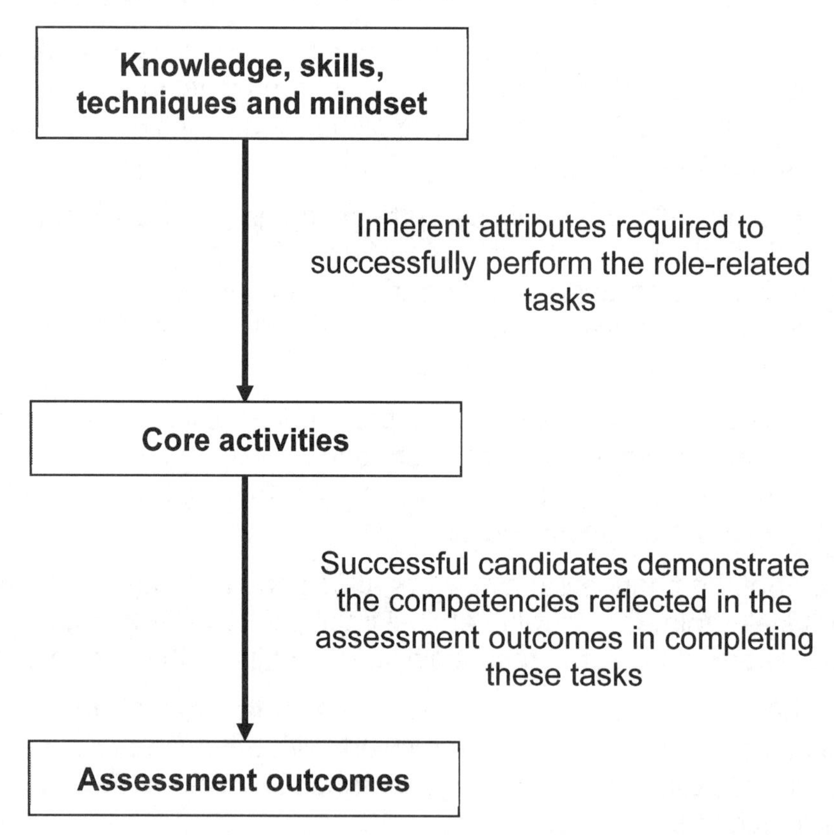

All core activities will be assessed in each form of the examination in line with the weightings. A sample (but not all) of the related assessment outcomes will be tested in any particular exam.

4.2 Core activities

The blueprint defines the following core activities:

	Core Activity	Weighting
A	Prepare costing information for different purposes to meet the needs of management.	12–18%
B	Prepare budget information and assess its use for planning and control purposes.	17–25%
C	Analyse performance using financial and non-financial information.	17–25%
D	Apply relevant financial reporting standards and corporate governance, ethical and tax principles.	12–18%
E	Prepare information to support short-term decision-making.	17–25%
F	Prepare information to manage working capital.	7–13%

As stated above, **all** core activities will be assessed in **each** variant of the examination in line with the above weightings.

Given the blueprint requires 17 – 25% for core activities B, C and E, this means that there will often be two separate tasks for each of budgeting, performance analysis and decision-making.

At first sight it may seem that core activities A, B, C and E are driven mainly by P1 knowledge and activities D and F by F1. Given this, you may wonder how E1 fits into this framework and the answer is that, in addition to discussing KPIs in Core Activity C, other aspects of E1 are embedded within the other activities. This is seen more clearly when we look at the underlying assessment outcomes below.

4.3 Assessment outcomes

Assessment outcomes translate core activities into a range of "I can" statements that, in case study, effectively give you the basis of the wordings for exam tasks.

Given this, it is vital that you look at the assessment outcomes below and make sure you feel confident that you could answer a task worded in this way. If necessary, then go back to your P1, F1 or E1 notes and revise the appropriate technical content.

The full list is as follows:

	Core Activities	Assessment outcomes
A	Prepare costing information for different purposes to meet the needs of management.	I can use appropriate technologies to gather data for costing purposes, from digital and other sources. I can apply different costing methods to produce costing information suitable for managers' needs. I can explain costing information to operational and senior management using appropriate formats and media. I can compare different costing methods and systems to determine the most suitable for use by the organisation for different purposes. I can identify the cost information required for digital cost objects.
B	Prepare budget information and assess its use for planning and control purposes.	I can use appropriate technologies to gather data from digital and other sources to co-ordinate budget preparation. I can explain and use different forecasting methods to assist in budget preparation. I can use different approaches to produce information for use by managers when preparing budgets. I can explain budget information to managers using appropriate formats and media. I can apply various techniques to determine the effect on budgets of changes to variables. I can explain to functional managers how budgets are used for planning and control purposes. I can discuss the behavioural implications of budgetary planning and control. I can compare alternative approaches to budgeting to determine their suitability for the organisation and for different purposes.

C	Analyse performance using financial and non-financial information.	I can identify information that can enable managers to review performance. I can interpret variances to review functional and organisational performance. I can identify appropriate KPIs for different functions of the organisation. I can explain company performance using KPIs. I can prepare performance reports for use by different functions and for different purposes in appropriate formats and media.
D	Apply relevant financial reporting standards and corporate governance, ethical and tax principles.	I can apply relevant IFRS in a given context, to facilitate the preparation of financial statements. I can apply the principles of corporate governance and ethics. I can identify the impact of tax regulation on transactions, decisions and profits.
E	Prepare information to support short-term decision-making.	I can identify relevant costs and benefits. I can apply appropriate techniques that support short-term decision-making. I can prepare information to support operational decisions. I can explain factors that could influence short-term decisions. I can apply appropriate techniques to deal with situations where there is risk and uncertainty.
F	Prepare information to manage working capital.	I can identify appropriate sources of short-term finance and methods of short-term investments. I can explain how to manage and control working capital. I can explain working capital ratios in comparison to prior periods or to other organisations. I can identify the impact of changing working capital policies.

5 The exam process

5.1 Overview

The examination is three hours long. A 15-minute tutorial is available before the start of the examination to allow candidates to familiarise themselves with the test driver.

The examination has four sections (tasks), which are equally weighted (i.e. 45 minutes long). After this time, you be automatically moved on to the next section. You may also choose to finish a section early and move on to the next but cannot return to previous sections in the time remaining.

There may be more than one sub-task within each section and an indication of how long to spend on each sub-task will be given to allow candidates to manage their time.

For example, the first exam variant of the sample prototype paper shows the following instructions:

Section (task)	Time for section (minutes)	Number of answer screens	Number of sub-tasks	% time to spend on each sub-task
1	45	1	2	(a) 48% (b) 52%
2	45	1	2	(a) 52% (b) 48%
3	45	1	2	(a) 36% (b) 64%
4	45	1	2	(a) 60% (b) 40%

More than one core activity will normally (but not always) be assessed in each section/task and the order of core activities and assessment outcomes in the blueprint does not reflect how these might be structured in the examination.

For each sitting there are a number of variants, so different students will not necessarily face the same exam tasks. You are not permitted to discuss any aspects of the variant you sat until after the exam window has finished. The marking and moderation processes ensure that no advantage is gained from sitting one particular variant rather than another.

5.2 The pre-seen

The exam is based on:

- pre-seen material issued in advance of the exam day, supplemented by
- additional, previously unseen material given to you in the exam room.

One pre-seen will be used over two exam windows, giving candidates the opportunity to resit using the same pre-seen. The pre-seen will be shared as follows:

- May/August
- November/February

CIMA releases the pre-seen material approximately seven weeks before the first examination. This is posted on the student area of the CIMA website (www.cimaglobal.com) and it is your responsibility to download it.

The pre-seen material is an introductory scenario to set the scene for the case study, together with accounting and financial information. The pre-seen material is an extended scenario consisting of approximately ten exhibits giving information about a business organisation.

You will be taking on the role of a management accountant who works for the organisation, and your responses to the tasks will usually be addressed to your superior.

5.3 The unseen

In the examination you will be provided with the following.

- An on-screen version of the pre-seen material
- Additional new unseen material, which contains both triggers (new information) and tasks (what you need to do)
- Space to complete your answers
- An on-screen calculator (although candidates are permitted to take their own calculators as long as it's a CIMA approved model.)
- Reference materials (Present value tables, Cumulative present value tables and Normal distribution tables)
- A notepad and pen for planning and workings along with an on-screen scratch pad.

The unseen material will be a continuation of the pre-seen and will usually bring the scenario up to date. In many cases there is a 'twist' in the unseen i.e. a development that students might not have anticipated from the pre-seen. The unseen may focus on a number of issues that appeared in the pre-seen or it may just focus on one or two; either way it will provide the basis for the content of your answers.

A common mistake made by weaker students is that they place too much emphasis on their analysis of the pre-seen material and do not develop the information in the unseen material adequately. The key points to be referred to in your answer should be driven by the new information in the unseen material.

5.4 Triggers and tasks

Each section in the unseen material will begin with a **trigger**.

This will be information provided as an introduction to the work that you are required to complete.

The information may be in the form of a briefing by your superior, a newspaper article, some financial information or extracts from internal reports. You will be expected to integrate this new information with the analysis you have performed on the pre-seen material to produce a coherent and well informed response.

Within each section of the examination, there will then be a **task** or sub-tasks that you will be asked to perform, usually by your superior. These tasks will require different types of response, although usually reports, briefing notes and emails.

Word processing capabilities will be provided within the test driver to allow the formatting and presentation of responses in a professional manner. From 2019, this included the ability to use tables to put together a response. For full details of the word processing functionality and to try this in advance of the examination, a tutorial is available on cimaglobal.com.

There is a time limit attached to each section and you will have a clock showing the time remaining in the corner of your screen. Once you have submitted a section (or the time limit is reached, whichever is sooner) you will not be able to return to that section. This should reduce the problem of not completing the paper but does mean you will need to be disciplined when attempting each section.

If you feel that you do not need all of the time on an earlier section, then moving forwards prematurely will not allow you extra time on later section – the extra time will be lost. Given this, it is always advisable to use the full time allocated to each section to recheck that you have answered the question requirement in full and that you have related your response to the specific context of the case.

A walkthrough of the prototype sample exam will be carried out in chapters 2 to 4.

5.5 Calculations

Examination tasks will not be set that require specific calculations.

However, candidates should, wherever possible, show how they have used and interpreted data from the pre-seen and the new information presented during the examination and/or undertook analysis or calculations to support their responses.

6 Marking and feedback

6.1 'Three level' marking

The Case Study Examinations are human marked using a holistic 'three level' approach for each task, enabling markers to give credit for all relevant points, even if not mentioned in the indicative answer.

For example, in the February 2020 exam, task 1(a) of variant 1, worth 9 marks, asked students to do the following:

"Explain the advantages and disadvantages to Lottie Graphite of using a participative approach to budget setting in these circumstances. Please also explain whether you think participative budgeting would be an appropriate method for setting the budgets for the operations in Feland."

The published indicative answer was accompanied by the following marking grid:

Trait			
Participatory budgets	**Level**	**Descriptor**	**Marks**
		No rewardable material	0
	Level 1	Explains a limited number of points without application to the context of the scenario.	1–3
	Level 2	Explains a reasonable number of points that include both advantages and disadvantages. Some limited application to the context of the pre-seen and/or scenario. May not contain consideration of whether participative is an appropriate approach.	4–6
	Level 3	Explains fully both the disadvantages and advantages and applies the detail provided in the pre-seen and scenario to illustrate the points made in context. Contains a clear consideration of whether participative is an appropriate approach.	7–9

Markers will first assess which level to place your answers in, and then decide how many marks it is worth within the level concerned.

The lessons to be learned

The key differences between the levels are

- Number of points made.
- Degree of application to the context of the pre-seen and/or scenario.
- The extent to which you answered the question set – in this case, pros/cons **and** whether participative budgeting would be appropriate in the situation given.

Make sure your answers address these issues.

6.2 The 'marginally competent candidate' and scaled scores

The pass mark is set by identifying the 'marginally competent candidate'.

The process

(1) A panel of experts debates the tasks within a variant to decide what should be expected from a student deemed competent for this task. This debate does not focus on a perfect answer but, instead, asks what would be expected of a CIMA student (or member) in practice – what is the minimum expected if we were considering employing them, for example.

(2) A sample of student scripts is then discussed and the scripts ranked. This is repeated and refined until the "marginally competent candidate" is identified. This student deserves to pass (but only just!) as they would be employable and have the skills expected of a CIMA student or member in the real world.

(3) The marks earned by this script are then used to set the pass mark for that variant, which is then 'scaled' so it becomes equivalent to a score of 80 out of 150. This is then equated across the other variants, ensuring that students are not disadvantaged if they sit a "harder" variant. The scaled score is required because otherwise the pass mark would change from one window to another.

The lessons to be learned

When answering a task in the exam, you could imagine that this was part of a job interview and ask yourself what would be required to get the job.

Your employer would be less impressed by you showing off knowledge but much more impressed that you can answer a question asked, apply your comments to the company's specific circumstances and make practical, relevant suggestions. Make sure your answers do this!

6.3 Feedback and 'grade descriptors'

Feedback on performance against each core activity will be provided so that learners know their areas of weakness for further study. (Note: there is no requirement to obtain a pass or meet a minimum threshold for each core activity – it is the overall mark that matters.)

In addition to the wording of core activities and assessment objectives, CIMA has published 'grade descriptors' to give you more insight into the skills required to pass. It is these that are used to feedback performance to students.

For example, the grade descriptors for core activity A are as follows:

Core activity	**Assessment outcome**	*If you met the exam level passing standard for each of the core activities, you can generally be described using some or all of the following characteristics:*
A. Prepare costing information for different purposes to meet the needs of management	1 I can use appropriate technologies to gather data for costing purposes from digital and other sources. 2 I can apply different costing methods to produce costing information suitable for managers' needs. 3 I can explain costing information to operational and senior management using appropriate formats and media. 4 I can compare different costing methods and systems to determine the most suitable for use by the organisation for different purposes. 5 I can identify the cost information required for digital cost objects.	• Communicates costing information with clarity. • Demonstrates understanding of the business model and its environment, including digital ecosystems, in gathering cost information and when applying costing methods. • Applies professional judgement when gathering data for costing purposes and when applying costing methods. • Demonstrates technical understanding when applying costing methods. • Applies professional scepticism when comparing different costing methods. • Demonstrates business awareness when preparing costing information to meet the needs of management.

Note that the verbs used in the third column (grade descriptors) are different from those in the second (assessment outcomes). This is designed to show how the 'softer skills' enable and support the achievements of the assessment outcomes and core activities within the simulation. It's intended to draw out the importance of these skills to support producing the best, most applied and plausible answers within the simulation.

The two columns are complementary and should be read in conjunction.

If in the exam, you score enough marks for the tasks relating to core activity A, then your feedback will show that you are 'proficient'.

On the other hand, if you fail to develop your answers sufficiently, then the feedback will show the following:

Core activity	**Rating**	*You were below the passing standard for this core activity. This is because you did not demonstrate some or all of the following characteristics:*
A. Prepare costing information for different purposes to meet the needs of management	Not proficient	• Communicates costing information with clarity. • Demonstrates understanding of the business model and its environment, including digital ecosystems, in gathering cost information and when applying costing methods. • Applies professional judgement when gathering data for costing purposes and when applying costing methods. • Demonstrates technical understanding when applying costing methods. • Applies professional scepticism when comparing different costing methods. • Demonstrates business awareness when preparing costing information to meet the needs of management.

The lessons to be learned

Make sure your answer demonstrates the 'soft skills' shown in the final column:

- Have you communicated clearly?
- Have you related your comments to the specific circumstances of the company in the scenario, thus demonstrating 'business awareness' and an 'understanding of the business model'?
- Have you evaluated the extent to which the technique being discussed, such as participation, is useful for the company in the scenario, thus demonstrating 'professional scepticism'?

7 Topic areas tested to date

Up to and including the February 2022 sitting, the following topics have been examined under the current syllabus.

(Note: "S" refers to which of the two sample/prototype papers and "V" to the variant in the exam sitting where the topic arose):

	Sample papers	**F20**	**M20 A20**	**N20 F21**	**M21 A21**	**N21 F22**
A – Costing						
ABC			V1,5	V3	V1	V1
CGMA cost transformation			V4	V6	V6	
Costing digital objects		V3	V2	V2,5	V3,4	V2,6
Costing other objects			V3	V4	V5	
Digital costing	S1	V2	V6	V1		V5
Direct v indirect costs	S2				V3,4	V4
Marginal / absorption costing		V1		V1		V3
Throughput		V1				
Other Apportionment					V2	
B – Budgeting						
ABB		V2	V4	V2		V2
Beyond budgeting	S1	V3	V4		V3	
Feedback vs feedforward	S2		V5	V3	V6	
Fixed v flexible budgets			V3		V5	
Forecasting – regression				V4		
Forecasting – time series		V1,3	V1,6	V1	V3,5	V1,6
Importance of budgeting				V6		
ZBB			V4,5	V1	V2,6	V5
Participation vs top down		V1	V3	V2	V1	V5
Producing budgets - general				V6		
Responsibility accounting	S2		V3	V5		V3,5
Rolling budgets			V2		V1	V3,4
Sources of data	S1				V4	V4
What-if / sensitivity / stress testing	S2	V2	V2	V3,5	V2,4	V1,6
Operating gearing					V2	

	Sample papers	F20	M20 A20	N20 F21	M21 A21	N21 F22
C – Performance appraisal						
KPIs – business unit/product	S1			V2	V3,4,5	
KPIs – customer			V3,6			
KPIs – dashboard				V5	V1,2	V1
KPIS – marketing						V2
KPIs – distributor				V6		
KPIs – equipment	S2					
KPIs – maintenance				V1	V6	
KPIs – production				V3		
KPIs – recycling				V4		
KPIs – sales	S1,2	V1	V1,5			V4,6
KPIs – supplier		V2,3				
KPIs – warehouse			V4			V3
KPIs – IT support						V5
Variances – fixed OH		V2	V2,5	V1,6	V6	V1,3
Variances – var OH						V1
Variances – labour			V2,6	V3		V1,5
Variances – materials		V2	V2			V1
Variances – P&O			V1	V4,5	V5	
Variances – sales		V1,3	V1,3,4,6	V2,4	V2,3	V2,4,6
Variances – ABC					V1	

	Sample papers	F20	M20 A20	N20 F21	M21 A21	N21 F22
D – FR, governance & ethics						
Assets held for resale	S1	V2	V5		V6	V1,4
Inventory valuation		V1	V2,6	V5	V6	V2,3
Events after reporting period		V2			V3	V2
NCAs – depreciation + UL		V3		V1		V1
NCAs – disposal		V3				V3
NCAs – initial expenditure		V3	V3,5,6	V2,6	V1,4,5	V1,4,5,6
NCAs – impairment			V6		V5	
NCAs – leasing		V1	V1	V3,4	V2,4,5	V2,6
NCAs – revaluation	S2			V1		
NCAs – subsequent exp.			V4	V3	V3,5	V3,5
Governance	S2					
Taxation		V2,3	V5	V2, 6	V4	

	Sample papers	F20	M20 A20	N20 F21	M21 A21	N21 F22
E – Decision making						
Relevant costing	S1		V1,2,4	V1.2,5, 6	V1,2,4	V3,6
Risk – Decision trees	S2		V5	V1, 6	V4	V5
Risk – Expected values		V1,2,3	V4,6	V3, 4	V2	V1,2,4,6
Scarce resources – Key Factor Analysis	S1	V1				
Scarce resources – Linear Programming			V3,6	V3,5	V3,6	V3,5
Uncertainty – minimax, maximin, etc.		V2	V2,3		V3,5,6	V1
Multi product CVP		V3	V1	V2,4		V2
PV chart					V1,5	V4
Operating gearing					V1	
F – Working capital						
Dealing with a cash deficit	S1		V1			V5
Investing surplus cash			V3	V2		V4
Approaches to WCM (aggressive, conservative)				V6	V2	V3
Evaluating a supplier's WC ratios	S2	V2	V2	V4	V3,5	V1
Evaluating customers using WC ratios						V6
General inventory management			V4			
Inventory – EOQ			V5	V3	V6	
Inventory – JiT						V3
General payables management						
General receivables management		V1,3	V6	V1	V4	V2
Receivables – factoring				V5	V1	
Working capital cycle				V6		

8 Summary

You should now have a basic understanding of how the case study works. All of the ideas presented in this chapter will be developed further in the remainder of this textbook.

Next steps:

(1) It is a good idea to register with Pearson Vue to see the online version of the "Question tutorial" exam as this will allow you become more familiar with the look and feel of the exam. All the relevant material from the "Question tutorial" exam has been reproduced in this textbook but it is important to recognise that the CIMA case study examinations are dynamic and shouldn't be viewed as equivalent to a static paper exam.

(2) Think about the date on which you will sit the exam and work backwards to create a sensible and achievable study timetable.

(3) You need to ensure that your technical knowledge is up to date/full especially if the OTQ exams were sat a while ago.

It might be worth locating and gathering together any materials you already have from the supporting technical subjects (E1, P1 and F1).

When doing this, make sure you are led by the blueprint "I can" statements to give focus. We will show you in later chapters how you may need to use these materials.

(4) In the following chapters we do a complete walkthrough of the prototype sample paper issued in June 2019, illustrating how to analyse the pre-seen information and how to answer exam questions.

(5) In chapter 6 we refine our exam technique further by looking at how to answer the more challenging tasks from the May/August 2020 exam variants.

(6) Finally, in chapter 7, you have more tasks from the February 2020 exam variants to practice, grouped by core activity.

Chapter

2

Walkthrough of the 2019 Prototype exam – pre-seen information

0 Introduction

The Case Study Examinations are like no other CIMA exam; there is no new syllabus to study or formulae to learn. The best way to be successful at this level is to practise using past case study exams and mock exams based on your real live case study. By reviewing previous case studies alongside your current case you will improve your commercial thought processes and will be more aware of what the examiner expects. By sitting mock exams, under timed conditions you can hone your exam techniques and, in particular, your time management skills.

This textbook is therefore based on this principle. It presents the prototype case study and uses this to demonstrate the skills and techniques that you must master to be successful. The prototype case, GymFit, will be used to walkthrough the processes and approach. The remainder of this chapter contains the GymFit pre-seen material.

We would advise that you skim read this now before moving on to Chapter 3 where you will be provided with more guidance on how to familiarise yourself with the pre-seen material.

1 Extract from job description

You are a Finance Officer for GymFit. Your main role is to support Steven Potter, the Finance Manager. Your tasks include the production of the annual budget, producing the monthly management accounts and providing information to management as required. You also assist with the preparation of the financial statements and deal with any queries regarding financial reporting.

2 Company Information

GymFit, is a fast growing, leading provider of low-cost gyms and one of the pioneers of the low-cost gym model, which is based on relatively low gym membership fees and a 'no-frills' service concept. It now has 102 gyms with 486,000 members based in major towns and cities throughout Celtland, Europe. The company was founded in 2005 using finance from venture capitalist, Land Ventures. It is currently listed in the Celtland stock exchange and uses the C$ as its home currency.

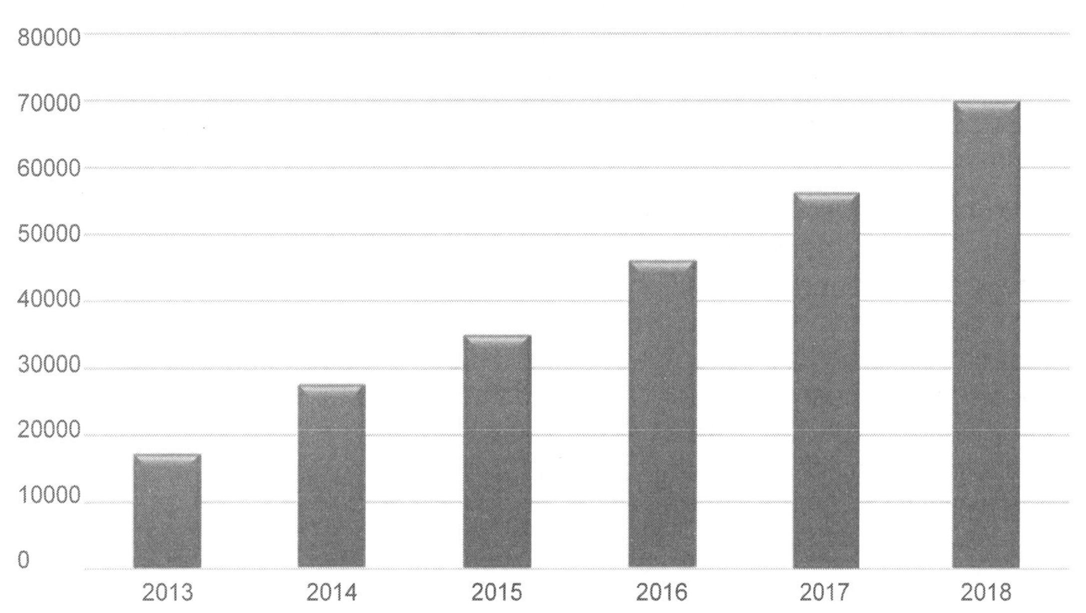

The company has grown rapidly from sales revenue of C$17.8 million in 2013 to C$73.1 million in 2018. The number of gyms it operates has also increased during the same period from 26 gyms to 102. The rapid increase in the number of gyms has been through a mixture of organic growth and acquisition of existing gym groups. The company is now the 2nd largest operator of low-cost gyms in Celtland.

GymFit's business model offers 24/7 gym operating hours and a no-contract membership i.e. there is no fixed membership period. The high specification gym equipment used is eco-friendly. In order to offer low membership fees, their model is based on a no-frills concept, meaning that facilities are restricted to the gym equipment, there are no wet facilities e.g. saunas or pools, and no café or bars that you would expect to find in a traditional health club.

The low-cost model used by GymFit is dependent on advanced technology. Prospective GymFit members can join using a simple online process that can be completed in minutes. Members can also manage their accounts, view class timetables and book classes online.

The use of technology results in an efficient staffing model with, for example, no need for dedicated in-gym sales and marketing teams.

Membership

GymFit membership is on a no-contract basis i.e. it does not involve a fixed membership period and members are free to cancel their membership at any time without penalty. There are three types of membership: solo gym membership, where the member is able to access only one chosen gym; two gym membership, where the member can access two chosen gyms and bundle membership where the member can access gyms nationwide. These types of membership require payment of a monthly fee. In addition, it is possible to access gym facilities on a daily basis by purchasing a day pass. Membership fees vary depending mainly on the location of the gym. Occasional marketing campaigns are run offering discounted membership to all new members. Student members also receive a discount.

Each member is provided with a unique personal identification number (PIN) code which is used to provide electronic access to the gym and its facilities.

Members have access to high quality fitness equipment, work-out areas and some free fitness classes. Other classes such as Pilates, yoga and dance fit are available on payment of an additional fee. All new members are offered a free induction session and these are provided by the fitness instructors. The member can also, on payment of an additional fee, arrange for individual coaching from a fitness instructor. These additional fees are paid directly to the instructors and are a private arrangement between the gym member and the instructor. Other facilities offered include showers, changing areas, lockers and vending machines.

The People

Staff

The average number of employees, during 2018, was 254. A typical gym has two employees, a manager and an assistant manager, who manage the running of the gym. The remaining staff are employed at head office in various functions including IT, HR, Finance and Marketing. These employees are complemented by a number of freelance fitness instructors who are hired on a zero-hours contract where the instructors are not guaranteed to be offered work in any one week. The fitness instructors are paid a relatively low hourly rate but are able to supplement their income with fees from individual coaching sessions.

All fitness instructors are trained fitness experts. Their main role is to assist members with using the equipment, run induction sessions for new members, lead some group classes, and provide general exercise and fitness advice. They are also expected to carry out simple preventative maintenance and testing the equipment. They can generally resolve most of the simple problems arising with the equipment, anything they cannot deal with is referred to the contracted maintenance company. In addition to this, they also refill vending and water machines and, where possible, attend additional training sessions related to equipment use, fitness or health and safety.

Gym managers are empowered to independently run their own sites, including the setting of membership fees, with bonus targets linked to gym performance. Other employees are given competitive remuneration including a defined contribution pension scheme and the opportunity to share in the company's success through share incentive plans.

The need for reception staff is eliminated due to the use of the electronic entry system and the online membership and class booking system, other staffing needs such as cleaning, security and non-routine machine maintenance are outsourced which means that gym staff (managers and fitness instructors) are free to concentrate on the core activities of the gym.

The Senior Management Team

The company's senior management team bring to the company a wide range of previous experience mainly in the leisure and retail industries. The team is relatively young, highly enthusiastic and engenders a 'can do' culture throughout the organisation.

The details of the company's executive directors are given below:

Bertram Durand (42) Chief Executive Officer (CEO)

Bertram was appointed as CEO in 2014 and brings to the company extensive experience in the leisure and fitness industry.

Nicola Collette (45) Chief Financial Officer (CFO)

Nicola was appointed as Chief Financial Officer in 2015. She is a professionally qualified accountant. She has been with the company since it started operations in 2005 and was responsible for the company's flotation on the Celtland stock exchange.

Jessica Treewood (38) Marketing Director

Jessica has been with the company since 2014. She holds a BA in Marketing from Celtland University. She previously worked as Marketing Director for a competitor company in the fitness club sector.

Ethan Henson (38) Operations Director

Ethan was appointed Operations Director in 2016. He has responsibility for the running of the gyms and the HR function. He was previously a fitness trainer and has worked his way up through the ranks of the company to become Operations Director.

Gerard Fischer (46) Property Director

Gerard joined the company in 2011 as Property Director. He is responsible for the company's portfolio of properties. He is a qualified civil engineer and has vast experience in property management mainly gained in the hotel industry.

Gemma Schneider (36) IT Director

Gemma joined the company in 2010 as an IT technician and was appointed IT Director in 2017. She holds a MSc in Information Technology. She is keen to further develop GymFit's IT systems with the assistance of her team of innovative and highly qualified staff.

ORGANISATION CHARTS

Executive and non-executive directors

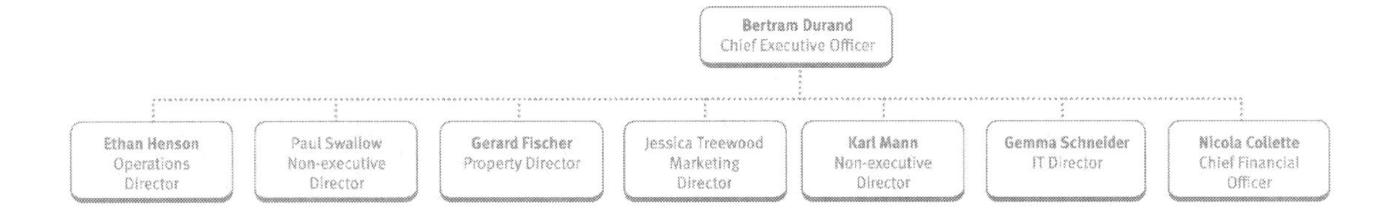

Finance Department

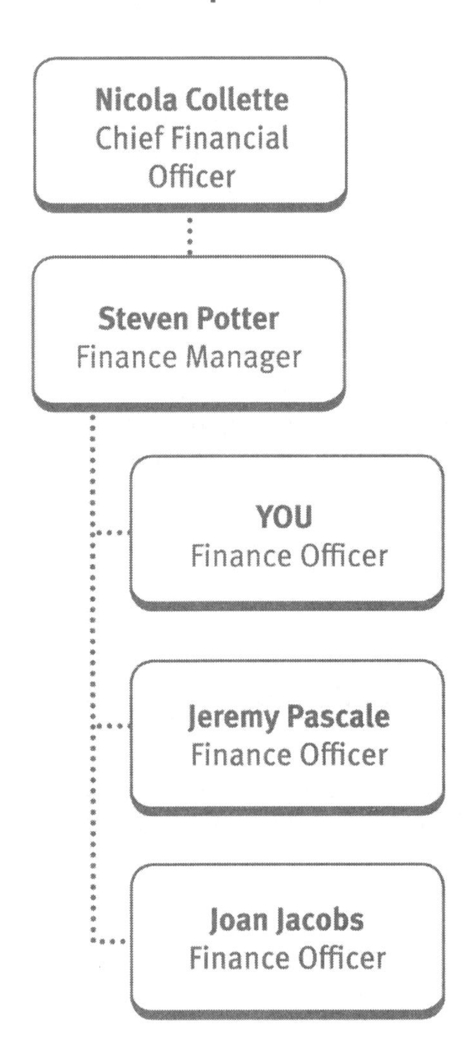

Company Operations

The Gyms

Each gym has more than 150 items of high specification equipment and free weights for members to use. The fitness equipment is eco-friendly with around 70% of the machines using no electricity and are powered by the user instead. Each gym offers a range of cardio machines including running, cycling and step machines and weight machines of various types to help flex every muscle in the body.

The low-impact workout areas give members an opportunity to warm-up or stretch out. Equipment available includes exercise balls and yoga mats.

Each gym contains studios for use by the fitness instructors when leading fitness classes including yoga, Pilates and Dancefit. There are also showers and changing facilities available and vending machines selling bottled drinks and other fitness related items such as sweat bands, protein powder and health bars.

Information Technology (IT)

The IT department runs and manages the company's website and is responsible for website development. The company's operations are driven by technology and the IT department is constantly looking for new ways to utilise IT to improve the member proposition and to achieve cost efficiencies.

GymFit offers a simple online joining process that requires a valid email address and other personal data. Membership and class fees can be paid by credit card, debit card and direct debit and members can manage their accounts, view class timetables and book classes using computer, tablet or mobile. GymFit maintains a customer database which can be used to communicate with members.

Gyms are open 24/7 but only staffed for around 16 hours of the day. The gyms have automated access control and CCTV which is monitored on a 24-hour basis and is enhanced by the use of 'panic buttons' throughout the gym. It is the use of this technology which enables 24/7 operation of the gyms whilst keeping costs low.

The use of technology also results in an efficient staffing model, with no need for dedicated in-gym sales and marketing teams. The staffing model means managers are freed from many traditional health club tasks and can focus on running successful gyms and serving the needs of members.

The extensive use of information technology brings other considerations in terms of system failure, data security and privacy. GymFit's membership system, data processing, account payments, gym access, customer safety and customer marketing, are all dependent on the IT systems. The systems hold a significant amount of confidential customer data including email address, home address and bank details. A breach of data security would constitute a significant risk to the company's reputation and brand.

Marketing

The marketing team's main activities are market research; the promotion and advertising of new and existing gyms; raising brand awareness and advising on pricing strategies. The Marketing team works closely with the IT and Properties department. Marketing efforts are directed at both existing members, to try to ensure member retention, and the recruitment of new members.

The marketing team uses the website to provide members with details of classes being operated each week and any other news or member offers. The customer database is also used to communicate electronically with members using email and SMS.

Regular marketing campaigns ensure that the awareness of the brand is high. A recent campaign featuring a leading Olympic athlete, Johnny Wren, resulted in a 2% increase in member numbers.

Finance

The financial information system produces monthly management accounts and both half-yearly and annual statutory accounts. It also generates daily and weekly sales revenue and membership number information for management to monitor actual results against budgets.

The Finance team also carries out ad-hoc projects including investment appraisal and investigations, along with ongoing decision support. Some areas, including all internal audit work, are delivered by external experts.

Budgets are produced annually using incremental budgeting for sales and cost items. All budgets are broken down into monthly periods, with the exception of the sales budget which is broken down into weekly periods.

Properties

The company has significant experience of developing and managing properties and has been able to use that expertise and its close relationships with suppliers to reduce its fit-out and property management costs.

Growth of the company is dependent on being able to find suitable properties for the new gyms. The company has plans to develop between 15 and 20 properties per year. The majority of properties are leased, for periods of up to 15 years, whilst a small number are owned by the company.

Properties need to be large enough to accommodate the fitness equipment and offer studio space for exercise classes. The ideal property is between 1,000 and 2,000 square metres, over a maximum of two floors. Properties need to be either located within a dense population catchment area to ensure sufficient potential local members or in highly visible locations with easy car parking facilities or access to major transport hubs.

Company Strategy

The company's long-term objective is to deliver long-term profitable growth through improvements in operating efficiency, offering a strong member proposition and by focusing on its people.

It plans to achieve growth through the selective acquisition of existing gym groups, and the lease and fit-out of new properties. The company has a rigorous approach to site selection, with flexible fit-out arrangements allowing the use of a wide variety of building types. It aims to reduce gym fit-out costs through the use of a competitive tender process, negotiating improved terms with suppliers and value engineering the fit-out specification to avoid unnecessary cost.

It plans to achieve improvement to operating efficiency through economies of scale, use of data and technology and also by managing its cost base. The outsourcing of support functions will also enable cost reduction and allow the company to focus on core operations.

In order to continually improve the member proposition, the company will pursue innovative low cost ways to differentiate itself from its competitors. Improvement of member satisfaction, reflected in strong member satisfaction ratings, is a key aim which is dependent on having knowledgeable, well-trained staff. The company strongly believes that attracting, motivating and training people of the highest calibre is key to the company's continued success.

3 The Health and Fitness Industry in Celtland

Celtland health and fitness gym sector is a rapidly growing sector of the health and fitness industry. It has estimated sales revenue of C$7 billion in 2018, an increase of 6.3% on 2017. There are now over 9.7 million people in Celtland who are members of a gym.

This sector experienced modest growth until 2011 thereafter the growth in the market accelerated rapidly, mainly driven by the low-cost segment. Prior to 2011 the market comprised of two main segments: public gyms funded by local government and private gyms funded and operated by commercial enterprises. The rapid increase in low-cost gyms since 2011 has fragmented the market by creating a third segment, low-cost (or budget) gyms, representing 12% of total private gym numbers in 2018.

Gyms are differentiated by a number of factors, including price and contract terms, quality, scope of services and facilities, as well as whether they are part of a larger network.

These can be broadly grouped into:

- Low-cost (or budget) gyms: these are private gyms and differentiate themselves by offering access to gym facilities for a lower price, normally below (depending on the location sometimes well below) C$20 per month. To contain costs, these gyms generally do not offer access to 'wet facilities' (e.g., saunas, steam room, pools), operate large venues (above 1,000 square metres) and can generally be joined online. Also, they will normally transparently advertise their prices online and offer monthly rolling contracts as an option.
- Mid-range and premium gyms: these are also private gyms but are more (or much more) expensive than low-cost gyms. They may, however, offer access to better facilities (e.g. wet facilities or a higher quality environment). These gyms can vary considerably in size, from very small facilities to very large ones. Some gyms will offer monthly rolling contracts and advertise their prices transparently online, others only offer longer-term contracts (e.g. minimum six months or one year) and sometimes require customers to contact the gym to obtain a quote.
- Public gyms: are owned and/or operated by, or on behalf of, local government. The quality of the facilities offered by public gyms can vary considerably. In many instances, public gyms also offer access to wet facilities, including a pool. Their pricing policy also varies considerably. Some business models in the operation of public gyms are similar to those in the categories above.

Recent government initiatives in Celtland, such as the 'GetupGo' campaign, have increased consumers awareness of the negative impact of an inactive lifestyle. The Society of Medical Practitioners have made physical activity one of its top priorities hailing physical activity as the best cure for lifestyle related diseases.

Societal trends have also brought active lifestyles more prominence through the use of Facebook, Instagram and Twitter. These trends have mainly influenced the younger generations who are consequently more health conscious than their predecessors.

Membership profile and customer demand

There are a number of determinants of gym membership with the most important being age; income and educational level.

Previous research studies have shown that the highest percentage of gym members are in the 18–35 age group however the fastest growing sector is the 36–55 age group. Income is a major determinant with households earning $75,000 or more per annum being more likely to have gym membership. However, within the high earners segment ($75,000 and above) educational level was a significant factor with around 25% of those with degree level education having gym membership compared to less than 12% of those who did not go to University or College.

The overall penetration rate in Celtland is 14.3% but demand will be influenced by the members' proximity to the gym with most gym members being within 12 minutes driving time of the gym. Proximity to good road or rail network will be a contributing factor. The extent of competition in the specific areas will also be an important factor in estimating potential demand.

Competitive Situation

Within the low-cost gym sector in Celtland there are four major players including GymFit. GymFit is the second largest operator in the sector in terms of number of gyms. The largest operator Gym4All has grown mainly through the acquisition of other smaller gym groups. A number of smaller gym groups, typically operating between ten and thirty gyms, still remain.

The rising star in the Celtland market is Fit4Life which has ruthlessly marketed itself as a lifelong alternative to the other low-cost gyms. Fit4Life offers members a lifelong membership fee which will not increase provided the customer remains a member. Its rapid growth has also been driven by its use of specialised fitness apps which have been developed using data analytics. These apps provide members with tailored personal training advice and programmes which they can access at home.

Future Outlook

Growth in the Celtland health and fitness gym market is strong and steady and is expected to continue for the next few years driven by technology changes and government initiatives to improve health and fitness.

The Celtland health and fitness gym market is relatively immature compared to similar markets in Europe. Norway, Sweden and the Netherlands all have mature markets with penetration rates of 19.4%, 16.7% and 16.4% respectively. These penetration rates indicate that there is potential for a strong increase in overall member numbers compared to Celtland's current penetration rate of 14.3%.

Whilst membership numbers are growing, operators still face the challenge of member retention. Technology can minimise cancellations by making the gym experience more enjoyable and rewarding, but operators must work to provide a service that members can't get from exercising alone or by going elsewhere.

The increasing presence of virtual reality (VR), immersive experiences and video-on-demand (VOD) is one way health and fitness clubs can achieve member retention. These technologies allow gym operators to provide content in multiple locations at once, while freeing up instructors. From a member perspective, VOD fitness can be accessed anywhere and at any time thus eliminating the need to be at a gym at a certain time, or at all. Apps and online channels also offer operators a way to help member's access VOD fitness classes at home or away.

4 Extract from GymFit's 2018 Consolidated Financial Statements

Statement of Profit or Loss for the year ended 31 December	2018 C$000	2017 C$000
Revenue	73,102	58,831
Operating expenses		
Gym operating costs	(20,389)	(16,384)
Lease costs	(13,840)	(10,800)
Staff costs	(10,561)	(7,955)
Head office costs	(7,280)	(5,840)
Depreciation	(11,524)	(10,154)
Amortisation	(940)	(1,154)
Total operating expenses	(64,533)	(52,287)
Operating profit	8,569	6,544
Finance Income	12	12
Finance costs	(612)	(633)
Profit before tax	7,969	5,923)
Taxation	(1,616)	(990)
Profit/(loss) for the year	6,353	4,933

Statement of Pro Financial Position as at 31 December	2018 C$000	2017 C$000
Non-current assets		
Intangible assets	49,653	48,974
Tangible assets	107,150	69,352
Investment	200	200
	157,003	118,526
Current assets		
Inventories	158	127
Trade receivables	7,229	4,651
Cash and cash equivalents	366	3,858
Total Assets	7,753	8,636
	164,756	127,162
Equity and Liabilities		
Share capital	48	48
Share premium	79,027	79,027
Retained earnings	17,632	12,357
Total equity	96,707	91,432
Non-current liabilities		
Borrowings	32,071	8,325
	32,071	8,325
Current liabilities		
Trade payables	35,320	27,298
Bank loans and overdraft	0	0
Current tax liabilities	658	107
	35,978	27,405
Total Equity and Liabilities	164,756	127,162

Statement of Cash Flows or the year ended 31 December	2018 C$000	2017 C$000
Cash flows from operating activities		
Profit/(loss) before tax	7,969	5,923
Depreciation	11,523	10,154
Amortisation	940	1,154
Net finance costs	600	621
(Increase)/decrease in inventory	(31)	(30)
(Increase)/decrease in trade and other receivables	(2,578)	(128)
Increase/(decrease) in trade and other payables	8,022	6,862
Cash generated from operations	26,445	24,556
Interest paid	(612)	(633)
Tax paid	(1,065)	(882)
Net cash generated from operating activities	24,768	23,041
Cash flows from investing activities		
Purchase of tangible assets	(49,321)	(21,374)
Purchase of intangibles	(1,619)	(818)
Interest received	12	12
Net cash used in investing activities	(50,928)	(22,180)
Cash flows from financing activities		
Increase/(repayment) of long-term borrowings	23,746	966
Dividend paid	(1,078)	(257)
Net cash from/(used in) financing activities	22,668	709
Net increase/(decrease) in cash and cash equivalents	(3,492)	1,570
Cash and cash equivalents at beginning of the year	3,858	2,288
Cash and cash equivalents at the end of the year	366	3,858

5 Budget information 2019

Membership Fee Budget 2019

		City	Town	Total
Number of gyms		30	86	116
Average number of members per gym	Full-fee	3,660	3,107	3,250
	Student	1,396	1,199	1,250
	Total	5,056	4,306	4,500
Average membership fee per month (C$)	Full-fee	21.96	12.14	15.00
	Student	17.59	9.73	12.00
Total membership fees per year (C$000)	Full-fee	28,934	38,926	67,860
	Student	8,840	12,040	20,880
	Total	37,774	50,966	88,740

Sales Budget 2019

Number of gyms	116		
Average number of members per gym	4,500		
Total sales revenue (C$000)	92,394		
	Per member C$	Number of members per gym	Total C$000
Average membership fees	170.00	4,500	88,740
Classes	5.28	4,500	2,756
Vending machine income	1.45	4,500	757
Day passes			141
Total sales revenue			92,394

Operating Profit Budget 2019

	Total		Per gym	
	$000	$000	$000	$000
Sales revenue		92,394		796
Operating expenses				
Gym operating costs	(23,920)		(206)	
Lease costs	(16,991)		(146)	
Staff costs	(11,822)		(102)	
Head office costs	(8,221)		(71)	
Depreciation	(14,616)		(126)	
Amortisation	(1,040)		(9)	
		(76,610)		(660)
Operating profit		15,784		136

GymFit Key Statistics

	Budget 2019	Actual 2018	Actual 2017	Actual 2016
Total number of gyms	116	102	71	59
New gym openings	14	31	12	15
*Number of mature gyms	71	59	44	32
Total number of members	548,100	485,600	358,400	300,800
Average number of members	522,000	422,586	344,066	283,908
Average number of members per gym	4,500	4,143	4,846	4,846
Total sales revenue (C$000)	92,394	73,101	58,831	47,983
Sales revenue per member per year	$177	$173	$171	$169
Total number of operational employees	225	198	138	114

*Mature gyms are those gyms which have been operating for more than 2 years.

6 The Tax Regime in Celtland

Corporate Profits:

- The corporate tax rate applicable to taxable profits is 20%.
- The sales tax rate is 20%.
- Unless otherwise stated below, accounting rules on recognition and measurement are followed for tax purposes.
- The following expenses are not allowable for tax purposes:
  - accounting depreciation; o amortisation
  - entertaining expenditure
  - donations to political parties; and
  - Taxes paid to other public bodies.
- Tax depreciation allowances are available on items of plant and machinery (including vehicles used for business purposes) at a rate of 25% per year on a reducing balance basis.
- Tax losses can be carried forward to offset against future taxable profits from the same business.

Fitness Monthly

16 January 2019 No. 78 C$4.70

Is data analytics the future for the fitness industry?

Georgio Duccatti – **Business Correspondent**

We live in a world driven by technology. The fitness industry is no exception, as the opportunity to use technology and data promises a step change in the gym experience. We are beginning to see collaborations between brands that have created connectivity between a wide variety of fitness equipment, devices, wearable technology and healthcare apps.

These collaborations offer us a much broader view of fitness, health and preferences. The resulting data has the power to fundamentally change our behaviour. It is no surprise then that the market for connected gym equipment is growing at an incredible rate, estimated at over 40% per year.

Imagine tracking changes in important body statistics, working through an automated training programme that has been designed based on your likes, dislikes, goals and progress.

The gym benefits too. By understanding your profile and preferences, the gym can align their offer, for example adapting classes and facilities. This increases member loyalty and reduces churn.

The amount of data that could be created is huge, along with the possibilities. It is still relatively early days but the size of the opportunity is clear.

Fitness Monthly

6 February 2019 No. 78 C$4.70

The battle to beat inactivity – are we winning?

Georgio Duccatti – **Business Correspondent**

According to a recent report by the Celtland Heart Disease Research Foundation the answer is a resounding 'No'.

The report suggests that more than 20 million people in Celtland are physically inactive and the charity warns that inactivity increases the risk of heart disease.

The Celtland government recently announced its GetupGo initiative to try to encourage both adults and children to exercise on a regular basis.

GetupGo heralds a new approach which shifts the balance of investment, for the first time, to focus more on encouraging inactive and under-represented groups to become more active. It is believed that this is where the greatest individual, community and economic gains can be made.

The government is encouraging community group, health care providers, employers and local authorities to take action to support the initiative.

Private sector companies in the health and fitness sector are also being encouraged to target new members from these under-represented groups.

So, if you're not already a member of a gym then maybe it's time to 'get up and go' down to your local gym. You might be pleasantly surprised at the offers available!!

Chapter

3

Walkthrough of the 2019 Prototype exam – analysing the pre-seen

Chapter learning objectives

- to understand various techniques and models that can help familiarisation with the pre-seen.

1 The importance of familiarisation

The pre-seen material is released approximately seven weeks before you sit the exam and one of your first tasks will be to analyse the context within which the case is set. Although your responses in the exam will be driven by the unseen material, you will only be able to fully assess the impact of each event on the organisation if you have a sufficient depth of knowledge and awareness of both the organisation and the industry in which it operates.

The purpose of the pre-seen material is to allow you to gain that knowledge and awareness. Remember, you will be acting in the position of a management accountant who works for the organisation in a finance officer role. It will therefore be expected that you will have the same level of familiarisation as someone fulfilling that role.

It is extremely important that you study the pre-seen material thoroughly before you go into the examination. There are two main reasons for this:

- It will save time in the examination itself if you are already familiar with the pre-seen material (especially in relation to how any costing information is presented).
- It enables you to develop a view of the situation facing the organisation in the case study.

You will not be able to respond to the examination tasks from the pre-seen material alone; the unseen material given to you in the examination will present significant new information that may alter the situation substantially. Even so, a major step towards success in the examination is a careful study, exploration and understanding of the pre-seen material.

Each set of pre-seen material is different but as a general rule, you can expect the following:

- Industry background
- History of the business
- Key personnel
- Current business/industry issues
- Management accounting information, such as costing schedules
- Financial Statements
- Tax regime

Each of these areas will need reviewing in detail.

You should question what each piece of information tells you, and why the examiner may have given it to you.

2 Exhibit by exhibit analysis

The purpose of this initial stage is to lay a foundation for further analysis. It's more about asking questions than finding solutions. Before you do anything else, you should read the pre-seen material from beginning to end without making any notes, simply to familiarise yourself with the scenario.

Read the material again, as many times as you think necessary, without making notes. You can do this over a period of several days, if you wish.

When you think you are reasonably familiar with the situation described by the material, you should start to make notes. By making notes, you will become more familiar with the detail of the scenario.

- Try to make notes on each paragraph (or each group of short paragraphs) in the pre-seen material.
- Ask yourself "why might the examiner have told me this?"
- Try to make your questions as broad as possible; consider as many different stakeholders as possible and try to put yourself in different positions (say the CEO, a customer, an employee, etc.) to consider the information from different perspectives.

Illustration 1 – GymFit: Introductory overview

Given below is an example of some questions you could ask yourself relating to the second exhibit of the "question tutorial" exam pre-seen information.

Question	Potential response
What does GymFit do?	Low cost, no frills, no contract approach to running a gym.
Is GymFit a major player?	2nd largest operator of low cost gyms in Celtland.
What is GymFit's pricing strategy?	Gym managers can set their own fees. If clients want additional lessons with fitness instructors, say, then they negotiate these with the instructor.
How important is IT to GymFit?	Critical – clients join/pay on the website, clients can view schedules on mobile devices, electronic entry to gyms, etc all these allow the company to employ fewer staff.
What are the key elements of the company's strategy to deliver growth?	(1) Improvements in operating efficiency, (2) Offering a strong member proposition and by, (3) Focusing on its people.

3 Note taking

When you're making notes, try to be as creative as possible. Psychologists tell us that using conventional linear notes on their own use only a small part of our mental capacity. They are hard to remember and prevent us from drawing connections between topics. This is because they seek to classify things under hierarchical headings.

Here are some techniques that candidates find useful. See which ones work for you as you practise on the "question tutorial" case in this text.

Spider diagrams

Spider diagrams (or clustering diagrams) are a quick graphic way of summarising connections between subjects. You cannot put much detail into a spider diagram, just a few key words. However, it does help you to 'visualise' the information in the case material. You must expect to update your spider diagram as you go along and to redraft it when it starts to get too messy. It is all part of the learning process.

Timelines

Timelines are valuable to make sense of the sequence of events in the pre-seen and to understand where the company in the case study presently stands. The case study exam takes place in real time, so you need to be clear how long is likely to elapse between the data in the pre-seen and the actual exam. This is the time period during which the issues facing the company can be incorporated into the unseen material.

Colours

Colours help you remember things you may want to draw upon in the exam room. You could write down all your financial calculations and observations in green whilst having red for organisational and blue for strategic. Some candidates use different colour highlighter pens to emphasise different aspects of the pre-seen material perhaps using the same colour coding suggestion.

Additionally, sometimes making notes in different colours helps you to remember key facts and some of the preparation that you have done using the pre-seen material.

Use whatever colours work for you – but it does help to make notes on both the pre-seen material and the research you do. DO NOT just read the material – you must take notes (in whatever format) and if colours help you to understand and link your research together then use colours.

4 Technical analysis

Now you're reasonably familiar with the material it's time to carry out some technical analysis to help you identify and understand the issues facing the company.

A good starting point is to revise any 'technical' topics that might be relevant. The pre-seen material might make a reference to a particular 'technical' issue, such as possible constraints in production/operation, costing or pricing issues, budget approach, performance issues, financial reporting issues and so on. Anticipate exam tasks by asking yourself how you would apply these models in the context of the live case.

If you lack confidence on any topic that might be relevant, go back to your previous study materials and revise it if necessary.

Exercise 1 – GymFit: P1 topic analysis

Typical P1 topic areas (that could be applied to any case) include the following.

1 Discuss which costs are fixed and which variable.

2 Discuss how useful overhead absorption is to GymFit in terms of (a) splitting costs between gyms and (b) splitting costs within gyms.

3 How useful do you think ABC would be to GymFit?

4 Discuss whether an incremental or ZBB approach would be most suitable for GymFit.

5 Suggest four variances that would be of most use to GymFiT. Justify your choices.

5 Financial analysis

You will almost certainly be given some figures in the pre-seen material. These might relate to the company's profits or losses, or product profitability. There might be statements of profit or loss and statements of financial position for previous years, future business plans, statement of cash flows, capital expenditure plans, and so on.

A key part of your initial analysis will be to perform some simple financial analysis, such as financial ratio calculations or a cash flow analysis. These might give you a picture of changes in profitability, liquidity, working capital management or cash flows over time, and will help ensure you have a rounded picture of the organisation's current position.

If a statement of cash flows is not provided, it may be worth preparing a summary of cash flows. You may have to make some assumptions if the detailed information isn't provided but even with these, there is great value in appreciating where the money has come from, and where it is being spent.

Profitability ratios

You might find useful information from an analysis of profit/sales ratios, for:

- the company as a whole
- each division, or
- each product or service.

Profit margins can be measured as a net profit percentage and as a gross profit percentage. You can then look at trends in the ratios over time, or consider whether the margins are good or disappointing.

Analysing the ratio of certain expenses to sales might also be useful, such as the ratio of administration costs to sales, sales and marketing costs to sales or R&D costs to sales. Have there been any noticeable changes in these ratios over time and, if so, is it clear why the changes have happened?

Working capital ratios

Working capital ratios can be calculated to assess the efficiency of working capital management (= management of inventory, trade receivables and trade payables). They can also be useful for assessing liquidity, because excessive investment in working capital ties up cash and slows the receipt of cash.

The main working capital ratios are:

- "inventory days" or the average inventory holding period: a long period might indicate poor inventory management
- "receivable days" or the average time that customers take to pay: a long period could indicate issues with the collection of cash, although would need to consider this in light of the entity's credit terms and industry averages
- "payable days" or the average time to pay suppliers: a long period could indicate cash flow difficulties for the entity, although would need to consider in light of credit terms.

You should be familiar with these ratios and how to calculate the length of the cash cycle or operating cycle.

Cash flow analysis or funding analysis

If the main objective of a company is to maximise the wealth of its shareholders, the most important financial issues will be profitability and returns to shareholders. However, other significant issues in financial strategy are often:

- cash flows and liquidity, and
- funding.

A possible cash flow problem occurs whenever the cash flows from operations do not appear to be sufficient to cover all the non-operational cash payments that the company has to make, such as spending on capital expenditure items.

An analysis of future funding can be carried out by looking at the history of changes in the statement of financial position.

Exercise 2 – GymFit: Ratio Analysis

Complete the following table and answer the questions below.

Ratio	*2019 (budget)*	*2018*	*2019*
Growth in revenue			
Growth in gym operating costs			
Growth in lease costs			
Growth in staff costs			
Growth in head office costs			
Growth in depreciation			
Growth in operating profit			
Operating margin			
Inventory days			
Receivables days			
Payables days			
Length of operating cycle			

Questions

1. Did GymFit perform well in 2018?
2. Why had revenue increased in 2018?
3. Comment on the increase in costs between 2017 and 18.
4. Had the working capital position worsened or improved? Explain.
5. Comment on GymFit's financial gearing.
6. Comment on GymFit's cash flow.
7. Discuss whether the 2019 budget is realistic.

6 Industry analysis and research

The relevance of industry research

There is little credit in the exam for real world comments and, at the operational level, the idea of the pre-seen is that you will have everything you need to know. If you know this inside out and have the technical knowledge at your fingertips in the exam to apply to the task, then you are giving yourself the best chance of passing.

Furthermore, a review of examiner's comments reveals that it is much more important to ensure you have revised the technical content from P1 and F1, than it is to do extensive background research.

Given the above, you could question whether any industry research is worthwhile. The purpose of doing at least some research is as follows:

- To help you develop a better understanding of the problems (and opportunities) facing companies in this industry and so prioritise issues.
- To give you greater reassurance that you understand the industry and haven't missed anything important in the pre-seen.
- By considering the strategies followed by real world companies and whether they could be adopted by the company in the pre-seen will help you analyse possible exam scenarios.
- This should mean that you will be able to understand, analyse and answer exam tasks more quickly and confidently.
- Hopefully, it will also stop you from making unrealistic comments in your answer on the day of the exam.

Ultimately it is a matter of achieving a balance between revising technical aspects and performing additional research that will help you put yourself in the position of the finance officer.

How to conduct industry research

As stated above, at operational level you will not be expected to undertake vast amounts of your own research into the industry. Having said that, such research will help you to more fully understand some of the issues affecting the organisation and to put yourself in the shoes of the person that you will need to be in the exam room. Therefore this section will give you some ideas and tools to help with this research.

Your research could incorporate any of the following sources of information:

- *Personal networks/experience*

  It may be that you have been a customer in the industry described. For the sample paper, many students would have had experience of being a gym member and so would appreciate some of the issues involved.

- *Using the Internet*

  This is the most convenient and commonly used method of researching the industry, but as noted above, try to target the information you're looking for in order to avoid wasting time. Generally, you will be looking for the following sorts of information:

  – Websites of firms similar to the one(s) in the pre-seen material. This can help you learn about the sorts of products and competitive strategies they follow.
  – Articles on the industry in journals and newspapers. These will keep you up to date on developments.

Illustration 2 – GymFit: Real world websites

Relevant websites for the gym industry include the following:

Industry in general:

https://www.theguardian.com/lifeandstyle/shortcuts/2017/may/08/the-budget-gym-boom-how-low-cost-clubs-are-driving-up-membership - looks at the rise of low cost gyms

https://www.moneysavingexpert.com/deals/cheap-gym-membership - gives idea of promotional activities used by gyms

Budget gym operators:

https://www.puregym.com/

http://www.fitness4less.co.uk/

7 Ethical analysis

Before the exam, you should take some time to remind yourself of CIMA's Guidelines on ethical conduct. Although these are useful, you must remember that the ethical issues in the exam are not necessarily ethical issues facing the management accountant, but more issues facing the business as a whole.

Ethical issues could this relate to any of the following areas:

- corporate social responsibility
- personal ethical behaviour of individuals in the case
- business ethics.

Illustration 3 – GymFit: Real world ethical issues

Online research into gyms quickly reveals ethical (and legal) issues related to onerous membership contracts. For example,

http://www.independent.co.uk/news/business/news/gym-group-may-have-legal-questions-to-answer-over-contracts-says-gig-economy-law-firm-that-a8036346.html

8 Position audit

Once you've analysed all of the above you're ready to carry out a position audit.

CIMA defines a position audit as:

Part of the planning process which examines the current state of the entity in respect of:

- resources of tangible and intangible assets and finance,
- products brands and markets,
- operating systems such as production and distribution,

- internal organisation,
- current results,
- returns to stockholders.

What you should be attempting to do is stand back so you can appreciate the bigger picture of the organisation. You can do this by considering four main headings – Strengths, Weaknesses, Opportunities and Threats. This is usually referred to as a SWOT analysis.

In general terms, threats and opportunities (and even weaknesses) can help you see where the scenario for the business might go and hence what the scenarios in the cases might be and therefore likely tasks.

More specifically, within your SWOT analysis you should look for:

- Threats homing in upon weaknesses – the potential for failure.
- Threats linked to strengths – should be able to defend against it but remember competencies slip.
- Opportunities linked to a strength – areas they should be able to exploit.
- Opportunities linked to weaknesses – areas where they could exploit in the future if they can change.

Exercise 3 – GymFit: SWOT analysis
Perform a SWOT analysis for GymFit.

9 Main issues and précis

In addition to preparing a SWOT analysis, it is useful to prepare a two-three page summary of your analysis. Try not to simply repeat information from the pre-seen but add value by including your thoughts on the analysis you've performed.

Once you've prepared your summary you are finally able to consider the key issues facing the organisation. Your conclusion on the main issues arising from the pre-seen will direct your focus and aid your understanding of issues in the exam.

Once you've got a list of the main issues, give yourself more time to think. Spend some time thinking about the case study, as much as you can. You don't have to be sitting at a desk or table to do this. You can think about the case study when you travel to work or in any spare time that you have for thinking.

- When new ideas come to you, jot them down.
- If you think of a new approach to financial analysis, carry out any calculations you think might be useful.

Remember, all of the above preparatory work enables you to feel as if you really are a management accountant working for this organisation. Without the prep, you're unlikely to be convincing in this role.

Illustration 4 – GymFit: Summary

The pre-seen information concerns a company called GymFit that offers low-cost gym membership in the country of Celtland.

Business model

GymFit offers low-cost, no-frills gym membership with no contracts. Despite having low fees, the company provides high quality gym equipment. The 'no-frills' aspect is that they do not provide swimming pools, saunas, restaurants or bars.

Key to low fees is keeping costs low (e.g. through competitive tendering when fitting out new gyms), outsourcing non-core aspects such as security and the use of technology to reduce staffing needs. Each gym typically has two employees – a manager and an assistant manager. A key aspect of staffing is the use of freelance fitness instructors on zero-hour contracts.

Growth has involved a mixture of organic growth and acquisition.

This strategy has been successful to date and the company is now the second largest low-cost gym in Celtland with 102 gyms and turnover in excess of C£73 million.

Competition

There are four major players in the low-cost sector in Celtland. The largest, Gym4All has grown primarily by acquisitions but the main threat comes from Fit4Life, who offers lifelong membership and has developed specialist fitness apps to enhance the customer experience.

Given the above, customer retention is now seen as a critical success factor in the industry.

Financial performance

Revenue grew by 24% from 2016 to 2017, resulting in an increase of 31% in operating profit. This also increased operating margins from 11.1% to 11.7%.

The overall level of investment in non-current assets grew substantially (55%), reflecting aggressive growth plans by the Board.

In terms of working capital and liquidity, cash fell by C$3.5 million and borrowing increased by C$24, reflecting the fact that considerable finance was needed to fund expansion and that, even with the additional debt, the company had a net cash outflow of C$3.5m. It is questionable how future growth will be financed.

Inventory days and receivables increased significantly, indicating that the company may be struggling to cope with the high growth experienced.

Future prospects

The market is expected to continue to grow, fuelled by low penetration rates compared to other European countries, government initiatives such as 'GetupGo' and technological developments.

It is vital that GymFit capitalises on these developments and does not get left behind.

Stated strategy

GymFit wants to continue to grow through a mixture of new gyms and acquisition.

In addition it wants to improve operating efficiency through economies of scale, outsourcing and the use of data and technology.

Finally, it wants to improve member satisfaction, linked primarily to having knowledgeable, well-trained staff.

Budgeting

Budgets are prepared on an annual basis GymFit adopts a participative approach to price setting, which should give better ownership of budgets but may result in budgetary 'slack' and 'padding', especially as gym managers have a bonus system linked to gym performance.

Budgeted sales for 2018 give an increase in revenue of 26% over 2017, which is higher growth than achieved last year, despite opening fewer new gyms. Overall the budget looks overly optimistic.

10 Summary

You should now understand what you need to do in order to familiarise yourself with the pre-seen sufficiently.

Test your understanding answers

Exercise 1 – GymFit: P1 topic analysis

1 Discuss which costs are fixed and which variable.

Costs that vary with the number of customers/members are likely to be

- An element of energy costs – e.g. heating water for showers
- An element of water costs if charged for usage
- An element of cleaning costs, although this may be totally fixed within the cleaning contract
- An element of the cost of providing free fitness classes
- An element of the maintenance cost of equipment.

Costs that vary with the number of gyms

- Most gym operating costs such as lighting, the fixed element of water bills, aspects of cleaning costs, etc
- Gym lease costs
- Gym staff costs.

All other costs, such as head office rent, will be fixed.

2 Discuss how useful overhead absorption is to GymFit in terms of (a) splitting costs between gyms and (b) splitting costs within gyms.

It may be that head office costs are split between gyms (p18) for performance evaluation purposes but it is unclear whether they actually do this and, if so, how. In any case, unless such costs are directly attributable to the gym's existence, then they should not be included when assessing the gym. Similarly, unless the costs are in some way controllable by the gym manager, then they should not be included for their performance appraisal. Either way, it is unlikely that splitting costs between gyms is very useful.

There is also no indication that they do any overhead absorption within gyms and, again, it is probably of little use to them:

- Inventory valuation – they are a service provider rather than a manufacturer, so don't have to determine the full cost (including overheads) of goods for inventory purposes.
- Pricing – they only have one basic revenue stream (membership) so there is no need to split costs between different sources within gyms in order to help price them – e.g. fees for trainers are paid directly to trainers.
- There is no indication that the gyms are broken down into different cost centres as the no-frills concept means that the usual cost centres of a restaurant, bars, pool, etc, do not exist.

The only exception to the above could be a need to apportion costs to classes in order to determine how much to charge for them, but classes only account for 3% of total revenue (p17).

3 How useful do you think ABC would be to GymFit?

The main benefit of ABC is that it gives a more useful split of costs between products/cost centres. For the reasons given above in the answer to Q2, not very.

4 Discuss whether an incremental or ZBB approach would be most suitable for GymFit.

GymFit currently does incremental budgeting.

Incremental budgeting is generally seen to be appropriate when there is no change in product range – this is true for GymFit.

Incremental budgeting is also useful where there is no change in customers or target markets. This is less true as 31 new gyms were opened in 2018 with plans for an additional 14 in 2019 (p19). Every time there is a new gym, then it could be argued that a ZBB would be more appropriate.

Furthermore, GymFit has grown by acquisition. Again ZBB will be more useful here as GymFit will want to make changes to gyms acquired and may not be able to trust previous budgets.

5 Identify four variances of use for GymFit.

Sales mix variances – GymFiT charges lower fees to students (p17) so management would want to see how the mix of customers varies from budget.

Lease cost expenditure variances – A key element of growth is finding suitable new premises, many of which are leased. Lease costs are the second largest cost category after operating costs (p18) so it is vital that management can see if leases on new gyms are more expensive than expected.

Cost expenditure variances for out-sourced operations such as cleaning and security – The company strategy (p11) includes a need to reduce costs. These cost variances could indicate the extent to which outsourcing is delivering such reductions.

Gym operating cost expenditure and efficiency variances – Operating costs are the largest category of cost (p14) and , as stated above, the company is looking to improve efficiency.

Exercise 2 – GymFit: Ratio Analysis

Complete the following table and answer the questions below.

Ratio	*2019 (budget)*	*2018*	*2019*
Growth in revenue	26.4%	24.2%	
Growth in gym operating costs	17.3%	24.4%	
Growth in lease costs	22.8%	28.1%	
Growth in staff costs	11.9%	32.8%	
Growth in head office costs	12.9%	24.6%	
Growth in depreciation	26.8%	13.5%	
Growth in operating profit	84.2%	30.9%	
Operating margin	17.1%	11.7%	11.1%
Inventory days		3	3
Receivables days		36	29
Payables days		311	302
Length of operating cycle		–	–

Notes:

1 Inventory days have been calculated using gym operating costs. Ideally we would have the purchases figure for vending machine items. Bottled water, etc, so the figure calculated will be too low.

2 Payables days have been calculated using gym operating costs + lease costs + head office costs. However, the figures that result seem extremely high, suggesting that 'trade creditors' includes more than what is owed to external cleaning, maintenance and security suppliers and utilities providers. It probably includes amounts owed for new gym equipment, for example.

3 Given the above, the resulting operating cycle figures are not likely to be very meaningful.

Questions

1 Did GymFit perform well in 2018?

Positives

- Overall profit for the year up 29% from C$4.9m to C$6.4m
- Revenue up 24%
- Operating profit up 31%
- Operating margins up from 11.1% to 11.7%
- Significant investment in new gyms and equipment

Negatives

- Many costs went up by more than revenue
- Significant drop in cash balances
- Significant increase in long term borrowing
- Significant increase in both receivables and payables

2 Why had turnover increased in 2018?

- Total number of gyms went up 44% from 71 to 102
- Average number of members went up 23% from 344k to 423k
- Average revenue per member went up 1% from $171 to $173
- This will be the result of a strong member proposition, a commitment to opening new gyms and successful advertising
- Note – the average membership per gym fell from 4,846 to 4,143

3 Comment on the increase in costs between 2017 and 18.

As discussed above, many costs are likely to be fixed per gym rather than fixed for the business as a whole. Therefore, each time a new gym is opened we should expect these costs to increase (gym operating, lease, staff etc). From 2017 to 2018 the number of gyms increased by 44%, so we would expect a 44% increase in these costs. However, this was not the case:

- Gym operating costs increased 24%
- Lease costs increased 28%
- Staff costs increased 33%

This either indicates that new gyms are becoming less expensive to open and operate, or that GymFit has gained costs efficiencies in existing gyms in line with their stated intent of cost cutting in their strategy.

4 Had the working capital position worsened or improved? Explain.

Worsened

- Cash fallen by C$3.5m
- Receivables increased by C$2.6m
- Receivables days increased from 29 to 36 days

5 Comment on GymFit's financial gearing.

Increased significantly

- Long term borrowings up by C$23.7m
- This means higher gearing risk for shareholders

6 Comment on GymFit's cash flow.

Positives

- Cash generated by operations increased to over C$26.4m
- Able to invest C$49.3m in new tangible assets
- Able to pay C$1m dividend, a significant increase on 2017

Negatives

- Net cash outflow – spent C$3.5m more cash than raised/generated
- Had to increase debt and reduce cash balances to finance growth – is this sustainable?

7 Discuss whether the 2019 budget is realistic.

Aspects that seem realistic/reasonable

- Average sales revenue per member only increasing by 1%
- Only opening 14 new gyms in 2019 compared with 31 in 2018
- 14 new gyms (14%) are planned to be opened in 2019, so would expect many gym related costs to increase by this amount. Gym lease costs are expected to increase by 23% possibly implying that new leases are more expensive. Similarly operating costs are expected to increase by 17%, which, if anything might be seen to overly pessimistic rather than optimistic.

Aspects that seem to be over-optimistic

- 26% growth in revenue compared to 24% in 2018 seems high, especially given that we are only opening 14 new gyms vs 31. The growth must therefore be heavily dependent on retaining existing customers and winning new ones for existing gyms as well as looking for growth by opening gyms. This is seen in the average gym membership increasing from 4,143 to 4,500 but it is unclear how such confidence can be justified, particularly as average gym membership fell from 2017 to 2018.
- As stated above, would expect many gym related costs to increase by 14% but staff costs are expected to increase by 12%. While this could indicate over-optimism, it is more likely to be due to planned reductions in staff costs and/or the fact that some gyms would not have been open for the full year.
- Operating margin increasing from 11.7% to 17.1%
- Operating profit increasing by 84%

Overall, the budget looks optimistic/challenging.

Exercise 3 – GymFit: SWOT analysis

Strengths

- Gyms are located with excellent access to public transport links and/or good parking
- Wide range of high-specification, eco-friendly gym equipment (70% use no electricity)
- 24/7 gym operating hours – attractive to members
- No-contract membership with option of pay-as-you-use basis
- Historic growth is forecast to continue
- Simple functional structure which suits the company's size/lack of diversification
- 2nd largest operator of low-cost gyms in Celtland
- One of the pioneers of the low-cost gym model
- Listed on the Celtland stock exchange
- Some free classes, free induction session
- Gyms have showers, changing areas, lockers and vending machines
- Advanced technology
- Members can join, manage their accounts, view class timetables and book classes online
- Simple online joining process
- Efficient staffing model, no need for receptionists (PIN entry system), in-gym sales, etc
- Fitness instructors are trained experts
- Experienced, highly enthusiastic senior management team (e.g. in developing and managing properties)
- Knowledgeable, well-trained staff
- 'Can do' culture throughout the organisation
- Gym managers have bonus targets linked to gym performance
- Competitive remuneration for employees, including pension scheme and opportunity to take part in a share incentive plan
- Recognise the need for continued investment in marketing
- Customer database used to communicate with members
- CCTV, panic buttons in the gyms
- Well-used website e.g. details of weekly classes
- Regular marketing campaigns ensure high brand awareness
- Healthy financials – revenue, profit increased.

Weaknesses

- No wet facilities e.g. saunas/pools
- No cafes/bars
- Fitness instructors may be dissatisfied with zero hours contracts
- Extensive use of IT leads to associated risks of system failure, data security and privacy. This can impact the company's reputation.
- High levels of receivables
- May be trying to grow too quickly as evidenced by a large fall in cash and increase in debt to finance new gyms

Opportunities

- Develop app-based technology, similar to Fit4Life to provide tailored personal fitness advice
- Use VR and VOD to improve member retention
- Collaboration to create connectivity between fitness equipment, devices, wearable technology and healthcare apps
- Harness data from such collaborations/ connected gym equipment to help understand customers' preferences, adapt classes and facilities etc.
- Work with the Celtland government to encourage under-represented groups to exercise more
- Organic growth in Celtland – increase number of gyms each year
- Merger with/acquisition of budget gym competitors
- Expand outside Celtland
- Further use of a celebrity to promote brand (Sir Chris Hoy is an 'ambassador' for PureGym in the UK)
- Offer corporate membership to businesses
- Open boutique gyms (under a different brand?)
- Ladies only facilities?
- Link with sportswear company to promote product through GymFit website/premises
- Improve operating efficiency through economies of scale, use of data and technology and managing its cost base
- Pursue innovative low cost ways to differentiate from competitors

Threats

- Increased competitive pressure from rivals – especially FiT4Life and Gym4ALL.
- Gym membership is discretionary (non-essential) spending, so overall demand may be heavily influenced by the state of the economy.
- Failure of IT systems – membership enrolment, account management, payment processing, gym access and customer communications are all dependant on the successful operation of information systems.
- Breach of data security – unauthorised access or loss of information could lead to legal claims, disruption to operations and reputational damage.
- The loss of key staff, both at gym level and managerial level could lead to a lack of experienced and motivated staff which would impact on the customer experience and on other central business functions.
- Failure to provide customers with a high quality, affordable and accessible service would result in a decrease in customer numbers and revenue and would also damage GymFit's reputation.
- Health and safety – serious injury to a member whilst no staff present results in litigation/loss of reputation.
- GymFit outsources a number of our non-core business processes, such as security, maintenance and cleaning. Failure to meet the high standards expected of these outsourced operators would impact on the customer experience and potentially their overall safety in the gyms. This could result in a reduction in customer numbers and a loss of revenue.

Note: you could then use the above analysis to envisage possible exam storylines, scenarios and tasks.

For example, taking the threat of competitive rivalry, one scenario could be that some gyms are underperforming, so the Board are considering whether to close them.

An exam style task could then be to discuss how you assess the performance of gyms anyway?

- What KPIs would you focus on and
- What sources of information would you look at?

Alternatively, how would you make the decision whether to close a particular gym?

- Hopefully you recognise that such a decision should be made by reference to relevant costing principles, so any head office recharges should be excluded, for example.
- Obviously the impact on sales is a relevant cash flow but how would you estimate this? Do you think customers would be lost or would some use a nearby gym instead?

This analysis can then prompt you to revise the relevant technical areas if you are unsure of any.

Chapter

4

Exam day techniques

Chapter learning objectives

- To develop a carefully planned and thought through strategy to cope with the three hours of exam time.

1 Exam day strategy

Once you have studied the pre-seen, learnt the three subject syllabi thoroughly and practised lots of exercises and mocks, you should be well prepared for the exam.

However, it is still important to have a carefully planned and thought through strategy to cope with those three hours of exam time.

This chapter takes you through some of the key skills to master to ensure all your careful preparation does not go to waste.

2 Importance of time management

Someone once referred to case study exams as "the race against time" and it's difficult to imagine a more accurate description. Being able to do what the examiner is wanting is only half of the battle; being able to deliver it in the time available is another matter altogether. This is even more important than in previous exams you may have faced because each section in the real exam is now timed and that once that time is up you will be moved on. Case study is not like a traditional exam where you can go back to a question if you get extra inspiration or feel you have some time left over. You have to complete each task within the time stated.

For this reason, time management is a key skill required to pass the Case Study Examination.

Successful time management requires two things:

- A tailored time plan – one that plays to your personal strengths and weaknesses; and
- Discipline in order to stick to it!

Time robbers

There are a number of ways in which time can be wasted or not used effectively in the Case Study Examination. An awareness of these will help to ensure you don't waste time in your exam.

Inactive reading

The first part of each task must be spent actively reading, processing the information and considering the impact on the organisation, how the issues link together and what could be done to resolve them. You may not have time to have a second detailed read and so these thoughts must be captured first time around.

Too much time spent on presentation

You will be writing your answer in software with some similarities to Microsoft Word however the only functions available are

- Cut
- Copy
- Paste
- Undo
- Redo
- Bold
- Italic
- Underline

While there are no specific marks for presentation, candidates need to be mindful that the better presented the answer is in terms of headings, sub-headings and so on, the easier the job will be for the marker. So, presentation is important, but not to the point of wasting time using fancy formatting for its own sake.

Being a perfectionist

Students can often spend such a long time pondering about what to write that over the course of a 3 hour exam, over half of it is spent staring into space.

As you are sitting a computer exam you not only spend time pondering, but also have the ability to delete so can change your mind several times before settling on the right word combinations. Just focus on getting your points down and don't worry about whether they could have been phrased better.

Although do bear in mind that the marker has to be able to read and understand your answer, so do write in clear English.

Too much detail on earlier parts of the requirement

As we've said earlier, not finishing answers is a key reason for failing the Case Study Examination. One of the main reasons why students fail to finish a section is a lack of discipline when writing about an issue. They feel they have to get all of their points down rather than selecting the better points and moving on. If a task requires you to discuss three different areas it is vital that you cover all parts adequately.

Too much correction

Often students can reread paragraphs three or more times before they move on to writing the next part of their answer. Instead, try to leave the read through until the final few minutes of the task and try to correct as many obvious errors as possible. The CIMA marker will be reading and marking your script on screen and it is harder to read and understand the points you are making if there are many typing errors.

3 Assimilation of information

One of the most challenging things to deal with in a case study examination is the volume of information which you have available. This is particularly difficult when you have both pre-seen and unseen information to manage and draw from. It is important that you refer to relevant pre-seen information in your responses as well as incorporating the unseen information.

The key things that you need to do to assimilate the information effectively and efficiently are:

- Read about and identify each event
- Consider what the issue is
- Evaluate the impact of the issue. Who is affected, by how much are they affected and what would happen if no action was taken?
- Determine the most useful and relevant exhibits from the pre-seen

Capturing all of your thoughts and ideas at this stage can be difficult and time consuming.

The following section on planning your answer will show you how to do this effectively without wasting time or effort.

4 Planning your answers

In section 2 of this chapter we saw how important it was to manage your time in the exam to ensure you're able to complete all of the necessary stages in the preparation of your answer.

One important aspect of your exam is planning your answer. Sitting the Case Study Exam is not as straight forward as turning up, reading the requirements, and then writing your answer.

If you do attempt to write without any form of content plan, your response will lack direction and a logical flow, it won't fully address the key points required and any recommendations will lack solid justification. It is for this reason that time should be specifically allocated to planning the content of your answers.

Given the preparation you've done before the exam, reading the unseen can often feel like a firework display is happening in your brain; each new piece of information you read about triggers a series of thoughts and ideas.

The planning process must therefore begin as soon as you start reading the unseen information. Every second counts within the case study exam and so it's important to use all of your time effectively by capturing the thoughts as they come to you.

To make sure the time spent now is of use to you throughout the task, you will need consider carefully how best to document your thoughts. You will be provided with an on-screen notes page ('scratchpad') as well as a wipe-clean laminated notes page and marker pen. Any method you adopt to plan must be concise whilst still allowing you to capture all of your ideas and see the bigger picture in terms of how the issues interrelate with one another.

Furthermore, the method must suit you! Everyone is different and what might work for one person could be a disaster for another. For example, some people prefer to work with lists, others with mind maps.

Most people find that some form of central planning sheet (to enable the bigger picture to be seen) is best. How you prepare the central planning sheet is a matter of personal preference and we've given illustrations of two different methods below. Practise each one to find out which you prefer and then tailor it further to settle on something that works for you.

Method 1 – planning within the answer box (highly recommended!)

This process is ideally suited to people who prefer lists and structure and is most easily done within the answer box using the exam software.

Step 1:

- Begin by reading everything in the task exhibit.
- Ensure you have identified all aspects of the requirements, paying particular attention to the verbs used, and then write the requirements out as headings and sub headings within your answer box.

  For example, if asked to evaluate a proposal, then you would want arguments for and against, so these could be added as sub-headings at the very start.
- Brainstorm how you would answer the task, bringing in technical knowledge.

  For example, if deciding whether to close down a gym, you could jot down "use relevant costing".

Step 2:

- Read everything in the wider exhibit and associated reference materials, making notes under the relevant task headings and sub-headings.

  For example, if asked to explain why a sales mix variance is adverse, then you may find that the examiner has already given you two specific operational issues within the exam that can be addressed in your answer.

Step 3:

- Review your notes and headings to identify any linkages to information provided in the pre-seen and note under the relevant heading.

Step 4:

- Convert your rough notes into a finished answer.
- This will involve a mixture of deleting some points, developing others and in some cases, generating new ideas under headings that are lacking. The beauty of the word processor is that things can be deleted or expanded upon very easily.

Method 2 – The extended mind map

This process is ideally suited to those who prefer pictures and diagrams to trigger their thoughts.

Step 1:

- Read the unseen information and identify the key tasks required.
- As you read, write each task in a "bubble" on your wipe-clean laminated notes page.

Step 2:

- Keep adding each new part of the task you identify to your sheet. At the end you should have a page with a number of bubbles dotted about.

Step 3:

- Review your bubbles to identify any linkages to the trigger information or pre-seen exhibits. Add any relevant information to your planning sheet in a bubble attached to the appropriate part of the task.

Step 4:

- Review the task bubbles and brainstorm any relevant knowledge which you can use in responding to the task. Add this to bubbles attached to the task.

With detailed information provided in the exam it would be very likely that your brain would think of a wide range of ideas which, if left uncaptured, would be forgotten as quickly as you thought of them.

This is where mind mapping comes in handy. You would not of course need to draw one as neat as this and feel free to add colours or graphics to help your thought processes.

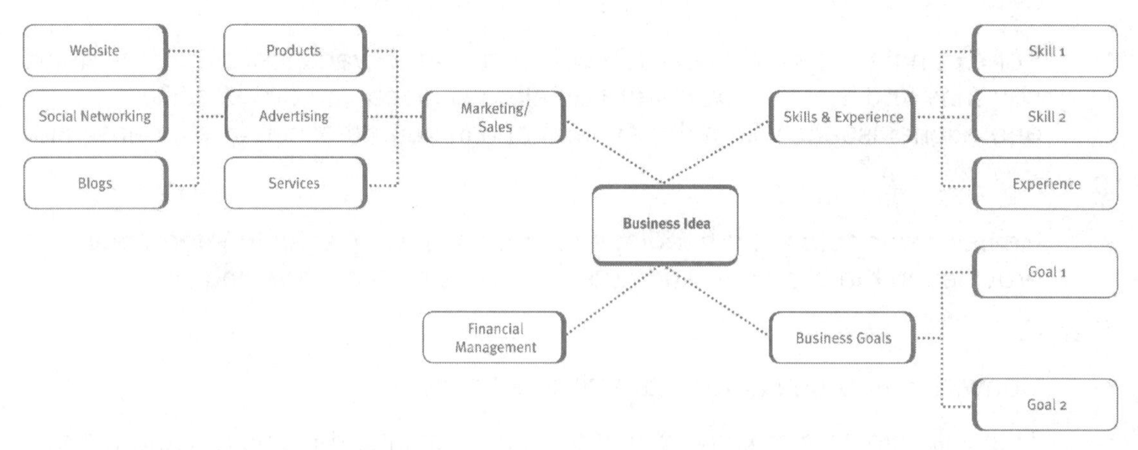

Have a go!

Some additional guidance

(1) This is perhaps the hardest part of the exam; as soon as you tell your brain it needs to come up with some ideas, it very often refuses to cooperate! Practice makes perfect so working through the exercises in Chapter 6 and attempting mock exams will really help your brain to deliver ideas when you need it to.

(2) Don't simply view technical models as something that must be included to tick a box if explicitly requested in the requirements. Instead use the models to help analyse the issues, suggest solutions or generate ideas. They were developed to be useful!

(3) If you start looking at one of the task requirements and are stuck for ideas, don't waste time staring into space. Move on to the next part of the task (but not onto the next task itself as you won't be able to return) and you'll find the creative juices soon start flowing.

5 Presentation and communication

The Case Study examinations aim to test a wide range of skills and you may be required to communicate in many different ways to various different audiences, each with different information needs. In the exam, you will be given a blank answer box with no headings, so you need to ensure that you include the basic presentation elements required as shown below, both in terms of headings and the use of tables. However, rather than worrying about different formats in excessive detail, the key is to communicate clearly so that the marker can understand what you are saying.

An email

A requirement to draft an email may be in response to a specific question raised by an individual within the unseen information, or perhaps even in response to an email that is presented within the unseen.

Illustration 1 – Email

In the real world, a typical layout for an email would be:

Email

To: **Finance Director**
From: **Finance Officer**
Date: **Today**
Subject: **RE ....**

Content...

However, in the exam, there are no marks for such headings, so it is more important to focus on the content of your response. If you are asked to write an email, then you should write short sentences (the number of which may well be specified in the requirement) that directly address the requirements.

A report

In the exam a commonly requested format is a report. Alternatively, you might also be asked for sections of a report and not the whole thing.

Illustration 2 – Report

In the real world, a typical layout for a report would be:

> **Title: A report on the implementation of Total Quality Management**
>
> Introduction
>
> Brief background/context for requirement
>
> Main report content broken down using further sub-headings
>
> Conclusion
>
> Key conclusions and recommendations

However, with a report, an introduction and conclusion/ recommendation is probably not advised as this could just waste time. The key thing always is that you answer all aspects of the question clearly and logically with headings. At the operational level you don't need to waste time with formal report structures.

Slide presentation

If a slide presentation is called for, your answer need only consist of the bullet points that would appear on each slide. Read the requirement carefully as guidance will be given on how many slides to prepare and the maximum number of bullets on each slide. Most likely this would be 2 slides, with a maximum of 5 bullets on each slide (or you may just be asked for 10 bullet points in total).

Illustration 3 – Slides

A typical layout for the presentation of slides would be:

> Slide 1
>
> Title
>
> - XX
> - XX
> - XX
> - XX
> - XX

You will not need to prepare speaker notes.

As with emails, do not worry too much about presentation – you do not need to layout your answer as a slide (e.g. you don't need to draw a box). Simply using the heading "Slide 1" and noting the bullets will be sufficient.

A letter

Exactly the same as for an email but laid out in letter format. That means you should include a space for an address, a date, state to whom the letter is addressed and a summary of what the letter is regarding.

The letter should be signed off in the normal business fashion, unless you are told otherwise.

Illustration 4 – Letter

A typical layout for the presentation of a letter should be:

Address

Date

Dear X

Title

Content of your answer to the requirement using short sentences or bullet points as instructed.

Yours sincerely,

A Management Accountant

6 Writing style

Introduction

Writing style is something that develops over time. It is influenced by your education and experiences. To some it comes easily, they enjoy words – but remember, you are not looking to win any prizes in literature. It's about putting facts, ideas and opinions in a clear, concise, logical fashion. Some students get very worried about their writing styles. As a general rule you should try to write as you would talk.

Logical flow

A typical point starts with a statement of fact, either given in the case or derived from analysis – 'what?'

This can then be followed by an interpretation – 'so what?'

This can then lead to an implication – 'now what?', or 'what next?'

For example:

(1) What? – The net relevant cash flow for the project is positive.

(2) So what? – Suggesting we should go ahead with the project.

(3) Now what? – Arrange board meeting to discuss strategic implications.

A similar structure can be obtained using the Socratic approach – what, why, how?

- So what?
- Why should we use it?
- How does it work?

Who is reading the response?

Failure to pitch the level correctly will inevitably result in failure to communicate your ideas effectively, since the reader will either be swamped with complexity, or bored with blandness. The recipients of the report should also dictate the level of tact required.

Tactless	*Tactful*
The directors have clearly made errors	There were other options open to the board that, with hindsight, would have been beneficial
The marketing director is responsible for this disastrous change in strategy	The board should consider where this went wrong? It would appear that the marketing department may have made some mistakes

Making your response easy to read

To ensure that the marker finds your answers accessible and easy to read, you should try to do the following:

- Use short words, short sentences, short phrases and short paragraphs. If you are adopting the 'what, so what, what now' approach, then you could have a paragraph containing three sentences. The next point can then be a new paragraph, also containing three sentences.
- Use the correct words to explain what you mean! For example, students often get confused between:
  - recommendations (what they should do – actions) and options (what they could do – possibilities).
  - objectives (what we want to achieve – the destination) and strategies (how we intend to achieve them – the route).
- Avoid using vague generalisations. Too often students will comment that an issue will "impact" on profit rather than being specific about whether profit will increase or decrease (or even better still, trying to quantify by how much). Other common phrases which are too vague include "communicate with" (you need to say specifically what should be discussed) and "look in to" (how should an option be looked in to?)
- Avoid unnecessary repetition. This can either be of information from the exam paper (pre-seen or unseen), of discussion within the report (in particular between what is said in one section and another) or can relate to the words that you use.

Some students fall into the trap of thinking that writing a professional report means simply writing more words to say the same thing! The issue is quality not quantity.

For example, compare the following:

- 'I, myself, personally' OR 'I'
- 'export overseas' OR 'export'
- 'green in colour' OR 'green'

- Watch your spelling – this may seem a small and unimportant point, but poor spelling makes a document seem sloppy and may convey an impression that the content is as loose as the general appearance! Poor spelling interrupts the marker as they read your report, so there is the danger that they conclude that it did not have a logical flow.
- Recommendations – be decisive – do not 'sit on the fence' or ask for more information. Make a clear recommendation based on the information you have and justify why you have chosen that course of action.

Exercise 1

This exercise will get you thinking about what makes a well written script. The technical content of the requirement is not relevant – we are focusing on writing style and flow.

The risk committee of X plc met to discuss a report by its risk manager. The report focused on a number of risks that applied to a chemicals factory recently acquired in another country.

The Risk Manager explained that the new risks related to the security of the new factory in respect of burglary, the supply of one of the key raw materials that experienced fluctuations in world supply and also an environmental risk.

The environmental risk was with respect to the possibility of poisonous emissions from the new factory. Vincent Ng, the CEO who chaired the risk committee, said that the factory was important to him for two reasons. First, he said it was strategically important to the company. Second, it was important because his own bonuses depended upon it. He said that he knew from the report what the risks were, but that he wanted somebody to explain to him what strategies they could use to manage the risks. 'I don't get any bonus at all until we reach a high level of output from the factory,' he said. 'So I don't care what the risks are, we will have to manage them.'

You have been asked to outline strategies that can be used to manage risk and identify, with reasons, an appropriate strategy for each of the three risks facing the new venture.

Requirement:

Consider these two responses and note the positive and negative aspects of each.

Answer 1

Introduction

Risk can be managed using the following strategies.

- **Transfer** the risk to another organisation for example by buying insurance. This is usually cost effective where the probability of the risk is low but the impact is potentially high.
- **Avoid** the risk altogether by withdrawing completely from the risky activity. This is done where the risk is high probability and high frequency and so it is too costly to reduce the risk sufficiently.
- **Reduce** the risk by implementing controls or by diversification.
- **Accept** the risk without taking any further steps to mitigate it. For this to be acceptable the frequency and the impact of the risk must place the risk within the risk appetite of the company.

Risk of burglary

It is usual to insure against burglary an example of the transfer strategy. This is because of the high impact of burglary.

It is also usual to put safeguards in place such as security guards because of the probability of burglary. This is an example of risk reduction.

Raw materials supply fluctuation

Depending on the cost benefit analysis the company could chose to transfer the risk by entering into forward contracts to purchase the materials.

There will be a cost associated with this and it will lower but not remove the risk associated with supply and price fluctuations. They may choose to accept the risk as part of the operational risk associated with their industry.

Environmental risk

The company should take reasonable steps to reduce the chance poisonous emissions. It should use appropriate technology and controls to reduce the risk.

Risks cannot be completely eliminated so if the poisonous emissions could give rise to significant costs it should also purchase insurance and transfer the risk.

Answer 2

Risk is managed by this:

(1) Identify the risk. This is by brainstorming all the things that the risk can be.

(2) Risk assessment. We won't know this properly until afterwards.

(3) Risk Profiling. This is decided on consequences and impact.

(4) Risk quantification. This can be average loss or it can be largest loss.

(5) Risk consolidation which will depend on the risk appetite and diversification.

The risks at the factory are:

- The main risk at the factory is environmental risk. You can't do anything about this risk because global warming is because of everyone.
- The big risk is that the CEO is "I don't care what the risks are" this will need to have the risk awareness embedded in and the tone at the top.
- The other risk is that the CEO could manipulate the output levels to get his bonus. This needs to be looked at seriously because he is also on the risk committee and the remuneration committee and he is not independent and that should be a NED.

7 Summary

You should have an appreciation of some of the issues you may encounter in the exam and some possible techniques to overcome these.

Next steps:

(1) In the next two chapters we will present the unseen and guide you through the process of producing an answer. It is worth ensuring you can log on to the Pearson Vue site now and make sure you have registered for the practice case study exam. It is advisable to familiarise yourself with the software as much as possible.

(2) As you are about to embark on a full attempt at the "question tutorial" paper it is a good time to revisit previous chapters and ensure you are comfortable with all of the material so far before proceeding.

Test your understanding answers

Exercise 1

The first solution has several positive aspects:

- Brief introduction linking to requirement
- Overview of model with explanation and clear examples
- Specific points from scenario addressed
- Headings clearly signpost the answer
- Appropriate language

There are some areas which could be improved:

- Specific reference to the company name
- More explicit use of the information from the scenario

The second solution is not as strong as the first. Some of the main criticisms:

- Main options available are not clearly explained
- No attempt to introduce the answer
- Inappropriate language for a formal report/response
- Lack of tact regarding the CEO – the intended audience!!

As a piece of writing there is not much to say from a positive perspective except:

- Clear structure
- Writing is concise (but probably a bit too brief)

Chapter

5

Walkthrough of the 2019 Prototype exam – answering variant 1

Chapter learning objectives

- To gain experience trying to answer a case study exam.

1 Introduction

The aim of this chapter is to give you a chance to practise many of the techniques you have been shown in previous chapters of this study text.

This should help you to understand the various thought processes needed to complete the full three hour examination. It is important that you work through this chapter at a steady pace.

Don't rush on to the next stage until you have properly digested the information, followed the guidance labelled 'Stop and Think!' and made your own notes. This will give you more confidence than simply reading the model solutions. You should refer to the unseen produced in the previous chapter as you proceed through these exercises.

2 First screen

The opening screen of the exam shows you how many sub-tasks you have to deal with and how to allocate your time within tasks:

Section (task)	Time for section (minutes)	Number of answer screens	Number of sub-tasks	% time to spend on each sub-task
1	45	1	2	(a) 48% (b) 52%
2	45	1	2	(a) 52% (b) 48%
3	45	1	2	(a) 36% (b) 64%
4	45	1	2	(a) 60% (b) 40%

The exam software will prevent you from spending more than 45 minutes on task 4, say, but you need to ensure that this is split 27 minutes on sub-task (a) and 18 minutes on sub-task (b).

3 Task 1

Understanding the context

The first screen of task 1 reveals that GymFit has purchased Fit4Life's gym portfolio:

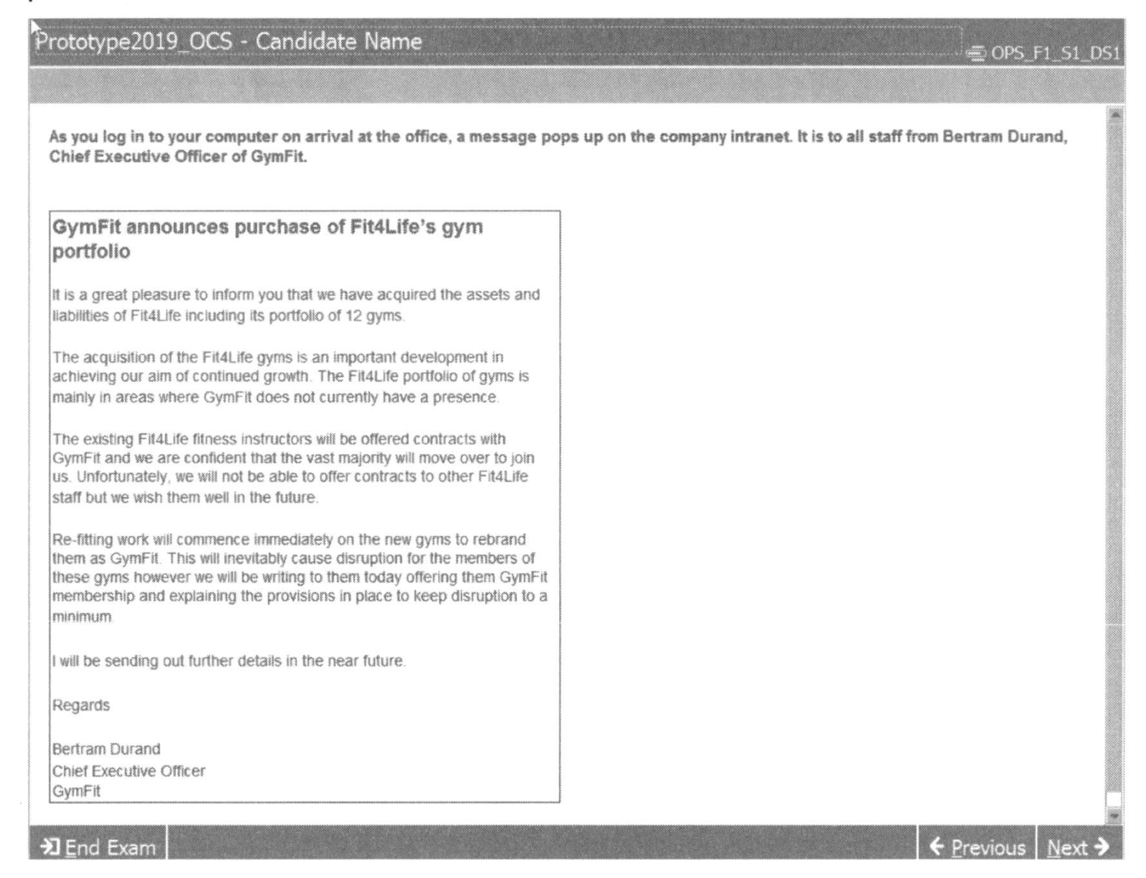

Prototype2019_OCS - Candidate Name

OPS_F1_S1_DS1

As you log in to your computer on arrival at the office, a message pops up on the company intranet. It is to all staff from Bertram Durand, Chief Executive Officer of GymFit.

GymFit announces purchase of Fit4Life's gym portfolio

It is a great pleasure to inform you that we have acquired the assets and liabilities of Fit4Life including its portfolio of 12 gyms.

The acquisition of the Fit4Life gyms is an important development in achieving our aim of continued growth. The Fit4Life portfolio of gyms is mainly in areas where GymFit does not currently have a presence.

The existing Fit4Life fitness instructors will be offered contracts with GymFit and we are confident that the vast majority will move over to join us. Unfortunately, we will not be able to offer contracts to other Fit4Life staff but we wish them well in the future.

Re-fitting work will commence immediately on the new gyms to rebrand them as GymFit. This will inevitably cause disruption for the members of these gyms however we will be writing to them today offering them GymFit membership and explaining the provisions in place to keep disruption to a minimum.

I will be sending out further details in the near future.

Regards

Bertram Durand
Chief Executive Officer
GymFit

End Exam | Previous | Next

Stop and think!

(1) Start thinking about the relevant information in the pre-seen. It's very important that your responses are applied to the scenario. For example, how much can you remember about Fit4Life? We were told in the pre-seen that

"The rising star in the Celtland market is Fit4Life which has ruthlessly marketed itself as a lifelong alternative to the other low-cost gyms. Fit4Life offers members a lifelong membership fee which will not increase provided the customer remains a member. Its rapid growth has also been driven by its use of specialised fitness apps which have been developed using data analytics. These apps provide members with tailored personal training advice and programmes which they can access at home"

(2) GymFit is acquiring the assets and liabilities, not buying the company – group accounting is not in the F1 syllabus.

(3) There could be integration issues relating such as rebranding but also HR issues (E1) relating to existing staff moving over to GymFit.

Answering the question set – understanding the requirements

The requirements (and further context) are given on the next screen:

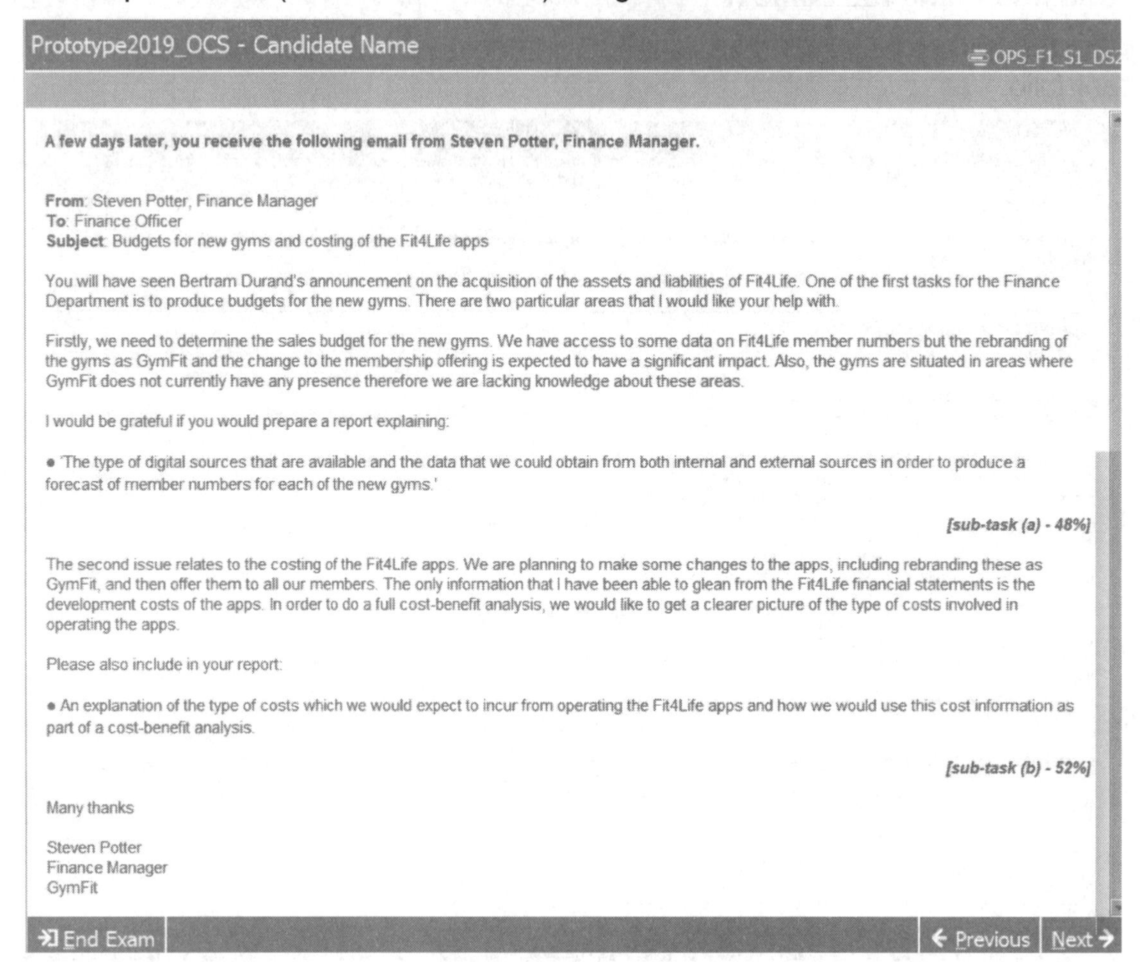

Prototype2019_OCS - Candidate Name

OPS_F1_S1_DS2

A few days later, you receive the following email from Steven Potter, Finance Manager.

From: Steven Potter, Finance Manager
To: Finance Officer
Subject: Budgets for new gyms and costing of the Fit4Life apps

You will have seen Bertram Durand's announcement on the acquisition of the assets and liabilities of Fit4Life. One of the first tasks for the Finance Department is to produce budgets for the new gyms. There are two particular areas that I would like your help with.

Firstly, we need to determine the sales budget for the new gyms. We have access to some data on Fit4Life member numbers but the rebranding of the gyms as GymFit and the change to the membership offering is expected to have a significant impact. Also, the gyms are situated in areas where GymFit does not currently have any presence therefore we are lacking knowledge about these areas.

I would be grateful if you would prepare a report explaining:

• 'The type of digital sources that are available and the data that we could obtain from both internal and external sources in order to produce a forecast of member numbers for each of the new gyms.'

[sub-task (a) - 48%]

The second issue relates to the costing of the Fit4Life apps. We are planning to make some changes to the apps, including rebranding these as GymFit, and then offer them to all our members. The only information that I have been able to glean from the Fit4Life financial statements is the development costs of the apps. In order to do a full cost-benefit analysis, we would like to get a clearer picture of the type of costs involved in operating the apps.

Please also include in your report:

• An explanation of the type of costs which we would expect to incur from operating the Fit4Life apps and how we would use this cost information as part of a cost-benefit analysis.

[sub-task (b) - 52%]

Many thanks

Steven Potter
Finance Manager
GymFit

End Exam | Previous | Next

It is vital that you understand the nature and scope of the requirements. Here you need to prepare a report which covers:

- "The type of digital sources that are available and the data that we could obtain from both internal and external sources in order to produce a forecast of member numbers for each of the new gyms"

  Make sure you answer the question set – we need to cover both **internal** and **external** sources but are only asked for forecasts for the **new** gyms (i.e. those previously owned by Fit4Life), not our existing gyms. Similarly we only want data that will specifically help us estimate membership **numbers,** not to forecast how much they typically spend, for example.

- "An explanation of the types of cost which we would expect to incur from operating the Fit4life apps and how we would use this information as part of a cost-benefit analysis."

  "To **explain**" is a higher level verb that "to list". You need to make clear further details about the costs – what is a 'digital' source, why this cost will arise and/or how it behaves and/or even try to quantify it.

  Separately you need to explain how each one would be used in CBA in the **context** of the decision to rebrand the apps.

Let's plan – Task 1(a)

If you prefer to plan within your answer box, then the above considerations will help you set up suitable headings and then start to populate them.

Alternatively, if you prefer to use your wipe clean whiteboard, then you could split your planning sheet into a grid to ensure all parts are covered:

Type of source	*Data GymFit could obtain*
External	
Internal	

Either way, you now need to brainstorm all the relevant points you can think of under the above headings, making sure you are bringing together your knowledge from the relevant syllabus as well as your analysis of the pre-seen information.

Let's think a bit more about these requirements by breaking them down into the component parts.

External sources – from your E1 studies you will know that secondary research can include looking at government reports on population and incomes, industry reports, websites and so on. The task does hint at looking at different "areas", so start with these.

Internal sources – we are told that we would have Fit4Life membership lists in order to email them and offer GymFit memberships but you could also think about existing GymFit data that could help as well, such as membership numbers for similar sized gyms in similar areas (e.g. near towns or business parks).

It is vital that each source has a corresponding comment on what information could be obtained and how this could help forecast membership numbers.

Task 1(b)

Again you could set up headings within your answer or use a planning sheet:

Type of cost	*Use within CBA*

From your P1 knowledge, you will be aware that digital products, such as apps, have a wide range of cost types, including IT support and infrastructure costs, and that the timing and frequency of costs will be difficult to estimate. Try to apply as many of your comments as possible to the fact we are talking about an app, rather than a manufacturer of baked beans!

As a rough rule of thumb you should spend about 15–20% of the time available for reading and planning. So for this section of the exam, where you are given 45 minutes, you should be spending approximately 7–8 minutes planning your answer before you complete the exercise below. This would leave you about 35 minutes to write your answer and a few minutes spare to check through what you have written.

Exercise 1

Prepare a response to the first task in the prototype exam GymFit.

4 Task 2

For task 2, the trigger and requirements are mixed together into one screen, together with reference material:

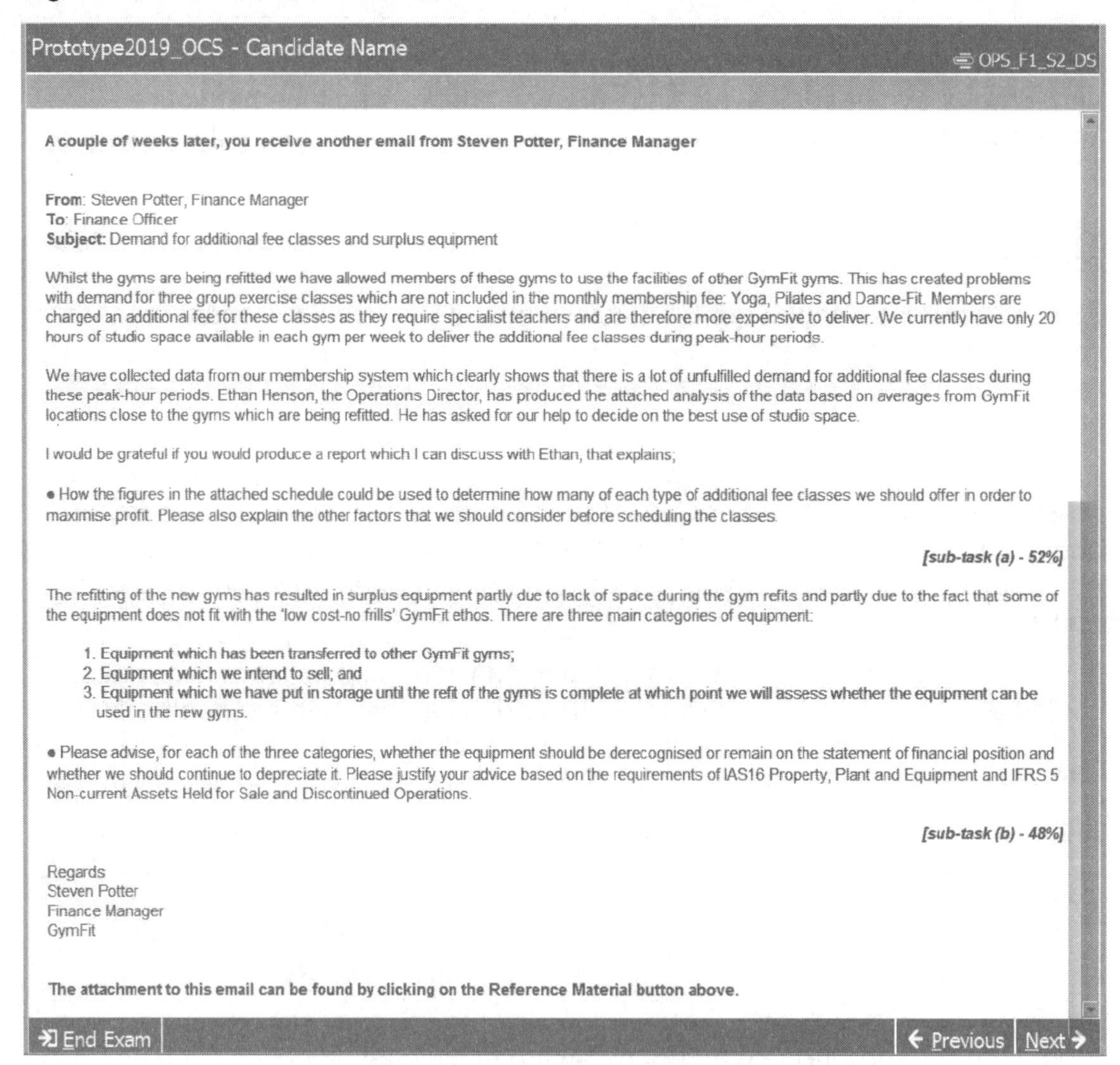

Prototype2019_OCS - Candidate Name

OPS_F1_S2_DS

A couple of weeks later, you receive another email from Steven Potter, Finance Manager

From: Steven Potter, Finance Manager
To: Finance Officer
Subject: Demand for additional fee classes and surplus equipment

Whilst the gyms are being refitted we have allowed members of these gyms to use the facilities of other GymFit gyms. This has created problems with demand for three group exercise classes which are not included in the monthly membership fee: Yoga, Pilates and Dance-Fit. Members are charged an additional fee for these classes as they require specialist teachers and are therefore more expensive to deliver. We currently have only 20 hours of studio space available in each gym per week to deliver the additional fee classes during peak-hour periods.

We have collected data from our membership system which clearly shows that there is a lot of unfulfilled demand for additional fee classes during these peak-hour periods. Ethan Henson, the Operations Director, has produced the attached analysis of the data based on averages from GymFit locations close to the gyms which are being refitted. He has asked for our help to decide on the best use of studio space.

I would be grateful if you would produce a report which I can discuss with Ethan, that explains;

- How the figures in the attached schedule could be used to determine how many of each type of additional fee classes we should offer in order to maximise profit. Please also explain the other factors that we should consider before scheduling the classes.

[sub-task (a) - 52%]

The refitting of the new gyms has resulted in surplus equipment partly due to lack of space during the gym refits and partly due to the fact that some of the equipment does not fit with the 'low cost-no frills' GymFit ethos. There are three main categories of equipment:

1. Equipment which has been transferred to other GymFit gyms;
2. Equipment which we intend to sell; and
3. Equipment which we have put in storage until the refit of the gyms is complete at which point we will assess whether the equipment can be used in the new gyms.

- Please advise, for each of the three categories, whether the equipment should be derecognised or remain on the statement of financial position and whether we should continue to depreciate it. Please justify your advice based on the requirements of IAS16 Property, Plant and Equipment and IFRS 5 Non-current Assets Held for Sale and Discontinued Operations.

[sub-task (b) - 48%]

Regards
Steven Potter
Finance Manager
GymFit

The attachment to this email can be found by clicking on the Reference Material button above.

End Exam | Previous | Next

Understanding the context

With tasks like this, you still need to appreciate the bigger context before launching into the specific requirements. Within the context of refurbishment, we have (a) decision making under constraints and (b) FR advice.

Stop and think!

(1) Using your P1 knowledge, consider how should they allocate scarce studio time (profit, contribution, contribution per hour, throughput...)?

(2) You won't be expected to do complicated calculations, so what you need should already have been done for you in the reference materials:

Analysis of contribution from additional fee classes during peak-hour periods

	Yoga	Pilates	Dance-Fit
Class capacity limit (number of participants)	15	15	20
Class length (hours)	1.50	1.00	0.75
Estimated demand per week (number of members)	150	90	80
Number of classes required per week	10	6	4
Number of hours required per week	15	6	3
Contribution per hour	C$35.00	C$45.00	C$65.00
Contribution per class	C$52.50	C$45.00	C$48.75

(3) Can you remember the financial reporting rules for which assets should be recognised/derecognised and the implications for depreciation?

Answering the question set – understanding the requirements

Given the above, the specific requirements are worded as follows:

"Produce a report ... that explains

- "How the figures in the attached appendix could be used to determine how many of each type of additional fee classes we should offer in order to maximise profit. Please also explain the other factors that we should consider before scheduling the classes."

  Note that you need to explain **how** the numbers will be used – i.e. explain the **methodology**, not just get to the right answer. Also you are asked for **other** factors.

- "Please advise, for each of the three categories, whether the equipment should be derecognised or remain on the statement of financial position and whether we should continue to depreciate it. Please justify your advice based on the requirements of IAS16 Property, Plant and Equipment and IFRS5 Non-current assets Held for sale and Discontinued Operations."

  Note that there are two elements here – should the assets be **derecognised** and should we continue to **depreciate** them.

Let's plan!

Task 2(a)

For P1 methodology type tasks the following approach is useful:

- **Explain** the method – why do you use contribution, why are fixed costs excluded, what is the scarce resource, how are products ranked (contribution per unit of scarce resource) and how is the resource then allocated?
- **Apply** the method – walk through the steps above applying them to the specific context – what is the scarce resource here, which class would be prioritised first, how much time does this use up, how much is left for the second choice and so on?
- **Go beyond** the method and discuss wider issues – here you are asked for "other factors" but previous tasks have asked for limitations, extra information required and so on.

Task 2(b)

For F1 financial reporting tasks use the following steps:

- **Identify** the relevant standards/topics – here we are told to use IAS 16 and IFRS5 and are given assets in 3 categories – those to be transferred, those held for sale and those where the future is unclear. The requirement emphasises whether assets should be derecognised and whether GymFit should continue to depreciate them.
- **State** the rules – for example, outline the criteria that have to be met for assets to be classified as "held for sale" and the implications for the financial statements if they are so classified.
- **Apply** the rules to the specific context – for example, do any of the assets held by GymFit meet the criteria for assets "held for sale"? If so, then what are the specific consequences?

Exercise 2

Prepare a response to the second task.

5 Task 3

As for task 2, the trigger and requirements for task 3 are mixed together into one screen, together with reference material:

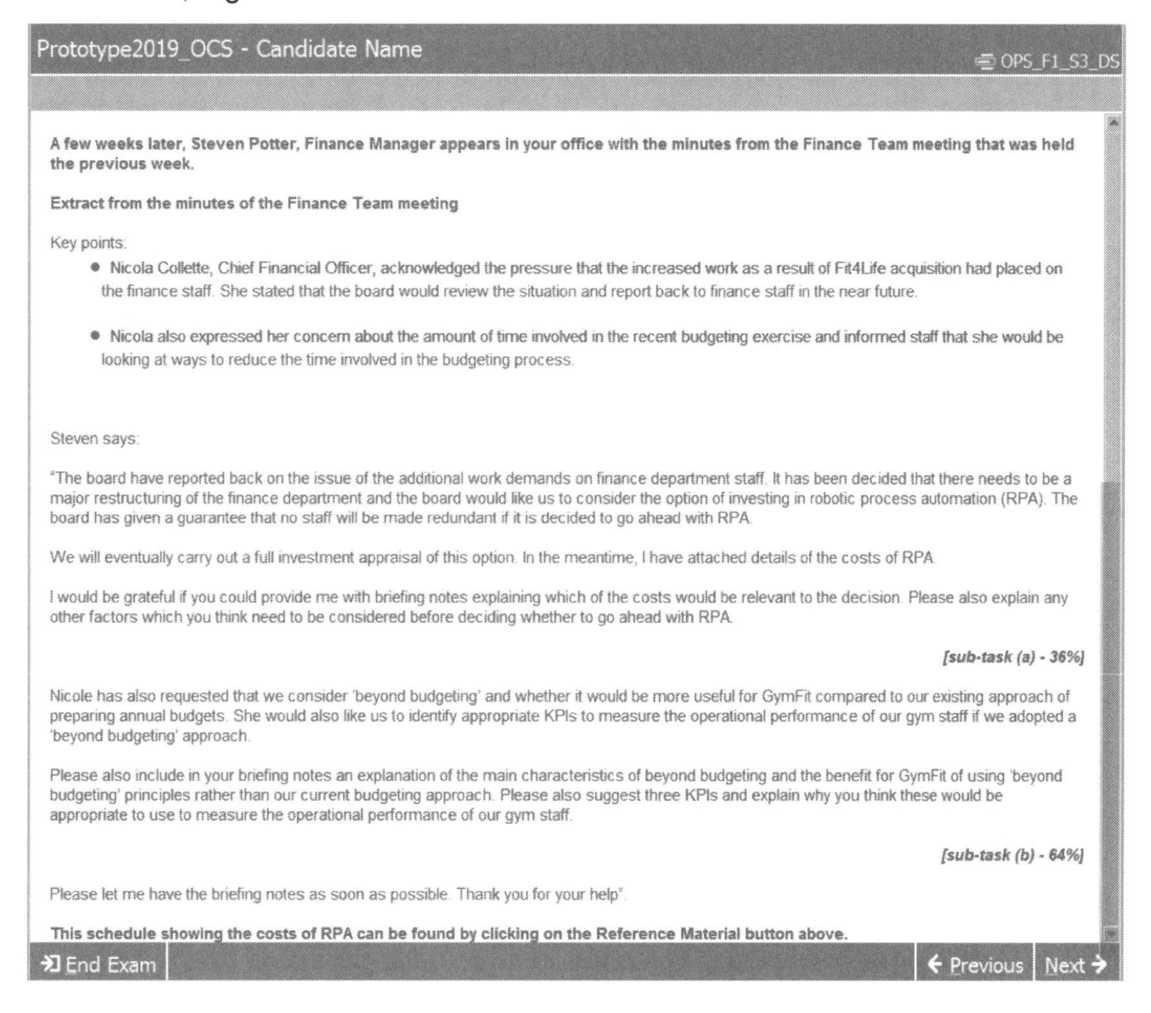
Prototype2019_OCS - Candidate Name

OPS_F1_S3_DS

A few weeks later, Steven Potter, Finance Manager appears in your office with the minutes from the Finance Team meeting that was held the previous week.

Extract from the minutes of the Finance Team meeting

Key points:

- Nicola Collette, Chief Financial Officer, acknowledged the pressure that the increased work as a result of Fit4Life acquisition had placed on the finance staff. She stated that the board would review the situation and report back to finance staff in the near future.
- Nicola also expressed her concern about the amount of time involved in the recent budgeting exercise and informed staff that she would be looking at ways to reduce the time involved in the budgeting process.

Steven says:

"The board have reported back on the issue of the additional work demands on finance department staff. It has been decided that there needs to be a major restructuring of the finance department and the board would like us to consider the option of investing in robotic process automation (RPA). The board has given a guarantee that no staff will be made redundant if it is decided to go ahead with RPA.

We will eventually carry out a full investment appraisal of this option. In the meantime, I have attached details of the costs of RPA.

I would be grateful if you could provide me with briefing notes explaining which of the costs would be relevant to the decision. Please also explain any other factors which you think need to be considered before deciding whether to go ahead with RPA.

[sub-task (a) - 36%]

Nicole has also requested that we consider 'beyond budgeting' and whether it would be more useful for GymFit compared to our existing approach of preparing annual budgets. She would also like us to identify appropriate KPIs to measure the operational performance of our gym staff if we adopted a 'beyond budgeting' approach.

Please also include in your briefing notes an explanation of the main characteristics of beyond budgeting and the benefit for GymFit of using 'beyond budgeting' principles rather than our current budgeting approach. Please also suggest three KPIs and explain why you think these would be appropriate to use to measure the operational performance of our gym staff.

[sub-task (b) - 64%]

Please let me have the briefing notes as soon as possible. Thank you for your help".

This schedule showing the costs of RPA can be found by clicking on the Reference Material button above.

End Exam | Previous | Next

Understanding the context

The acquisition has highlighted the need to improve the way the finance function operates. Suggested improvements are investment into RPA and a switch to beyond budgeting. Here the context is E1 based (the operation of the finance function) but the specific requirements are more P1 focussed (relevant costing and budgeting).

Also note the specific problems highlighted as you will want to ensure that you address these in your answer:

- **Pressure** that the increased workload has placed on staff
- The **time** involved in the recent budgeting exercise.

Stop and think!

- Can you remember the principles of relevant costing and the characteristics, pros and cons of 'beyond budgeting' from P1?
- Can you remember the pros and cons of RPA from E1?

Answering the question set – understanding the requirements

The requirements are worded as follows:

"Briefing notes..."

- "...briefing notes explaining which of the costs would be relevant to the decision. Please also explain any other factors which you think need to be considered before deciding whether to go ahead with RPA"

  Two aspects to this sub-task.

  Firstly you need to **explain** which off the costs are relevant. As mentioned before, the choice of verb is critical, so this involves more than just stating whether costs are or are not relevant but **justifying** your choice and **making it clear why**.

  Secondly you need to **explain** (again, not 'list') other factors to be considered.

- "...an explanation of the main characteristics of beyond budgeting and the benefit for GymFit of using 'beyond budgeting' principles rather than our current budgeting approach. Please also suggest three KPIs and explain why you think these would be appropriate to use to measure the operational performance of our gym staff".

  Again there are two aspects to this sub-task.

  Firstly to **explain** 'beyond budgeting' (what is it trying to achieve and why?) and the **benefit** (just the pros but not the cons) for GymFit of using it.

  Secondly to suggest KPIs for **gym** staff (not the over-worked finance staff!) with **justification**. The second aspect – the rationale for each KPI – is vital. If your justification is strong, then you still get credit even if your choices were 'unexpected'.

Let's plan!

Task 3(a)

As stated in the commentary on task 2, for P1 methodology type tasks the following approach is useful:

- **Explain** the method – briefly explain what we mean by 'relevant costs' (future, incremental cash flows)
- **Apply** the method – walk through the costs in the reference materials line by line and explain how the rules apply to each specific cost.

Prototype2019_OCS - Candidate Name OPS_F1_S3_RM

Robot Process Automation (RPA)		
Cost categories	**C$**	**Notes**
Depreciation and amortisation of hardware / software	(10,000)	(1)
Amortisation of development costs	(15,000)	(2)
IT maintenance costs	(37,000)	(3)
Licence fees	(8,000)	(4)
Staff training costs	(10,000)	(5)
Total costs	**(80,000)**	
Savings on salaries and benefits	120,000	(6)
Net benefit	**40,000**	

Notes:

1. The depreciation and amortisation of hardware and software is based on the assumption that the transaction processing operations will require two robots.
2. The development costs relate to the planning, assessment, design and testing of the RPA.
3. The IT maintenance costs relate to the costs of an existing employees who will be responsible for maintenance of the hardware and updates to the software.
4. Licence fees are payable to the provider of the software for the robots.
5. Staff training will be required for existing accounting and IT staff.
6. Savings on salaries and benefits relate to the expected cost savings from not having to hire additional accounting staff.

End Exam | Previous | Next

- **Go beyond** the method and discuss wider issues – here you are asked for "other factors" concerning the investment in RPA. Your comments can be derived from a number of sources:
  - The scenario (i.e. Will it reduce the pressure on finance staff? Will it speed up budgeting?),
  - From your P1 knowledge (e.g. relevant costing only includes factors that can be quantified in financial terms – what about non-financial issues such as staff morale?)
  - From your E1 knowledge – what are the pros and cons of RPA?

  With all of the above try to apply your comments to GymFit as much as possible.

Task 3(b)

The same answer approach to 3(a) can be applied here:

- **Explain** the method – briefly explain the characteristics of 'beyond budgeting'.
- **Apply** the method – the key aspect here is whether GymFit should switch from its current method. Beyond budgeting is great for some organisations but not others – which of these categories does GymFit fit into and why?
- **Go beyond** the method and discuss wider issues – here this is incorporated into the "apply" stage.

In terms of the KPIs you are only asked for three, so focus on what you think the key operational staffing issues are for a gym. For example, you may feel that quality is important (explain why!) and that one way of measuring this would be by looking at the number of customer complaints.

Exercise 3

Prepare a response to the third task.

6 Task 4

As for tasks 2 and 3, the trigger and requirements for task 4 are mixed together into one screen, together with reference material:

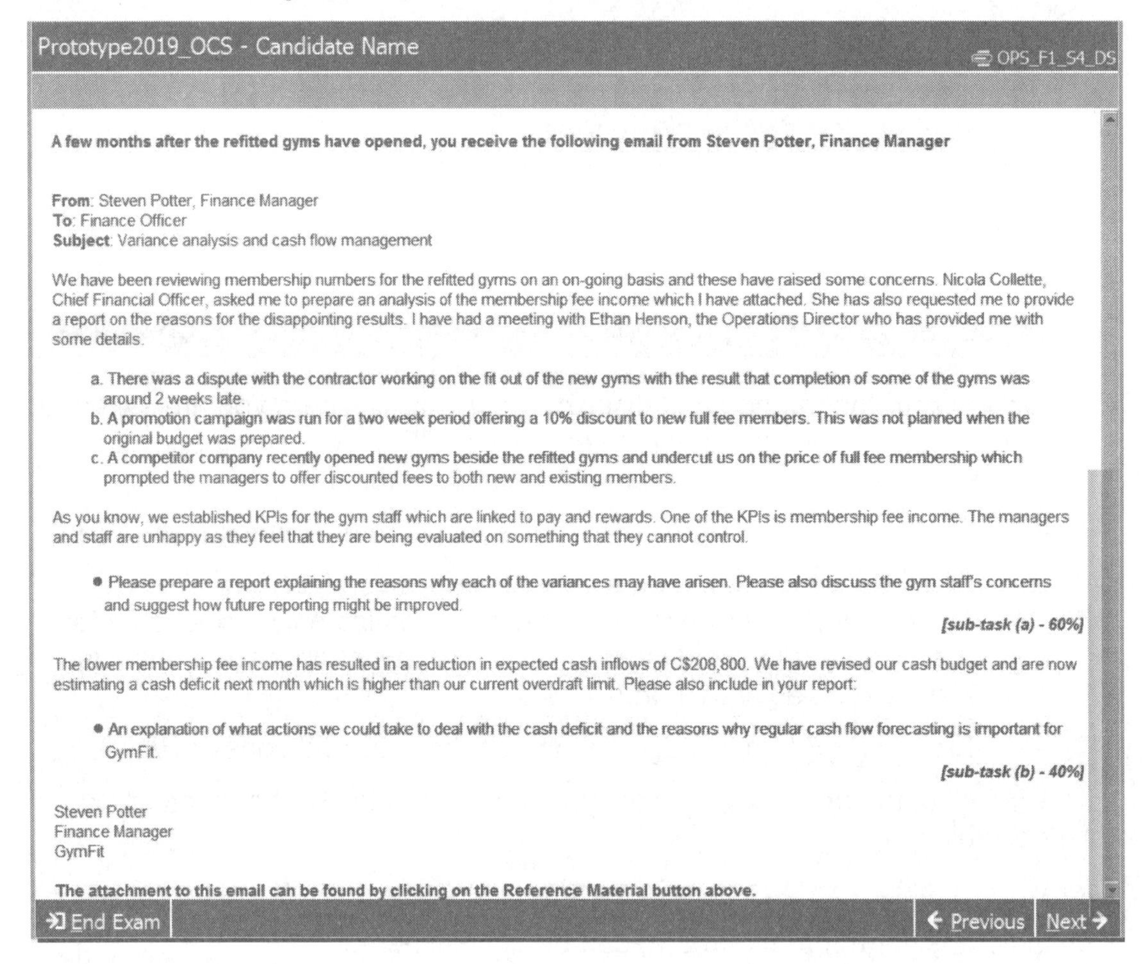

Prototype2019_OCS - Candidate Name

OPS_F1_S4_DS

A few months after the refitted gyms have opened, you receive the following email from Steven Potter, Finance Manager

From: Steven Potter, Finance Manager
To: Finance Officer
Subject: Variance analysis and cash flow management

We have been reviewing membership numbers for the refitted gyms on an on-going basis and these have raised some concerns. Nicola Collette, Chief Financial Officer, asked me to prepare an analysis of the membership fee income which I have attached. She has also requested me to provide a report on the reasons for the disappointing results. I have had a meeting with Ethan Henson, the Operations Director who has provided me with some details.

a. There was a dispute with the contractor working on the fit out of the new gyms with the result that completion of some of the gyms was around 2 weeks late.
b. A promotion campaign was run for a two week period offering a 10% discount to new full fee members. This was not planned when the original budget was prepared.
c. A competitor company recently opened new gyms beside the refitted gyms and undercut us on the price of full fee membership which prompted the managers to offer discounted fees to both new and existing members.

As you know, we established KPIs for the gym staff which are linked to pay and rewards. One of the KPIs is membership fee income. The managers and staff are unhappy as they feel that they are being evaluated on something that they cannot control.

- Please prepare a report explaining the reasons why each of the variances may have arisen. Please also discuss the gym staff's concerns and suggest how future reporting might be improved.

[sub-task (a) - 60%]

The lower membership fee income has resulted in a reduction in expected cash inflows of C$208,800. We have revised our cash budget and are now estimating a cash deficit next month which is higher than our current overdraft limit. Please also include in your report:

- An explanation of what actions we could take to deal with the cash deficit and the reasons why regular cash flow forecasting is important for GymFit.

[sub-task (b) - 40%]

Steven Potter
Finance Manager
GymFit

The attachment to this email can be found by clicking on the Reference Material button above.

End Exam | Previous | Next

Understanding the context

It is now a few months' later and membership numbers have been disappointing, giving rise to a number of adverse sales variances and poor results on KPIs that link to staff pay and rewards. Staff concerns over the controllability of a specific KPI – membership fee income – are highlighted.

Furthermore, this has also resulted in cash flow problems that may mean the overdraft limit will be breached.

Three operational factors are highlighted that will give key context for aspects of your answer:

- A dispute with a contractor
- An unplanned promotional campaign
- Activities of a competitor.

Stop and think!

- You will not be expected to calculate variances but can you remember the ideas behind sales mix and quantity variances and possible causes for them from P1?
- Using knowledge from P1 and E1, can you remember the issues around setting staff targets that they feel are not fully controllable by them and the implications for motivation?
- How many ways of addressing a cash deficit can you remember from F1?

Answering the question set – understanding the requirements

The requirements are worded as follows:

- "Please prepare a report explaining the reasons why each of the variances may have arisen. Please also discuss the gym staff's concerns and suggest how future reporting may be improved".

  You have to **explain** why each of three variances have arisen, meaning that simple list of generic factors and causes is not sufficient. Your answer must make it clear the likely causes in this case.

  You are then asked to **discuss** staff concerns. In order to discuss something, there normally needs to be an 'argument' with opposing viewpoints. Also, any discussion should, if possible, end in a conclusion. In this context the discussion is whether or not the staff concerns are valid. A good answer does not simply say "yes" or "no" but considers both sides of the argument and the extent to which it can it be said that the KPI of membership fee income is in or out of their control.

  Finally you have to **suggest** how reporting could be improved. The verb here would indicate that in-depth justification is not required (but some helps!)

- "An explanation of what actions we could take to deal with the cash deficit and the reasons why regular cash flow forecasting is important for GymFit".

  As with previous tasks the verb used here is "to **explain**", so your answer needs more than just a list of options. Try to apply your comments to the context and ensure they are worded as **actions** GymFit could take.

  Finally, you have to explain the reasons why regular cash flow forecasting is important for GymFit, so it is vital that your answers moves beyond generic reasons why cash budgeting is useful to specific reasons for GymFit, such as the fact that it has allowed us to anticipate breaching the overdraft limit, so action can be taken to avoid that outcome.

Let's plan!

Task 4(a)

With variance tasks such as this the following approach is useful:

- Briefly explain what each variance **means**. For example, an adverse price variance means that actual fees paid per customer per month were lower than budgeted. (Aside: how would you explain the adverse sales mix variance?)
- For each of the variances given, look for possible **causes**:

  Start with the three given in the exam – do any of them apply here?

  Next examine any financial data given. While you don't have to perform calculations, you may spot key areas by looking at the numbers. For example, examining the reference materials:

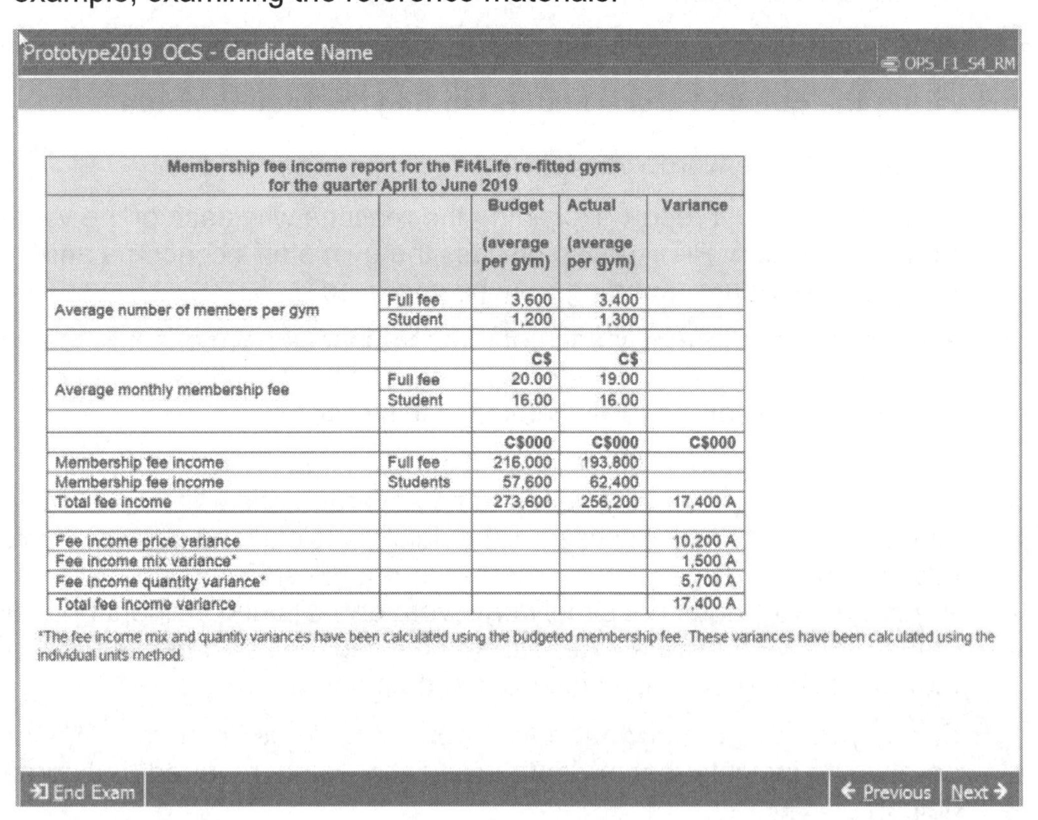

Prototype2019 OCS - Candidate Name

OPS_F1_S4_RM

Membership fee income report for the Fit4Life re-fitted gyms for the quarter April to June 2019				
		Budget (average per gym)	Actual (average per gym)	Variance
Average number of members per gym	Full fee	3,600	3,400	
	Student	1,200	1,300	
		C$	C$	
Average monthly membership fee	Full fee	20.00	19.00	
	Student	16.00	16.00	
		C$000	C$000	C$000
Membership fee income	Full fee	216,000	193,800	
Membership fee income	Students	57,600	62,400	
Total fee income		273,600	256,200	17,400 A
Fee income price variance				10,200 A
Fee income mix variance*				1,500 A
Fee income quantity variance*				5,700 A
Total fee income variance				17,400 A

*The fee income mix and quantity variances have been calculated using the budgeted membership fee. These variances have been calculated using the individual units method.

End Exam | Previous | Next

We can see that the actual price for students is the same as the budgeted figure, so any price variance is purely due to full fee members.

Can you remember anything in the pre-seen that might help?
For example, the reference materials distinguish full fee and student members but GymFit also offers three types of membership – one gym, two gym and 'bundle' membership – is this relevant to the variances?

As stated above, when discussing the staff concerns over KPIs you need to consider both sides of the argument, so you could split your planning into factors staff can control, factors they cannot and those with partial control or influence.

In terms of recommendations, you can keep your answer very practical in terms of suggesting new KPIs and/or ways of reporting variances, such as splitting between planning and operating variances.

Task 4(b)

To improve cash flow you could start by brainstorming as many possible options as possible and then prioritising your list, so that you write about the 'best' ideas first. For example, suggesting that GymFit discuss the issue with their bank to arrange an overdraft extension should be discussed before, say, a share issue to raise long term funds.

Finally try to address specific concerns over why cash flow forecasting is important first, such as to manage the risk of exceeding the overdraft, before resorting to generic ideas, such as helping the company reduce its cost of finance.

Exercise 4

Prepare a response to the fourth task.

7 Summary

You should now have a better understanding of how to approach the exam requirements and plan your answer. Although this chapter uses the "question tutorial" exam as an example, the techniques used can be applied to any set of exam tasks.

Next steps:

(1) As previously mentioned, you should attempt a written answer yourself to all of the tasks before reviewing the suggested solutions.

(2) Reviewing the solutions may highlight knowledge gaps which you may need to revisit.

(3) CIMA have produced two sample exams based on this pre-seen. You should try to attempt the second one at exam speed and using the exam software if possible.

Test your understanding answers

These answers have been provided by CIMA for information purposes only. The answers created are indicative of a response that could be given by a good candidate. They are not to be considered exhaustive, and other appropriate relevant responses would receive credit.

CIMA will not accept challenges to these answers on the basis of academic judgement.

Exercise 1

Digital sources and type of data

Digital sources are those that can be accessed by computers or other digital devices. Some of them are "born-digital," or originated in a digital form for example, pictures taken with a digital camera, web pages or twitter feeds, others were converted into digital files. Digital sources include e-books, e-journals, websites, blogs, online newspapers, online magazines and official government publications.

To determine the potential member numbers for each of the new gyms, we would need to establish the demographics of the local areas. This will involve accessing government statistics which will give us data on the size of the population within the local area. We know that the penetration rate for gym membership is 14.3% however that rate will vary depending on the demographics of the particular area. The government statistics will also provide us with further analysis of the population segmented by factors such as age; gender; income; disposable income; occupation and education level.

We can determine the profile of low-cost gym members from research reports which are available online. It is clear from previous research reports that the main determinants of gym membership are age; income and education level.

We can also access our membership database and, using data analytics, categorise our current membership. This will give us a better indication of the profile of the membership which is attracted by our current member proposition.

There will however be other factors that we would need to consider. Generally, gym members will live within 10 miles of the gym however a gym which is located close to an industrial area is likely to attract members from local businesses who will use the gym at lunchtime and after work. Access to good road or rail network may be an important factor in determining how far members may travel to access the gym. The proximity to a university may also be important in determining the mix of members between students and full fee members. The proximity of competitor gyms will also be a major factor in determining our member numbers.

All of these factors can be quantified by using data available via digital sources for example, government statistics or area maps.

Digital costing

Type of costs from operating Fit4Life apps

The cost of developing the apps whilst significant is not the only cost which needs to be considered. There are four main categories of costs associated with maintaining and operating apps post-development:

Functional services:

Functional services are those needed to execute the functionalities and features of the apps. While the apps developer will have provided a certain functionality, the apps will not work unless we subscribe to a service that will provide a delivery mechanism. This will allow functionality such as push notifications; social media and chat; SMS and email messaging.

Administrative services:

We will need an intuitive, powerful, accessible and user-friendly administration dashboard to enable us to effectively administer the apps. Administrative costs are the most difficult to anticipate as they will largely depend and differ based on each individual app. The administration dashboard will allow us to manage the content of the apps; manage the functional services detailed above; update the apps; manage user profiles; collect and analyse user behaviour; control access by users and enable data or user segmentation.

Infrastructure services:

These services include infrastructural components such as where the app is hosted, where data is stored and how the data is delivered. This will include the cost of servers (where the app is hosted); data storage; content delivery network (CDN) and images data.

IT support services:

Ongoing technical support is a critical component of any app deployment. We will need technical support to enable us to deal with iOS and Android updates; updates to application programming interfaces (APIs) and bug fixing. IT specific maintenance costs for infrastructure will also be required since servers, data storage, CDN and image data will all require some level of monitoring and maintenance.

Cost-benefit analysis

In order to carry out a cost-benefit analysis we will need to determine each of these costs and their frequency. Some of the cost will be paid regularly to suppliers such as the subscription costs associated with the apps' functionality. Other costs will require us to estimate the likelihood and extent of occurrence and the time involved with carrying out each task.

For example, we will need to estimate how often we will need to carry out iOS and Android updates or updates to APIs. Once we have established the time involved in each of these tasks, we can then determine the number of additional IT staff that would be required.

Some of the costs will be incurred on features or updates that are common to all the apps and an appropriate method will need to be determined to share the costs between the apps.

It will be necessary to establish the total costs over the lifetime of the app and then compare this to the expected benefits in terms of increased revenue. Determining the lifetime of an app can be very difficult particularly when there are rapid changes in technology as there is at the present time.

Exercise 2

Limiting factor analysis

How to use the figures in the schedule to decide on the mix of additional fee classes

The figures provided by Ethan could be used to determine the combination of classes which would maximise profit. It appears that time during peak periods is our scarce resource. It would require 24 hours to satisfy the demand for classes but only 20 hours are available. Ethan's analysis has provided contribution per class and contribution per hour for the three classes. Fixed costs are not considered since these would remain the same no matter which combination of classes are offered. Contribution per hour should be used to determine the optimum combination of classes since hours are the scarce resource and therefore we need to maximise the contribution from each hour.

In order to make a decision, we would rank the classes in descending order of contribution per hour and allocate the time available to satisfy the demand for the class that provides the highest contribution per hour first. Any remaining hours would be allocated to the class with the second highest contribution per hour. If any hours still remain, these would be used to satisfy as much as possible of the demand for the remaining class.

Dance-Fit is the top ranked class with C$65.00 contribution per hour and can be fully satisfied as only three hours of time are needed. Pilates has the second highest contribution per hour at C$45.00 and is therefore our second ranked class. Demand for Pilates classes can also be fully satisfied as these only require a further six hours. Yoga has the lowest contribution per hour at C$35.00 and therefore the remaining 12 hours would be used to run 8 Yoga classes.

Other factors to be considered

There are several other factors that could be considered which could potentially improve the decision. There are numerous assumptions and estimates contained in the analysis. It is possible, for example, that specialist teacher hours are also a constraint. There is an apparent assumption that there will be enough teacher availability but this may not be the case. It is also important to consider that demand is estimated and based on an average. Errors in the demand estimates could result in insufficient Dance-Fit or Pilates classes or even empty classes. It is also possible that some classes may not be full to capacity and this would change the contribution per hour. In addition, demand may vary for different locations and it would be better to make a decision based on the demand at each location.

We should also consider whether it is possible to increase capacity. There may be other larger studio spaces within each gym which could be used to reduce or remove the binding constraint. This could however potentially have consequences for the availability of places in the free classes. In addition, it may also be possible to change the length of the class. By reducing yoga to a one hour class, it may be possible to accommodate the vast majority of those who would like to take part in yoga.

We should also consider the impact of providing insufficient additional fee classes. This approach would leave insufficient provision for yoga, which could have significant implications for planned additional fee income in addition to customer satisfaction, retention and therefore membership income.

Financial accounting treatment of the surplus gym equipment

Equipment transferred to other gyms

The gym equipment is transferred to other gyms would remain on the statement of financial position under non-current assets and would continue to be depreciated in the normal way.

Equipment which we intend to sell

According to IFRS 5, non-current assets will be classified as 'assets held for sale' if their carrying amount will be recovered principally through a sales transaction rather than through continuing use.

In general, the following conditions must be met for an asset (or 'disposal group') to be classified as held for sale:

1 Management is committed to a plan to sell

2 The asset is available for immediate sale

3 An active programme to locate a buyer is initiated

4 The sale is highly probable, within 12 months of classification as held for sale (subject to limited exceptions)

5 The asset is being actively marketed for sale at a sales price reasonable in relation to its fair value

6 Actions required to complete the plan indicate that it is unlikely that plan will be significantly changed or withdrawn.

We clearly intend to sell the equipment and if management puts in place plans to find a buyer including actively marketing the equipment at a reasonable price, then the equipment would be treated as "held for sale" and would be held at the lower of the carrying amount and the fair value less costs of disposal. Assets held for sale will be shown in the statement of financial position under current assets and will no longer be depreciated.

Equipment held in storage

The equipment which we have decided to store until a final decision should remain on the statement of financial position. According to IAS 16, relating to de-recognition, an asset should only be removed from the statement of financial position on disposal or when it is withdrawn from use and no future economic benefits are expected from the asset. In this case, the equipment which is held in storage may be used in the future to generate economic benefits. The equipment would also continue to be depreciated since according to IAS 16, depreciation begins when the asset is available for use and continues until the asset is derecognised, even if it is idle.

Exercise 3

Investment in RPA

Relevant costs

The depreciation costs and amortisation costs are not relevant costs as they are not cash flows. However, the purchase costs of the hardware and software and the development costs will be relevant costs.

The IT maintenance costs will be irrelevant as they relate to the cost of an existing employee who will be paid whether the investment in RPA goes ahead or not.

The licence fees will be a relevant cost as these are incremental costs.

The training costs are relevant costs as these are future, incremental cash flows. However, they are not likely to occur on an annual basis but on an ad-hoc basis as it is likely that further training will be required in the future for new employees and in the event of any changes to the software.

The savings on salaries and benefit for staff is relevant. It is not intended to make any of the existing staff redundant however by investing in RPA we avoid having to hire additional staff.

Other factors

The use of RPA will free accounting staff to concentrate on value-added processes which require analysis and evaluation including supporting business managers with decision making.

An automated process is available around the clock, and is able to scale up or down quickly, according to demand. The ability to manage demand due to business growth or cyclical volume peaks is easily achievable when RPA is implemented. This will enable us to meet peaks in demand by dedicating more resource to any process without recruitment, training requirements or overtime costs.

RPA eliminates human error and it also brings 24/7 operation with no downtime. Robots also never give their notice therefore there is savings in recruitment costs.

Beyond budgeting

Characteristics of beyond budgeting

Under a 'beyond budgeting' approach, rolling forecasts on a monthly or quarterly basis, are suggested as the main alternative to annual budgeting. Instead of evaluating performance against budget targets these are replaced with relative external performance measures which are based on a comparison of key performance indicators with competitors and similar units within the company.

Beyond budgeting supports decentralisation and employee empowerment. It also places greater emphasis on team-based rewards rather than individual rewards.

Benefits of adopting a beyond budgeting approach

One of the main problems with our current annual budgeting system is that it is rapidly out of date. We are operating under fast changing market conditions with competitors open new gyms on a regular basis and changes to technology impacting on customer preferences. The use of rolling forecasts would provide more accurate information that reflects the latest estimates on economic trends and customer demand. This would enable our managers to determine strategies that adapt to the fast changing market conditions.

The use of relative performance measures will shift the focus from beating other managers for resource allocation to beating the competition by creating a climate based on competitive success. For example, we could use relative performance measures to compare the performance of the gym managers and/or staff across the company. The use of comparative measures will also ensure that our managers strive for continuous improvement rather than being content to meet budget targets.

Beyond budgeting will motivate our managers by giving clear responsibilities and challenges.

Authority will be devolved to our operational managers who are closer to the action and so can react quickly. The managers will be empowered to deliver key ratios rather than to keep to strict budget limits. Our managers will have wider discretion in making decisions and can obtain resources without being dependent on resource allocation as part of the budget process. This will enable our managers to react quickly to seize any opportunities that arise as a result of the changing environment.

By making rewards team-based it will eliminate dysfunctional behaviour. The success of our company does not rely on one individual but in everyone working together to achieve the same goals. The success of the operation of each of the gyms is not solely reliant on the gym manager but on all the staff. As part of the process we can establish customer-orientated teams and create information systems which provide fast and open information throughout the organisation.

KPIs for gym staff

The following are suggested KPIs which we could use to measure the performance of our gym staff:

Number of new members

As most of our costs are fixed it is important to grow our membership to obtain economies of scale. The gym managers and staff are able to influence growth in new members through price promotion and by ensuring that feedback from existing members is positive.

Average membership fee

It is important to grow the number of members but profitable growth is fundamental. Price promotions and discount should be used by the gym managers with care to ensure profitable growth and also to avoid a price war with other local competitor gyms.

Number of member complaints

This is a measure of customer satisfaction and could be linked to the number of members leaving and therefore income. Measuring the number of complaints will ensure managers take care to manage those areas of the business that can result in complaints such as a lack of available staff or delays in mending broken equipment. Furthermore, when presented with issues, managers and staff will be more careful to ensure that these are resolved to the customer's satisfaction wherever possible.

Exercise 4

Variance analysis

Fee income price variance

The adverse fee income price variance relates solely to the full fee members since the fee for student members was in line with budget. This is at least partly due the decision to offer discounted membership fees as this was not reflected in the original budget. It will also be partly due to the discounting of the full fee by gym managers of the gyms that have been affected by the competitor company opening nearby gyms.

Fee income mix variance

The fee income mix variance measures the effect on fee income of the sales mix being different than budget. The variance is adverse which reflects the split between full fee members and student members. There is a higher percentage of student members than budgeted and as student members have a lower average fee the variance is adverse. It would be helpful to discover why the mix is different to budget. It may be that the mix assumed in the budget was inappropriate and if so, the budget for future period should be revised or the variance separated into its planning and operational elements. A further breakdown of membership numbers in each of the gyms would be useful.

Fee income quantity variance

The fee income quantity variance measures the effect on fee income of the total quantity being higher or lower than budget based on volumes at the budgeted mix. The total number of members per gym are below budget which will be partly as a result of the late opening of the new gyms and partly due to the competition from the competitor who may have attracted some of our existing and potential members to its gyms. The discounted fees which have been offered to full fee members both through the sales promotion and by the gym managers has failed to have the desired impact on full fee member numbers. The number of student members however is above budget despite the fact that fees were not discounted. This suggests that our budget estimates of student numbers were potentially inaccurate and that there may also be scope to increase the fee for student members. The student fee offered by GymFit may be lower than that offered by the competitor firm and this needs to be clarified.

Gym manager and staff's concerns

The gym staff's concerns are valid since it is unfair that the company's reward system is based on factors that they cannot control. The gyms staff would not have been able to influence the late opening of the gyms. It could be argued however that the gym managers were able to influence the impact of the competitor opening nearby gyms since they have the authority to adjust fee levels.

However, we do not want to get into a price war with the competitor company and we need to take action to avoid this happening. We could stop the GymFit managers from using indiscriminate discounting and perhaps offer, for example, a price match guarantee to match the membership fee of any gyms within a 2 mile radius of our gyms. Other types of promotion should also be considered, for example, offering additional free classes.

In future reporting, it may be better to split the variances between their operational and planning elements. The operational variances would then reflect the position relating to factors that are within the control of the operational managers and would be a better basis for the reward system.

Cash flow management

Dealing with the cash flow deficit

There are a number of steps that we could take to plan for any cash deficit arising including:

(a) Approaching the bank to arrange additional short-term borrowings or to increase overdraft facilities.

(b) The statement of financial position as at 31st December 2018 shows investments of C$200,000. Assuming we have not already done so, we could sell these although we would need to consider any penalties that may be imposed as a result of early withdrawal/ sale.

(c) We could review the finance methods for our capital expenditure on gym equipment and /or the fit-out of new gyms. It may be possible to arrange different forms of finance or change/ renegotiate the payments dates on the finance. For example, we may choose to lease the equipment rather than buy the equipment outright.

(d) We could also consider the timing of our dividend payment to shareholders.

(e) We could consider postponing revenue expenditure such as advertising expenditure. We should be careful however as whilst advertising expenditure tends to be classified as discretionary expenditure a reduction or delay in the expenditure may result in reduced member numbers at a later date.

(f) It may be possible to bring forward the planned disposal of non-current assets. If the asset is not required, we could sell the asset sooner or perhaps arrange with the purchaser to pay a deposit.

Why regular cash flow forecasting is important for GymFit

Regular cash flow forecasting would ensure that the forecasts are more accurate, reflecting for example, the latest expectations of the new gyms. Adoption of a rolling budget approach would be particularly suited to cash flow forecasts which needs to be reviewed regularly.

It is important at GymFit not just to focus on profit but also to improve cash flow management. Our costs are mainly fixed therefore any changes to member numbers will have a major impact on profit but also on cash flow.

A rolling approach to cash flow forecasting will offer better visibility of cash flows and help to identify deficits, thereby ensuring appropriate financing arrangements are put in place to avoid a shortage of funds. Visibility of cash will also allow GymFit managers to adjust the timing of planned expenditure to avoid any cash flow shortages.

Where the cash flow forecasts are suggesting that there will be a surplus, GymFit managers can arrange to reinvest these funds to make further gains.

Chapter

6

Further advice on answering more challenging exam tasks

Chapter learning objectives

- To better understand how to answer more challenging exam tasks by looking at tasks from the May/August 2020 exam sittings.

1 Examiner feedback and a suggested approach to questions

1.1 Feedback via examiner's reports

After each pair of exam sittings CIMA publish the exams, suggested answers, marking grids and an examiner's report that discusses all variants from those sittings.

While many students are producing high quality scripts in the time available, there are common themes that have arisen where students can improve. Here are some typical comments:

- **Time pressure is not the main problem**

  "There was little evidence that time pressure caused any problems and most candidates completed answers for all tasks, although in some of the variants answers on specific elements of tasks were superficial or too brief... Often this seemed to be due to a lack of technical knowledge..."

- **No need for lengthy introductions**

  "Some candidates are wasting time giving extraneous information. There were often lengthy introductions to issues given which then meant that there was less time to address the actual task in hand. There are no marks for introductions or setting the scene; candidates need to address the task being asked and no more."

- **Planning answers is important**

  "When sitting an Operational level case study examination, it is important to take time to plan your answer so that you are able to apply your knowledge to the specifics of the case. I would suggest that for certain tasks you plan your answers in the answer screen itself.

  For example, if you are asked for the potential benefits and problems of a course of action, I would suggest that you first note down headings for benefits and problems. Then under each heading list your benefits and problems; these will become your sub-headings. Then you can write a short paragraph under each sub-heading.

  This will allow you time to think about all of the points that you want to make and will help to give your answer a clear format. Ultimately, it should save you time".

- **Apply models to the scenario**

  "There was evidence in a number of the variants of the erroneous use of learned models. In a case study the most important thing to do is to answer the task asked within the context of the business. The random inclusion of models with no application to the company, earned no marks."

- **Justify comments made**

  "Candidates also need to be conscious of unsupported assertions. Making statements such as, "this improves decision making", "this graph is essential" or "planning is enhanced" is not enough to gain any marks. Candidates must explain "how" the model or technique achieves these assertions. Wild enthusiasm is not enough without sound and reasoned explanation. As in November many candidate answers would have been improved if they added "because of ...." at the end of a sentence to explain why something is as it is."

- **Applying the more technical aspects of P1 and F1 is often the biggest discriminator between students**

  "Applying knowledge from P1 and especially F1 ... appeared to be more challenging."

  "Application to the scenario was generally good for tasks that linked to the E1 and P1 syllabi but often still poor in relation to F1 and the more technical aspects of P1."

1.2 Feedback via articles

In 2021 CIMA published an article, "A walkthrough of a real examination answer", where weak and strong student scripts were compared.

The article concluded with three keys to producing a passing answer for the Operational Case Study Examination:

- **Demonstrate technical understanding in the context of the scenario.**

  Information given (both pre-seen and unseen) should be, as far as possible, incorporated into answers.

  In other words, technical understanding is important but simple regurgitated knowledge scores poorly — it needs to be applied.

- **Ensure that your knowledge base is complete.**

  When there are knowledge gaps, application is not possible.

  You may use the 'Assessment Outcomes' in the blueprint as a useful checklist.

- **Read the requirements carefully and do exactly what the examiner asks you to do.**

  This is helpful for answer planning and time management.

1.3 A general approach to answering questions

In chapter 5 we answered exam tasks using an "Explain, Apply, Go beyond" approach. Given the above feedback this general approach to answering many exam tasks, but especially more challenging ones, could be developed further to involve the following steps:

1 **Read the question carefully and set up relevant headings in your answer.**

Students often fail simply because they do not answer the question set.

Pay particular attention to verbs used (e.g. 'explain') and scope (e.g. does the task require a discussion of both advantages and disadvantages or just one of these).

2 **Add relevant technical knowledge.**

It is vital that you demonstrate relevant technical knowledge. However, on its own, this is likely to limit your score to level 1 which will not be enough to pass. You must move to the next stage(s).

3 **Apply comments to the scenario / context.**

Technical knowledge must be demonstrated in the context of the scenario so points made in step 2 must be applied and illustrated using the information given in the pre-seen and/or new information given in the exam paper.

This is the most important step and should take your answer into level 2/ possibly level 3 on the marking grid.

4 **Think wider.**

This involves stepping back from the detail and considering the bigger picture, such as considering wider issues and implications, or exercising judgement/scepticism.

This gives a completeness to your answer and often takes you from a level 2 to a level 3 score on the marking grid.

While this approach applies for the most part, sometimes it may need adapting to suit particular exam tasks, such as questions on variances or those involving financial reporting standards. Examples of these are covered later.

In the rest of this chapter we apply this approach, with some modifications where necessary, to tasks from the May/August 2020 sittings that students struggled with.

2 Overview of the May/August 2020 pre-seen

Note: *While we have summarised the pre-seen and exam requirements to aid focus, you may also find it useful to download the full variants from the CIMA website, so you can see the tasks in context and have the full details of reference materials available if required.*

2.1 Introduction

The pre-seen information concerns a company called ChargeIT that develops, designs and manufactures cordless domestic electric products in Eastland in Northern Europe.

2.2 Business Model

Founded in 2001, the company has a reputation for producing quality products and being a reliable supplier.

The company makes two product ranges – floor care items (vacuum cleaners) and garden products (mainly lawnmowers and trimmers). What they all have in common is that they are cordless and rely on advanced, proprietary battery technology. Ongoing research and development is seen to be key to future growth.

Sales are made within Eastland (75%) and further afield, and involve B2C sales via the company website and B2B sales to major retailers. The latter are increasingly demanding better deals and lower prices, so managing customer power will be a major issue going forwards.

Despite developing new battery technology, the manufacture of the batteries is licenced to an external supply. Other aspects of manufacturing are kept in-house at the factory in Eastland.

Many other aspects of business are also kept in-house – the company maintains its own transport fleet, although local couriers are used for some website sales.

The company has a stated aim of new product developments and has invested heavily in new production machinery to facilitate future growth.

2.3 Industry trends

Sales overall in the market for vacuum cleaners has declined but handheld and robotic cleaners have seen positive growth.

In the gardening sector, sales of mowers and power tools have seen growth overall but, again, higher growth is seen for robotic devices.

The 2020 budget assumes significant growth in revenue of 15.1% but this is under half of that achieved in recent years. New products and markets are needed to achieve higher growth.

2.4 Financial performance

Revenue grew by 32.4% from 2018 to 2019, resulting in an increase of 59.3% in operating profit but a decrease in gross profit margins from 54.3% to 50.9%.

In terms of working capital and liquidity, cash increased by E$9.9 million, due partly to a zero dividend pay-out, but despite a net investment of E$2.2 million in non-current assets. This should mean that ChargeIT has the funds required to invest in new product lines should it wish to do so.

One concern, however, is that the overall investment in working capital increased by E$0.9 million, which combined with high growth, could indicate a risk of over-trading.

2.5 Specific management accounting details

- ABC - ChargeIT currently uses absorption costing based on a factory-wide rate based on direct labour hours. ABC could be relevant as ChargeIT is likely to want to increase its product range.
- Incremental budgeting - ChargeIT currently uses incremental budgeting and this appears to have served the company well to date. However, with a range of potential new products it could be argued that a switch to ZBB would be beneficial
- Budget participation - ChargeIT currently has a top-down approach with functional managers having little budgetary responsibility.
- Forecasting - given expansion plans and the nature of seasonality with garden equipment sales, time series analysis could be particularly useful.
- Organisational structure - ChargeIT is currently organised on mainly functional lines, whereas divisional structure may better facilitate growth.
- Variance analysis - ChargeIT operates a standard costing system, so it is highly likely that monthly operating statements are produced.

2.6 Specific financial accounting and governance details

- Statement of financial position – the SOFP shows both a revaluation surplus and a warranty provision, which may need explaining
- Governance - the company is owned by its founders. As such there has been little drive or need to ensure it complies with governance best practice, such as the separation of Chairman and MD, having non-executive directors or having a range of key committees (audit, remuneration and nomination). If it seeks a listing, then such issues will take on greater importance.

3 Core Activity A: Costing

3.1 Introduction

The May/August 2020 sittings examined the following tasks relating to Core Activity A (Costing):

- Variant 1 – Activity Based Costing (ABC).
- Variant 2 – Costing a digital cost object.
- Variant 3 – Cost drivers for warehouse activities.
- Variant 4 – CGMA cost transformation model.
- Variant 5 – Activity Based Costing (ABC).
- Variant 6 – Digital costing systems.

The tasks that caused the most difficulties for students related to ABC (variant 5) and costing a digital cost object (variant 2). These are discussed below.

3.2 Variant 5 – section 2 – ABC

Scenario

- The directors have decided to start selling the floor care and garden product ranges in Asia. Sales in Asia turn out to be better than expected.
- However, Gavin Mansell (MD) is concerned that fixed production overhead costs seem to be growing each month and wants more emphasis on cost control. In a bid to improve cost control, Ben Da Silva (FD) has suggested implementing ABC.
- Note: You were also given a flow chart and further notes on details of the injection moulding process.

Task

Students were asked to explain the following:

(1) How an ABC approach would affect the way that production overheads are allocated and absorbed compared to the current absorption costing system, with specific reference to the injection moulding part of the production process.

(2) Whether implementing an ABC system would be beneficial for cost control.

In terms of time allocations, you have 48% of 45 minutes = 21.6 minutes or 12 marks to complete both tasks without a split given between the two parts. It is too simplistic to simply divide the marks in two here, so you need to exercise judgement. The final marking grids gave 7 marks to the first sub-task and 5 to the second.

Suggested answer approach/structure

Once you are clear on the requirements, the next step is to set up headings in the answer box as suggested by the question.

1. How an ABC approach will differ from what we do now 2. Would implementing ABC be beneficial to our business for cost control?

Taking each of these in turn:

1 How an ABC approach will differ from what we do now

- Firstly, add relevant technical knowledge from P1 – explain how ABC is different from the current traditional approach of using labour hours. Comments could include:

Firstly, we would look at our overhead costs in a lot more detail by identifying production areas and then for each production area break it down into activities. Secondly, each activity would have its own cost centre (known as a cost pool) into which all the costs associated with the activity would be collated. Thirdly, we would not use direct labour hours as the basis for absorbing each of the overhead cost pools. Instead each cost pool would be absorbed on the basis of a cost driver that is the activity or action that drives or generates the cost.

- Either at the same time, or as a next step, try to apply and illustrate these points using the actual scenario given. This is the most important stage:

Firstly, we would look at our overhead costs in a lot more detail by identifying production areas and then for each production area break it down into activities. **For example, for injection moulding, production activities will include setting up the machinery each time a new mould is required, requisitioning raw materials from stores, loading of the plastic pellets into the melting vat, operating the machine and cleaning the machine each time a colour change is required.** Secondly, each activity would have its own cost centre (known as a cost pool) into which all the costs associated with the activity would be collated. **For example, cleaning the machine would include the cost of indirect labour, the cost of cleaning products and water used as well as a share of the cost of energy consumed in the cleaning process.** Thirdly, we would not use direct labour hours as the basis for absorbing each of the overhead cost pools. Instead each cost pool would be absorbed on the basis of a cost driver that is the activity or action that drives or generates the cost. **For example, the cost driver for injection moulding machinery cleaning could be the number of cleans because each time the machine is cleaned a cost is incurred: this is an example of a transaction driver.**

- Finally, try to develop points further. This could involve revisiting the question requirement to see if there is an angle you have missed, considering wider issues and implications, or exercising judgement/scepticism.

  Here the question asked for a comparison between ABC and the existing method. So far the answer has focussed exclusively on differences but are there any similarities that would be worth including? For example, we could add the following paragraph:

  > There are some activities though where direct labour hours may still be an appropriate driver. For example, the cost of operating the injection moulding machinery (largely energy, depreciation and maintenance) is going to be driven by the running time of the machine and hence a volume related driver such as direct labour hours or machine hours would be appropriate.

2 Would implementing ABC be beneficial to our business for cost control?

- As before, start with technical knowledge, but limit your answer to cost control aspects only and recognise that this sub-task needs to be written as an argument with justification:

  > Whether implementing ABC would be beneficial for our business ultimately depends on whether the benefits gained (in terms of improvements to profitability) exceed the significant costs (in terms of time) associated with its implementation.
  >
  > There is no doubt that the detailed information arising from implementing ABC would allow management to be better placed to control overhead cost. Knowing what each separate element of cost is within each production department and then establishing what drives each element of cost, means that management can more easily identify where cost savings are possible by controlling the cost driver.

- Then we can look to apply points to the specific scenario:

  > For example, it could be that by reviewing the injection moulding machinery cleaning costs, a more cost-effective process can be established whereby production is scheduled so that all plastic parts in a particular colour are moulded at the same time, meaning fewer cleans.

Marking grids

Trait			
How ABC differs	**Level**	**Descriptor**	**Marks**
		No rewardable material	0
	Level 1	Demonstrates some understanding of the differences between an ABC and an absorption costing approach with limited or no reference to the specific injection moulding production process.	1-2
	Level 2	Demonstrates a reasonable understanding of the differences between an ABC and an absorption costing approach with some reference to the specific injection moulding production process.	3-5
	Level 3	Demonstrates good understanding of the differences between an ABC and an absorption costing approach with good reference to the specific injection moulding production process.	6-7
Beneficial?	**Level**	**Descriptor**	**Marks**
		No rewardable material	0
	Level 1	Demonstrates some understanding of the benefits of ABC for cost control but with little reference to ChargeIT. Note that this question is specifically focused on cost control and therefore there is no credit for explanation of other benefits of ABC.	1-2
	Level 2	Demonstrates reasonable understanding of the benefits of ABC for cost control purposes with a reasonable attempt to explain within the context of ChargeIT.	3-4
	Level 3	Demonstrates good understanding of the benefits of ABC for cost control purposes with a good attempt to explain within the context of ChargeIT.	5

Examiner's comments

Very few candidates managed to score higher than a mid-level 2 for the first part of this. Most candidates could identify the main elements of ABC, such as cost pools and cost drivers, but fewer were able to explain these in any depth or to explain how this would change the way that costs were allocated and absorbed. Very few candidates applied their explanation to the injection moulding process given in the scenario.

For the part of the task about the benefits of ABC for cost control, many would have scored well if the question had asked for the benefits of ABC compared to absorption costing as many gave a list of these. However, few made reference to cost control and although explained that the set-up was costly did not try and compare this to the benefits it could bring.

3.3 Variant 2 – section 1 – Costing a digital cost object

Scenario

- The directors have decided to launch a new robotic lawn mower that can be operated using a mobile phone app.
- As this is the first time the company had developed a digital product, the senior management team is keen to understand how the costs differ from those of a physical product.

Task

You were asked to produce a report explaining the following:

(1) How the costs of a mobile phone app differed, in terms of type of costs and the timing of occurrence, compared to a lawn mower.

(2) The potential issues with determining the unit cost of the mobile phone app for planning and decision-making purposes.

In terms of time allocations, you have 52% of 45 minutes = 23.4 minutes or 13 marks to complete both tasks without a split given between the two parts. The final marking grids gave 7 marks to the first sub-task and 6 to the second.

Suggested answer approach/structure

Once you are clear on the requirements, set up headings in the answer box:

1. Types of costs 2. Potential issues in determining the unit cost of the app

Taking each of these in turn:

<u>1 Types of costs</u>

- Before starting an answer it is worth thinking what "types of cost" could mean. The question specifies timing (e.g. pre-launch v ongoing) but other classifications could include fixed v variable, direct v indirect, or labour v materials v overheads. Ideally your answer would try to incorporate as many different angles as possible.
- For example, suppose you start by making a distinction between pre-launch and post-development costs:

Pre-launch costs The majority of the costs of the app will be pre-launch: the costs associated with the design and development of the app. The costs of reproducing the app will be minimal compared to the costs of a physical product like the lawnmower. Post-development costs The cost of developing the app, whilst significant, is not the only cost which needs to be considered. There will be ongoing costs associated with maintaining and operating the app post-development.

- You could then add some more specific comments focussing on materials and labour costs, say:

> Pre-launch costs
>
> The majority of the costs of the app will be pre-launch: the costs associated with the design and development of the app. The costs of reproducing the app will be minimal compared to the costs of a physical product like the lawnmower.
>
> **The mobile phone app will have little or no material costs unlike the lawnmower for which material costs are a significant proportion of the total costs.**
>
> **For the mobile phone app, most of the staff costs will be specific as freelance staff were contracted to develop the app and will probably have been paid a fixed fee or a fee per day. Now the app has been developed these staff are no longer required. It means that, although there may be some permanent staff costs for preparing updates and providing product maintenance, the majority of staff costs are often upfront and pre-launch with very little ongoing post-launch costs.**
>
> Post-development costs
>
> The cost of developing the app, whilst significant, is not the only cost which needs to be considered. There will be ongoing costs associated with maintaining and operating the app post-development.
>
> **Most of these costs will be fixed in nature in contrast to the costs associated with the manufacture of the lawnmower which will include material, labour and variable overheads.**

- Finally you could add more examples to make it very clear to the marker that you have applied your comments to the scenario:

> Post-development costs
>
> ...
>
> **The ongoing costs will consist of: costs to provide functionality such as push notification or SMS and email messaging; costs to manage and update the app and collect data on users; costs associated with hosting the app, storing data and delivering data; IT support services to deal with updates of the operating system and the app and maintenance costs of the infrastructure.**

2 <u>Potential issues in determining the unit cost of the app</u>

- It is particularly important here to answer the exact question set. You are asked to discuss potential issues in determining a unit cost. To help identify these you may wish to think through the process for identifying a unit cost, such as apportioning costs, but your answer must address issues, rather than simply describing a process.

- Suppose you start with the basic elements of the process:

> The development costs of the app will initially be capitalised and then amortised over the life of the app.
>
> Whilst most of the design and development costs will be specific to an individual app, there may be elements which are shareable with other apps and a method of allocating these costs to the individual apps will be required.
>
> The ongoing costs of the app will be mainly fixed costs, which will need to be apportioned.

- Then we can look to apply points to the specific scenario:

> The development costs of the app will initially be capitalised and then amortised over the life of the app.
>
> **The lifespan of digital products can vary greatly. Determining the lifetime of an app can be very difficult particularly when there are rapid changes in technology as there are at the present time. Similarly, determining sales volumes over the lifetime of the app will also be difficult.**
>
> Whilst most of the design and development costs will be specific to an individual app, there may be elements which are shareable with other apps and a method of allocating these costs to the individual apps will be required.
>
> **In this case, we have only one app so all the costs will be direct, but this may change in future. Many product features or functions might also be shared amongst a number of products. We need to determine how to absorb these costs into each individual product. Determining the drivers associated with these costs may be difficult.**
>
> The ongoing costs of the app will be mainly fixed costs, which will need to be apportioned.
>
> **The amount and frequency of these costs will also need to be determined as will the estimated sales volume in order to calculate the cost per unit.**

- Finally step back to see if there are any bigger picture / related issues that could be added. For example, you could add the following as an opening paragraph:

> A major advantage of digital products is that there will be no inventory of the product. This avoids the need for inventory valuation by the accounting function. We will however want to establish the cost of the app for planning, control and decision making purposes.

Marking grids

Trait			
Type of costs	**Level**	**Descriptor**	**Marks**
		No rewardable material	0
	Level 1	Identifies very few types of costs of developing and operating the app and gives a limited explanation of when the costs arise or the cost behaviour.	1-2
	Level 2	Identifies a few types of costs of developing and operating the app and gives a reasonable explanation of when the costs arise and how the cost behaves compared to the lawn mower.	3-5
	Level 3	Identifies a number of types of costs of developing and operating the app and provides a good explanation of when the costs arise and how the cost behaves compared to the lawn mower.	6-7
Unit cost	**Level**	**Descriptor**	**Marks**
		No rewardable material	0
	Level 1	Demonstrates a weak technical understanding of how the unit cost would be determined. Does not explain any issues in trying to determine the cost.	1-2
	Level 2	Demonstrates a reasonable technical understanding of how the unit cost would be determined. Explains at least one potential issue in trying to determine the cost.	3-4
	Level 3	Demonstrates a good technical understanding of how the unit cost would be determined. Explains a few potential issues in trying to determine the cost.	5-6

Examiner's comments

This was answered with varying levels of competence, but few answers were excellent.

Higher performing candidates separated this into two sub-tasks and clearly identified the costs of the intangible app and the tangible lawnmower, and then were able to discuss the key points for determining the unit cost of the app.

Lower performing candidates confused these two criteria and tried to answer them together.

Candidate answers could have been so much better if time had been taken to read the task carefully. Few answers clearly compared the app and lawn mower costs, focussing instead on a list of costs incurred by the app.

4 Core Activity B: Budgeting

4.1 Introduction

The May/August 2020 sittings examined the following tasks relating to Core Activity B (Budgeting):

- Variant 1 – Time Series analysis.
- Variant 2 – What-if *analysis* and rolling budgets.
- Variant 3 – Flexible budgeting and participation in budget setting.
- Variant 4 – Activity Based Budgeting (ABB), and Beyond Budgeting.
- Variant 5 – Feedforward vs feedback control and Zero Based Budgeting (ZBB).
- Variant 6 – Time Series analysis.

The tasks that caused the most difficulties for students related to What-if" analysis (variant 2), ABB (variant 4) and ZBB (variant 5). These are discussed below.

4.2 Variant 2 – section 2 – What-if analysis

Scenario

- The directors have decided to launch a new robotic lawn mower.
- As this is the first time the company has budgeted for the new lawnmowers, there is uncertainty surrounding price, volumes and production costs. Given this, a spreadsheet giving a what-if analysis has been prepared

Task

Students were asked to produce a briefing paper explaining:

(1) The figures in the spreadsheet and what they tell about the impact on profit of potential changes to variables.

(2) The benefits and limitations of what-if analysis

In terms of time allocations, you have 28% of 45 minutes = 12.6 minutes or 7 marks for the first sub-task and 32% of 45 minutes = 14.4 minutes or 8 marks for the second sub-task.

Suggested answer approach/structure

Once you are clear on the requirements, the next step is to set up headings in the answer box as suggested by the question.

1. Explanation of figures in schedule
2. Benefits and limitations of what-if analysis

Taking each of these in turn:

1 Explanation of figures in schedule

- Firstly, add relevant technical knowledge from P1 – explain how what-if analysis is used. Comments could include:

  What-if analysis involves revising the budget on the basis of a series of varied assumptions. One or more variables can be changed at a time to determine the impact on the budgeted profit, cash flow or other aspects of the budget. When changing more than one variable it is better to use a spreadsheet to speed up the process.

  In this case, we have produced a spreadsheet to show the impact on profit of a different combination of selling price, variable costs and sales volume.

  We can use the spreadsheet to try to assess the impact on profit of different selling price and variable cost combinations.

- Either at the same time, or as a next step, try to apply and illustrate these points using figures from the spreadsheet:

  What-if analysis involves revising the budget on the basis of a series of varied assumptions. One or more variables can be changed at a time to determine the impact on the budgeted profit, cash flow or other aspects of the budget. When changing more than one variable it is better to use a spreadsheet to speed up the process.

  In this case, we have produced a spreadsheet to show the impact on profit of a different combination of selling price, variable costs and sales volume.

  We can use the spreadsheet to try to assess the impact on profit of different selling price and variable cost combinations.

  For example, a selling price of E$740 combined with variable costs of E$260 per unit would result in a profit of E$230,000 if sales volumes of 2,250 units are achieved.

  Alternatively, if our target profit was E$350,000, we can see from the spreadsheet that if sales volumes turn out to be 2,000 units that we will only achieve the target profit if selling prices are E$840 and variable costs are E$240.

  Furthermore, we can tell that at this level of sales volumes that we will make a loss if the selling price is reduced to E$640.

- Finally, try to develop points further. This could involve revisiting the question requirement to see if there is an angle you have missed, considering wider issues and implications, or exercising judgement/scepticism.

For example, we could add the following:

> However, the spreadsheet does not tell us the link between the different prices and volumes. If we were able to establish the price/volume relationship we could determine the potential profit.
>
> If we estimate for the budget that sales volumes would be 2,500 units at a price of E$740 and we knew, for example, that sales volumes would increase by 250 units for every reduction of E$100 in selling price, we can determine the revised profit figures for a combination of selling price of E$640 and sales volume of 2,750. It is clear from the spreadsheet that this combination of variables would result in a lower profit than the target.
>
> In contrast, a combination of sales volume of 2,250 and selling price of E$840 would result in a higher profit for all variable cost levels.

2 Benefits and limitations of what-if analysis

- As before, start with technical knowledge:

> *Benefits*
>
> What-if analysis provides us with more information about the budget's sensitivities to changes in different variables.
>
> It allows us to make a decision about whether we are prepared to accept the impact on profit of these potential changes.
>
> It will also allow us to decide whether it is worth spending time and money on further investigation of the market.
>
> We can also make contingency plans for the eventuality that the sales volume, for example, turns out to be much lower than expected.
>
> *Limitations*
>
> What-if analysis, however, is limited as it assumes that changes to variables can be made independently however many variables are interdependent. In reality, it is very unlikely that only one variable would change but more likely that there would be changes in a combination of variables.
>
> It also does not give us any indication of the likelihood or the probability of that change or scenario happening.

- Then we can look to apply points to the specific scenario. For example, taking the first limitation:

> What-if analysis, however, is limited as it assumes that changes to variables can be made independently however many variables are interdependent. In reality, it is very unlikely that only one variable would change but more likely that there would be changes in a combination of variables.
>
> **For example, it is highly likely that sales volumes are partly driven by selling prices, or that fixed costs may be stepped.**

- Finally, try to develop points further. For example, we could add the following to the final limitation:

> It also does not give us any indication of the likelihood or the probability of that change or scenario happening.
>
> **We could however determine the probabilities of different sales volumes and then calculate an expected value for both the sales volume and profit. However, this analysis is very dependent on the accuracy of the probabilities and, as this is a new market for us, these may be difficult to determine without expert advice**

Marking grids

Trait			
Figures	**Level**	**Descriptor**	**Marks**
		No rewardable material	0
	Level 1	Provides a limited explanation of the figures in the spreadsheet. Does not consider the impact on profit of changing variables.	1-2
	Level 2	Provides a reasonable explanation of the figures in the spreadsheet with some consideration of the impact on profit of changing variables.	3-5
	Level 3	Provides a good explanation of the figures in the spreadsheet and clearly explains the impact on profit of changing variables.	6-7
Benefits and limitations	**Level**	**Descriptor**	**Marks**
		No rewardable material	0
	Level 1	Explains at least one benefit or limitation of what-if analysis although the explanation lacks clarity.	1-3
	Level 2	Explains at least two benefits and/or limitations of what-if analysis but the explanations may lack clarity or depth and/or there may be limited application to the scenario.	4-6
	Level 3	Explains a range of benefits and limitations of what-if analysis. The explanations are clear and there is good application to the scenario.	7-8

Examiner's comments

> *First sub-task: Far too many candidate answers could only be awarded a level 1 because they simply described the figures in the reference material without adding any value; an explanation adds value to a description, and this was lacking in many answers. Better answers explained how as one input variable increased or decreased, profit increased or decreased.*
>
> *Second sub-task: Disappointingly, too many candidate answers were generic rather than applied and therefore did not score above a middle level 2. Answers that achieved a high level 2 were applied to the context of the case.*

4.3 Variant 5 – section 4 – ZBB

Scenario

- The directors decided to start selling the floor care and garden product ranges in Asia. Sales in Asia turned out to be better than expected resulting in a new goods assembly line, and new injection moulding equipment being installed.
- Given these changes, Ben Da Silva (FD) has suggested the use of ZBB for establishing maintenance costs for production machinery.

Task

Students were asked to produce a briefing paper explaining:

(1) How ZBB could be used to allocate funds to discretionary support activities. Please use the budget for production machinery maintenance to illustrate your explanation.

In terms of time, you have 48% of 45 minutes = 21.6 minutes or 12 marks.

Suggested answer approach/structure

- Firstly, add relevant technical knowledge from P1 – explain how ZBB is used (Note: not the benefits or weaknesses of using it!):

Step 1: Establish activities and objectives

The first stage of applying ZBB will be to decide on the discretionary support activities.

For each activity an objective is established.

Step 2: Establish decision packages

For each activity, there will be different ways in which its objective can be achieved or different levels of expenditure that could be incurred. These choices are reflected in decision packages which should be drawn up by those people closest to the activities.

Decision packages can either be mutually exclusive (different ways of achieving the objective) or incremental (different levels of service to achieve slightly different outcomes).

Step 3: Perform cost/benefit analysis and rank decision packages

After the decision packages have been fully developed with all of the costs quantified, a cost/benefit analysis needs to be performed.

Each decision package would need to be considered against these benefits and then ranked in order of preference.

Step 4: Allocate resources

After all decision packages across the business for support activities such as for machinery maintenance have been ranked, the whole budget is then considered and the resources available allocated to each part of the business accordingly.

- Either at the same time, or as a next step, try to apply and illustrate these points using the maintenance budget:

Establish activities and objectives

The first stage of applying ZBB will be to decide on the discretionary support activities. **One example of such an activity is maintenance of production machinery.**

For each activity an objective is established. **For example, the objective of production machinery maintenance could be to ensure that machinery breakdowns are limited.**

Establish decision packages

For each activity, there will be different ways in which its objective can be achieved or different levels of expenditure that could be incurred. These choices are reflected in decision packages which should be drawn up by those people closest to the activities.

Decision packages can either be mutually exclusive (different ways of achieving the objective) or incremental (different levels of service to achieve slightly different outcomes).

For machinery maintenance, mutually exclusive decision packages could be developed to either perform the maintenance in-house, with our own dedicated employees or we could outsource to an external specialist maintenance company.

Incremental decision packages can then be developed for each option, starting with the base package, which is the minimum level of machinery maintenance. We could decide in respect of this base package that none of the new machinery installed as part of the expansion needed any form of maintenance and that existing machinery had an annual check or was only maintained when there was evidence of issues.

Clearly this would be a potentially risky strategy as any breakdown in machinery, no matter how small could be costly in terms of lost production.

After the base package has been developed incremental packages will then build on this and add additional maintenance time and different activities that should be performed.

For example, it could be that the new machines are scheduled to have an annual service rather than having no service. Whilst this will generate additional cost (in terms of either the fee for a specialist maintenance company or the cost of the time for our own employees), it will help to ensure that the new machinery keeps working optimally.

Perform cost/benefit analysis and rank decision packages

After the decision packages have been fully developed with all of the costs quantified, a cost/benefit analysis needs to be performed.

Clearly, one benefit of spending money on machinery maintenance is to reduce the risk of breakdown, which if it happened could have a detrimental effect on the ability to produce.

There are other benefits though to maintenance in terms of keeping the machinery working optimally in order to safeguard throughput and the quality of production as well as prolonging the useful lives of machinery.

Each decision package would need to be considered against these benefits and then ranked in order of preference.

Allocate resources

After all decision packages across the business for support activities such as for machinery maintenance have been ranked, the whole budget is then considered and the resources available allocated to each part of the business accordingly.

Marking grids

Trait			
ZBB	**Level**	**Descriptor**	**Marks**
		No rewardable material	0
	Level 1	Demonstrates some understanding of how ZBB could be used to allocate funds to discretionary support activities. The explanation is likely to lack clarity and depth.	1-2
	Level 2	Demonstrates reasonable understanding of how ZBB could be used to allocate funds to discretionary support activities. The explanation may lack some clarity and / or depth.	3-5
	Level 3	Demonstrates good understanding of how ZBB could be used to allocate funds to discretionary support activities. The explanation is mostly clear and comprehensive.	6-7
Production machinery maint'nce	**Level**	**Descriptor**	**Marks**
		No rewardable material	0
	Level 1	Explains the use of ZBB with only limited reference to the activity of production machinery maintenance.	1-2
	Level 2	Explains the use of ZBB with reasonable reference to the activity of production machinery maintenance.	3-4
	Level 3	Explains the use of ZBB with good reference to the activity of production machinery maintenance.	5

Examiner's comments

Candidate answers tended to be one of two types. On the one hand, some candidates demonstrated a good general understanding of the ZBB process but often struggled to explain how ZBB could be used for preparing the production machinery budget. On the other hand, there were many answers where knowledge of ZBB was very poor, with little if any attempt at application.

Many candidates wasted time explaining the benefits and drawbacks of ZBB compared with incremental budgeting, which had not been asked for and scored no marks. Again, another example of candidates answering the question they wish they had been asked, rather than the task given.

4.4 Variant 4 – section 2 – ABB

Scenario

- The directors have commenced a review of operations following a decline in sales
- As part of this review, Ben Da Silva (FD) has suggested the use of ABB for establishing employee costs in the Finished Goods Distribution Warehouse, details of which were given in the reference materials.

Task

Students were asked to produce a briefing paper explaining:

(1) How a revised budget for the employee costs in the Finished Goods Distribution Warehouse could be established using an activity-based budgeting approach. Illustrate your explanation with reference to both of the activities of receiving finished goods inventory and placing of loaded pallets onto delivery trucks identified in the attachment.

(2) The benefits of using an activity-based budgeting approach for establishing the warehouse employee cost.

In terms of time, the question specified details for each subtask. You have 36% of 45 minutes = 16.2 minutes or 9 marks for the first sub-task and 20% of 45 minutes = 9 minutes or 5 marks for the second.

Suggested answer approach/structure

Once you are clear on the requirements, the next step is to set up headings in the answer box as suggested by the question.

1. Using Activity based budgeting (ABB) for warehouse employee costs
2. Benefits of using activity based budgeting for warehouse employee costs

Taking each of these in turn:

<u>1. Using Activity based budgeting (ABB) for warehouse employee costs</u>

- Firstly, add relevant technical knowledge from P1 – explain how ABB is used (Note: the question is asking for ABB not ABC)

Step 1: Establish activities

The first step to determine the hours required is to establish the activities that drive those hours.

Step 2: Establish required hours for each activity

The next step is to consider each activity separately, identify relevant cost drivers, and then determine the employee time that we expect to need for each of these activities during the budget period.

Step 3: Accumulate hours required and determine staff requirements

The next step is to accumulate all the hours required for each activity into a total number of hours required for the budget period.

This can then be used to establish how many staff are required based on the number of hours each staff member would be available for work during the budget period.

This would need to include any hours needed for training and allowances for sickness and employee holidays.

Step 4: Quantify cost

The final step would be to quantify this as a cost by applying the appropriate hourly rate for the employees required.

- Apply and illustrate these points using warehouse employee costs and the two activities specified in the requirement. For example, looking at steps 1 and 2:

Step 1: Establish activities

The first step to determine the hours required is to establish the activities that drive those hours.

For the finished goods warehouse these activities include receiving finished goods and placing pallets onto the delivery trucks.

Step 2: Establish required hours for each activity

The next step is to consider each activity separately, identify relevant cost drivers, and then determine the employee time that we expect to need for each of these activities during the budget period.

For example:

For receiving, each pallet of finished goods received from the production facility is moved into the correct location by forklift. Each time a pallet is moved, employee time is used to operate the forklift and therefore we can establish the total time needed as the number of pallets to be moved (which is the cost driver) in the budget period multiplied by the time taken to move each pallet. However, not all pallets will take the same amount of time to move because there are different locations in the warehouse.

However, we could split the warehouse into say three zones and establish an average time to move a pallet into each zone and calculate a total per zone and then an overall total.

For placing the loaded pallets onto delivery trucks, the number of hours required should be more straightforward to establish. Each truck has the same capacity and we know that on average each truck is loaded to 85% of this capacity. Therefore, we can establish the time it takes to achieve this. The total hours required will be the number of trucks loaded (which is the cost driver) multiplied by the time taken to load each truck.

- Finally, try to develop points further. This could involve revisiting the question requirement to see if there is an angle you have missed, considering wider issues and implications, or exercising judgement/scepticism.

  For example, here we could add an introductory paragraph making it clear how ABB fits into the wider process:

Introduction

The budget for warehouse employees during the budget period will be the hours needed for the level of activity expected multiplied by the rate of pay per hour.

The rate of pay per hour is relatively straightforward to establish as this will be the agreed rate with the employees. The number of hours required is less straightforward but will be calculated under ABB as follows:

Marking grids

Trait			
Application of ABB	**Level**	**Descriptor**	**Marks**
		No rewardable material	0
	Level 1	Demonstrates some understanding of an ABB approach. There may be an attempt to apply this to explain how to establish the budget, but this explanation is poor. Little or no reference is made to the activities suggested or to the scenario.	1-3
	Level 2	Demonstrates reasonable understanding of an ABB approach and makes a reasonable attempt to apply this to explain how to establish the budget. Explanation makes reference to the activities suggested, but the illustration lacks depth or clarity.	4-6
	Level 3	Demonstrates clear understanding of an ABB approach and applies this to explain how to establish the budget. Explanation is clearly linked to the activities suggested.	7-9

Trait			
Benefits of ABB	**Level**	**Descriptor**	**Marks**
		No rewardable material	0
	Level 1	Explains at least one benefit, but there is likely to be a lack of clarity in the explanation and little if any reference to the scenario.	1-2
	Level 2	Explains more than one benefit, but there may be a lack of clarity in the explanation. There is an attempt to link this to the scenario.	3-4
	Level 3	Explains with clarity more than one benefit with good reference to the scenario.	5

Examiner's comments

Using ABB to establish a revised budget

This task was not answered well, and most candidates only achieved level 1 or low level 2 scores. Many candidates still fail to differentiate between activity-based costing and activity-based budgeting. Most were able to achieve a level 1 answer by explaining some of the main features of ABC such as the need to establish cost pools and cost drivers. However, to do well in this task, candidates needed to use the information provided to consider how a budget would be established. Level 2 answers made reference to the activities and attempted to explain how to establish the time taken for each using the information. However, answers often then lacked the detail required to explain how this would be used to establish a budget.

The benefits of activity-based budgeting

Despite relatively limited answers on how to apply activity-based budgeting, most candidates were able to explain the benefits.

Higher performing candidates who achieved a level 3 score clearly focused the benefits on the budget for employee warehouse costs as opposed to discussing benefits of activity-based approaches more widely.

Lower performing candidates scoring at level 1 tended to discuss generic benefits with little or no reference to the scenario. Candidates are reminded to ensure that points made are sufficiently developed and applied.

5 Core Activity C: Performance appraisal

5.1 Introduction

The May/August 2020 sittings examined the following tasks relating to Core Activity C (Performance appraisal):

- Variant 1
  - Sales variances
  - Planning and operational variances
  - KPIs
- Variant 2 – Production cost variances
- Variant 3
  - Sales variances
  - KPIs
- Variant 4
  - Sales price, mix and quantity variances
  - KPIs
- Variant 5
  - Fixed production overhead variances
  - KPIs
- Variant 6
  - Sales and labour variances
  - KPIs

The tasks that caused the most difficulties for students related to sales variances (variant 4), and fixed production overhead variances (variant 5). These are discussed below.

5.2 Variant 4 – section 2 – Sales variances

Scenario

- The directors have commenced a review of operations following a decline in sales. As part of this review, sales variances have been analysed in more detail.
- Students were given a table of variances for the 5 months January to May 2020 for a specific model of lawn mower, an explanation of the basis of calculation (weighted average), and reference to specific events in the period under review: sales of garden products were disappointing despite an unbudgeted sales promotion of a 30% discount across all garden products if purchased online; and the loss of a large retailer in February, together with the gain of two smaller ones in March and April.

Task

Students were asked to produce a briefing paper explaining:

(1) What the sales price variances, sales mix profit variances, sales quantity profit variance and total variance in the schedule mean and the possible reasons for their occurrence

The question specified 44% of 45 minutes = 19.8 minutes or 11 marks for the task.

Suggested answer approach/structure

Once you are clear on the requirements, the next step is to set up headings in the answer box as suggested by the question.

> <u>Explanation of variances</u>
>
> 1. Sales price variances
>
> 2. Sales mix profit variances
>
> 3. Sales quantity profit variances
>
> 4. Total variance

When asked to "explain" variances, it may be useful to modify our general approach as follows:

- Rather than giving general definitions of variances, start by stating whether the specific variance is favourable or adverse and then use technical knowledge to interpret, in basic terms, what that means:

> <u>Explanation of variances</u>
>
> 1. Sales price variances
>
> The variance for the on-line sales channel is adverse which means that the average price achieved per lawnmower was less than budget.
>
> The variance for the retailer sales channel is favourable which means that the average price achieved for lawnmowers was higher than budgeted.
>
> 2. Sales mix profit variances
>
> The on-line sales channel is our most profitable channel (because we are dealing directly with the consumer at retail prices) and hence the favourable mix variance here indicates that we sold proportionately more to this, our most profitable customer group than we had expected.
>
> The sales mix variance is also favourable for the retailer sales channel, but because the average profit per lawnmower earned from retailers is lower than the weighted average this indicates that we sold proportionately less to retailers than expected.
>
> *[Note: the use of the weighted average method of calculation means that favourable or adverse is a combination of both whether we sold more or less than the standard mix would suggest, combined with whether that channel is more or less profitable than average]*

The total mix variance is favourable which means that for this lawnmower model the change in mix between the sales channels has resulted in additional profit.

3. Sales quantity profit variances

This variance is adverse, indicating that profit is lower than budgeted for the five-month period as a result of selling less of this lawnmower model than we expected to.

4. Total variance

The total variance is adverse and shows that for this model of lawnmower the impact of selling a lower quantity outweighs the impact of both a favourable move towards on-line sales rather than through retailers and a favourable change in the selling prices achieved from retailers.

- Either afterwards, or as you go along, give reasons from the scenario as to possible causes. The examiner will have told you key facts and events, so this should be a matter of matching the facts to the variance. With this type of requirement it is critical to focus on reasons in the scenario rather than using technical knowledge to give lists of generic reasons.

Explanation of variances

1. Sales price variances

The variance for the on-line sales channel is adverse which means that the average price achieved per lawnmower was less than budget.

This is a direct result of the 30% discount available to all online customers.

The variance for the retailer sales channel is favourable which means that the average price achieved for lawnmowers was higher than budgeted.

There were no price promotions for this type of customer, although there has been a change in retailers which will have changed the average selling price achieved across all the retailers compared to the budget. The major retailer that left had probably negotiated a significant discount, whilst the smaller new retailers have been secured at a higher selling price.

2. Sales mix profit variances

The on-line sales channel is our most profitable channel (because we are dealing directly with the consumer at retail prices) and hence the favourable mix variance here indicates that we sold proportionately more to this, our most profitable customer group than we had expected.

The sales mix variance is also favourable for the retailer sales channel, but because the average profit per lawnmower earned from retailers is lower than the weighted average this indicates that we sold proportionately less to retailers than expected.

This is likely the result of the 30% discount promotion in April and May, which will have encouraged the end consumer to purchase online with us rather than through our retailer sales channel.

The total mix variance is favourable which means that for this lawnmower model the change in mix between the sales channels has resulted in additional profit.

3. Sales quantity profit variances

This variance is adverse, indicating that profit is lower than budgeted for the five-month period as a result of selling less of this lawnmower model than we expected to.

Overall, despite the 30% discount for on-line sales during the period, sales based on standard mix across both sales channels are disappointing and perhaps reflect the increasing competitive pressures facing our garden range

4. Total variance

The total variance is adverse and shows that for this model of lawnmower the impact of selling a lower quantity outweighs the impact of both a favourable move towards on-line sales rather than through retailers and a favourable change in the selling prices achieved from retailers.

- Finally, try to develop points further.

For example, after the comment about total mix variances:

The total mix variance is favourable which means that for this lawnmower model the change in mix between the sales channels has resulted in additional profit.

However, this change in mix may only be temporary given that the 30% discount has now finished.

Alternatively the discussion of the total variance could be extended to consider the bigger picture:

The total variance is adverse and shows that for this model of lawnmower the impact of selling a lower quantity outweighs the impact of both a favourable move towards on-line sales rather than through retailers and a favourable change in the selling prices achieved from retailers.

However, it should be noted that this variance relates to only one lawnmower model and it's possible that the total of sales variances for other models is favourable which might indicate that there are issues of popularity for this model. Additionally, we need to consider the variances for this model in relation to all garden products because the 30% discount promotion will have had an impact across the range.

Marking grids

Trait			
Variances: technical	**Level**	**Descriptor**	**Marks**
		No rewardable material	0
	Level 1	Demonstrates limited technical understanding of what the sales variances represent, including the meaning of the adverse or favourable variances. There are technical inaccuracies.	1
	Level 2	Demonstrates reasonable technical understanding of what the sales variances represent, including the meaning of the adverse or favourable variances. There are some technical inaccuracies.	2-3
	Level 3	Demonstrates good technical understanding of what the sales variances represent and the meaning of the adverse or favourable variances	4
Variances: reasons	**Level**	**Descriptor**	**Marks**
		No rewardable material	0
	Level 1	Provides reasons for some of the sales variances, but the explanation lacks clarity and some of the reasons are likely to not be valid in respect of the variance explained.	1-2
	Level 2	Provides some valid reasons for the variances which are reasonably explained. Demonstrates limited understanding of the interrelationships between the variances but does reference the scenario.	3-5
	Level 3	Provides valid reasons for the sales variances which are well explained. Demonstrates good understanding of the interrelationships between the variances and the scenario.	6-7

Examiner's comments

Not all candidates were able to correctly explain the technical meaning of the variances. In particular, few candidates were able to articulate the mix profit variance, and many ignored the meaning of the total variance. It was common for answers to the mix variance to refer to mix of products as opposed to the mix of sales channels and very few answers made reference to the favourable mix variance relating to the retailers. This demonstrated a lack of technical understanding in relation to the weighted average method of calculating mix variances.

Candidates were much better at identifying reasons for the variances and many achieved at a least level 2 mark for this part. Lower performing candidates tended to reproduce pre-learnt reasons that did not relate to the scenario.

5.3 Variant 5 – section 2 – Fixed production overhead variances

Scenario

- The directors have decided to start selling the floor care and garden product ranges in Asia. Sales in Asia turn out to be better than expected.
- However, Gavin Mansell (MD) is concerned that fixed production overhead costs seem to be growing each month and wants more emphasis on cost control. As part of this he has requested an explanation of fixed production overhead variances and whether they are useful measure to help manage fixed production overhead costs.
- Students were given a table of fixed production overhead variances for July 2020, an explanation of the basis of absorption (direct labour hours), and reference to specific events in the period under review: the motor assembly line had been expanded in July by purchasing and hiring additional equipment and taking on new trainees; there hadn't been time to carry out formal training; additional off-site warehouse space had been hired; and most employees did overtime to help meet demand.

Task

Students were asked to produce a briefing paper explaining:

(1) The three fixed production overhead variances and possible reasons why each has occurred.

(2) The usefulness of these fixed production variances for managing fixed production overhead cost.

The question specified 52% of 45 minutes = 23.4 minutes or 13 marks for the two elements in total. The marking grid gave 9 marks for the first subtask and 4 for the second subtask.

Suggested answer approach/structure

Once you are clear on the requirements, the next step is to set up headings in the answer box as suggested by the question.

1. Explanation of fixed production overhead variances • Expenditure variance • Efficiency variance • Capacity variance 2. Usefulness of fixed production overhead variances

Taking each of these in turn:

1 Explanation of fixed production overhead variances

- As with the previous example, when asked to "explain" variances a good approach is to start by stating whether the variance is favourable or adverse and interpret, in basic terms, what that means:

<u>Explanation of fixed production overhead variances</u>

1. Expenditure variance

The fixed production overhead expenditure variance is the difference between actual fixed production overhead incurred in July 2020 and the budgeted fixed production overheads.

The variance is adverse which means that we incurred E$25,034 more fixed production overhead than we had budgeted.

2. Efficiency variance

The fixed overhead efficiency variance compares the actual hours used with standards hours for actual production. This difference in hours is then valued at the fixed production overhead absorption rate.

The variance is adverse which means that we used more direct labour hours to produce our products compared to standard. In other words, direct labour was not as efficient as it should have been

3. Capacity variance

The fixed overhead capacity variance is the difference between the originally budgeted direct labour hours and the actual direct labour hours for the month, multiplied by the standard absorption rate.

The variance is favourable which means that we have increased our capacity and were able to work more direct labour hours.

- Either afterwards, or as you go along, give reasons from the scenario as to possible causes. As before the key is to explain variances using the key events given to you by the examiner in the scenario:

<u>Explanation of fixed production overhead variances</u>

1. Expenditure variance

The fixed production overhead expenditure variance is the difference between actual fixed production overhead incurred in July 2020 and the budgeted fixed production overheads. The variance is adverse which means that we incurred E$25,034 more fixed production overhead than we had budgeted.

This is because:

- **We expanded the motor assembly production area at the start of the month resulting in the purchase of additional equipment. This will have resulted in additional depreciation costs which were not included in the original budget. There might also have been additional insurance costs as a result of the new equipment.**
- **We have had to hire off-site warehouse space to accommodate additional bought-in component inventory. This will have increased storage costs compared to our original budget.**

Also, we've paid more overtime than anticipated, and the overtime premium will have increased production overhead costs.

2. Efficiency variance

The fixed overhead efficiency variance compares the actual hours used with standards hours for actual production. This difference in hours is then valued at the fixed production overhead absorption rate. The variance is adverse which means that we used more direct labour hours to produce our products compared to standard. In other words, direct labour was not as efficient as it should have been.

In order to increase capacity, we took on additional trainees who learned what was required of them by watching others rather than through formal training. This is likely to have slowed down the rate at which our employees worked because they will have been explaining as they worked. In addition, once the trainees were operating, it is likely that because they were new to the process, they will not have worked as quickly as our experienced employees.

3. Capacity variance

The fixed overhead capacity variance is the difference between the originally budgeted direct labour hours and the actual direct labour hours for the month, multiplied by the standard absorption rate. The variance is favourable which means that we have increased our capacity and were able to work more direct labour hours.

This has arisen because we have taken on more trainees and allowed staff to do more overtime.

2 Usefulness of fixed production overhead variances

- Start by using your P1 knowledge to explain the usefulness of these variances in general terms:

Of the three fixed production overhead variances calculated, the only one that is potentially useful for cost control is the expenditure variance because this tells us the difference between what we incurred and what we planned to incur on fixed production costs.

The efficiency and capacity variances are components of the volume variance which measures the difference between the budgeted fixed production overhead and the fixed production overhead absorbed during the period. The volume variance therefore has little if any value in terms of controlling overhead costs as it just tells us that the level of activity was different to that budgeted.

- Then try to link these issues to the scenario:

> Of the three fixed production overhead variances calculated, the only one that is potentially useful for cost control is the expenditure variance because this tells us the difference between what we incurred and what we planned to incur on fixed production costs.
>
> **However, because we only calculate this on a total factory-wide basis, its usefulness is limited. We know that certain costs such as depreciation and equipment insurance will have increased, but we don't know how much of the expenditure variance as calculated relates to this.**
>
> **It could be that there are other factors affecting the variance, which are hidden because the variance is only one figure. It would be more useful to break this expenditure variance down into perhaps different areas of production to have a better idea of how each area is performing.**
>
> The efficiency and capacity variances are components of the volume variance which measures the difference between the budgeted fixed production overhead and the fixed production overhead absorbed during the period. The volume variance therefore has little if any value in terms of controlling overhead costs as it just tells us that the level of activity was different to that budgeted.
>
> **The efficiency variance does tell us about direct labour efficiency, but even this is of little use because it is not specific to any department or production area.**

Marking grids

Trait			
The variances	**Level**	**Descriptor**	**Marks**
		No rewardable material	0
	Level 1	Demonstrates technical understanding of at least one of the variances. The explanation may lack clarity and the reasons for the variances may be missing or not related to the scenario.	1-3
	Level 2	Demonstrates technical understanding of at least two of the variances, although the explanation may lack some clarity. Reasons for the variances will be given but may not always relate to the correct variance or be drawn from the information given in the scenario.	4-6
	Level 3	Demonstrates technical understanding of the three variances. The explanation is mostly clear and the reasons given relate to the specific variance and are drawn from the information presented in the scenario.	7-9

Trait			
Usefulness	**Level**	**Descriptor**	**Marks**
		No rewardable material	0
	Level 1	Demonstrates understanding that the expenditure variance is potentially useful, but explanation lacks clarity. Usefulness of volume related variances might not be addressed, or the explanation is inaccurate or vague. The issues with the fact that this is a factory wide absorption rate are unlikely to be considered.	1
	Level 2	Demonstrates reasonable understanding that the expenditure variance is potentially useful but that the volume related variances are not. The explanation may lack clarity or fail to address the factory wide overhead issues in any depth	2-3
	Level 3	Demonstrates good understanding that the expenditure variance is potentially useful but that the volume related variances are not. The explanation is clear and addresses the factory wide overhead issues.	4

Examiner's comments

Though production overhead variances has been tested many times before, candidate understanding of these variances is relatively poor.

Most candidates demonstrated understanding that the expenditure variance was the difference between actual and budgeted expenditure and gave clear reasons for the adverse variance which were relevant to the scenario.

However, the efficiency and capacity variances were often poorly explained, with a significant number of candidates failing to identify that the efficiency variance related to labour efficiency. The reasons given for these variances were often very limited with some candidates simply stating that the staff had been less efficient and that there had been an increase in capacity. Very few candidates managed to score a level 3 for this part of the task.

The usefulness of the variances was not answered well, if at all. It was clear that candidates did not really understand what these variances explained for the business. The idea of cost control was often referred to as comparing actual and budget with no indication of how only the expenditure variance concentrated on the costs. Few candidates scored above a level 1 here.

6 Core Activity D: Financial reporting, ethics and governance

6.1 Introduction

The May/August 2020 sittings examined the following tasks relating to Core Activity D (Financial reporting, ethics and governance):

- Variant 1 – IFRS 16 Leasing
- Variant 2 – IAS 2
- Variant 3 – IAS 16 Capitalisation of costs
- Variant 4
  - – IFRS 16 Leasing
  - – IAS 16 re: subsequent expenditure
- Variant 5
  - – IAS 16
  - – Tax depreciation allowances
  - – IFRS 5
- Variant 6
  - – Impairment
  - – IAS 16

The tasks that caused the most difficulties for students related to leasing (variant 4) and IFRS 5 (variant 5). These are discussed below.

6.2 Variant 4 – section 4 – IFRS 16 (Leasing)

Scenario

- The directors have commenced a review of operations following a decline in sales. As part of this review, it was decided to go ahead with installing robot process automation (RPA) in the finished goods warehouse with a view to leasing some of the equipment.
- Students were given a schedule containing various details, costs and timings for the leased equipment.

Task

Students were asked to produce a briefing paper explaining:

(1) How the asset that has been leased will be initially recorded and then subsequently measured in our financial statements for the year ended 31 December 2021 and future years.

The question specified 40% of 45 minutes = 18 minutes or 10 marks for the task.

Suggested answer approach/structure

In some respects, most Core Activity D tasks can be approached in the same way:

- Identify the relevant reporting standard(s)
- State the rules as concisely as possible without over-simplifying
- Apply the rules to the facts in the scenario

However, based on feedback in examiners' reports, it would seem that there are two issues that need to be addressed to score good marks:

- Some students clearly do not have sufficient technical knowledge concerning the accounting rules concerned.
- Students often fail to identify all of the accounting implications of a specified event and thus limit the scope of their answers. The best way to address this is to take time to plan your answer before launching into the detail

In the case of this task, planning could consider the following issues:

- Firstly check the question wording. The question makes a distinction between initial recording and subsequent measurement and asks for more than just the first year. Similarly, it refers to "financial statements", so consider both SOPL and SOFP aspects
- Then brainstorm what the phrases could mean. "Initial recording" involves looking at capitalising the leased asset but, thinking through the double entry, there will also be a lease liability to be set up.
- As part of "subsequent measurement", we will have to recognise that the asset will need to be depreciated. What is the method here, what would the UL be? Similarly, what will happen to the lease liability in subsequent years? Payments will need to be deducted but finance charges added.

Once you are clear on the requirements, the next step is to set up headings in the answer box. One option could be:

1. Introduction
2. "Right of use" asset
3. Lease liability

For this task let us address all three elements at the same time.

- As mentioned above, start by explaining the rules

Introduction
In accordance with IFRS 16, Leases, where equipment is leased, this gives rise to both a right-of-use asset and a liability. The right-of-use asset represents the fact that we have the right to use the equipment for the lease term. The liability reflects the fact that we have a future obligation to pay the lease payments over the lease term.

Right of use asset

The right-of-use asset will initially be measured at the initial measurement value of the liability plus the lease payment made at the start of the lease.

The right-of-use asset will need to be depreciated over the lower of the lease term and the life of the asset.

For the year ended 31 December 2021 this will result in a depreciation charge in the statement of profit or loss with initial value of the right-of-use asset reduced by the depreciation.

In subsequent years, there will be a further depreciation charge each year and further reductions in the right-of-use asset.

Lease liability

The liability will initially be measured and recorded at the present value of the lease payments that have not yet been paid.

For the year ended 31 December 2021, the lease liability will be increased by a finance charge. This will be charged to profit or loss.

In subsequent financial years the opening liability will be first decreased by the payment at the start of the year and then the interest charge will be added. This interest charge will also be charged to profit or loss and reflects that fact that leasing is essentially a form of finance.

- Then, either as you go along or afterwards, apply these rules to the asset in the scenario, making use of the figures and timings presented:

Introduction

In accordance with IFRS 16, Leases, where equipment is leased, this gives rise to both a right-of-use asset and a liability. The right-of-use asset represents the fact that we**, ChargeIT,** have the right to use the equipment for the lease term. The liability reflects the fact that we have a future obligation to pay the lease payments over the lease term.

For this lease there is an initial lease term of 10 years and then we have the option to extend for a further 5 years. IFRS 16 states that the lease term should be the period of non-cancellable payments plus any optional period if the option is reasonably certain of being exercised. In our case the lease term would appear to be the full 15 years.

Right of use asset

The right-of-use asset will initially be measured at the initial measurement value of the liability plus the lease payment made at the start of the lease **(E$25,000).**

The right-of-use asset will need to be depreciated over the lower of the lease term and the life of the asset, **which as noted above is the same at 15 years.**

For the year ended 31 December 2021 this will result in a **full year's** depreciation charge in the statement of profit or loss with initial value of the right-of-use asset reduced by the depreciation.

In subsequent years, there will be a further depreciation charge each year and further reductions in the right-of-use asset.

Lease liability

The liability will initially be measured and recorded at the present value of the lease payments that have not yet been paid.

This will include the nine payments of E$25,000 a year to be made from 1 January 2022 onwards and the further five payments of E$15,000 a year after that. The discount rate used to calculate the present value should be the interest rate implicit in the lease which is 10%.

For the year ended 31 December 2021, the lease liability will be increased by a finance charge **of 10% of the initial liability value**. This will be charged to profit or loss.

In subsequent financial years the opening liability will be first decreased by the payment at the start of the year and then the interest charge **at 10%** will be added. This interest charge will also be charged to profit or loss and reflects that fact that leasing is essentially a form of finance.

Marking grids

Trait			
Right of use asset	**Level**	**Descriptor**	**Marks**
		No rewardable material	0
	Level 1	Explains with technical accuracy some of the generic aspects of how the right of use asset will be initially and subsequently accounted for. Reference to the specific leased asset in the scenario and the financial statements might be missing or only briefly commented on.	1-2
	Level 2	Explains with technical accuracy most of the generic aspects of how a right of use asset will be initially and subsequently accounted for. Reference to the specific leased asset in the scenario might be limited, although there has been an attempt to explain the treatment in the financial statements for 2021, although future years may be missing.	3-4
	Level 3	Explains with technical accuracy how a right of use asset will be initially and subsequently accounted for with reference made to the specific leased asset in the scenario. The impact in the financial statements for 2021 is fully explained and future financial statements are also commented upon.	5

Trait			
Lease liability	**Level**	**Descriptor**	**Marks**
		No rewardable material	0
	Level 1	Explains with technical accuracy some of the generic aspects of how the lease liability will be initially and subsequently accounted for. Reference to the specific leased asset in the scenario and the financial statements might be missing or only briefly commented on.	1-2
	Level 2	Explains with technical accuracy most of the generic aspects of how the lease liability will be initially and subsequently accounted for. Reference to the specific leased asset in the scenario might be limited, although there has been an attempt to explain the treatment in the financial statements for 2021, although future years may be missing.	3-4
	Level 3	Explains with technical accuracy how a lease liability will be initially and subsequently accounted for with reference made to the specific leased asset in the scenario. The impact in the financial statements for 2021 is fully explain and future financial statements are also commented upon.	5

Examiner's comments

Most candidates were able to explain some elements of both the right of use asset and the lease liability, and in doing so achieve a level 2 score. However, although there were some very good level 3 answers, there were also many candidates who did not know how to account for leased assets. Common errors were failing to recognise that the right of use asset would be depreciated over 15 years and lack of clarity around which cash flows, would be included in both the lease liability and the asset. In answering financial reporting tasks clarity of answer could be improved by taking time to plan.

6.3 Variant 5 – section 3 – IFRS5

Scenario

- The directors have decided to start selling the floor care and garden product ranges in Asia. Sales in Asia turn out to be better than expected so the motor assembly line was expanded and plans made to sell the old assembly line equipment.
- Students were given a schedule detailing the plan for the old equipment:

  "The old assembly line will be used until 31 Oct 2020 when its accounting carrying amount will be E$35,000. It will be dismantled during November at a cost of E$4,500. On 1 Dec 2020 it will be advertised for sale at a price of E$50,000 and it is anticipated that a buyer will be found in early 2021."

Task

Students were asked to produce a briefing paper explaining:

(1) How the old assembly line should be reflected in the financial statements for the year ended 31 December 2020.

The question specified 24% of 45 minutes = 10.8 minutes or 6 marks for the task.

Suggested answer approach/structure

As stated above, most Core Activity D tasks warrant a little planning.

- Identify the relevant reporting standard(s). Here the issue is whether the old equipment constitutes an asset held for sale under IFRS 5.
- The task asks how the equipment would be reflected in the financial statements, so figures need to be discussed as well as classification. However, we don't know yet whether the equipment does satisfy the rules for an asset held for sale, so cannot say what the treatment in the financial statement is until we have done the first stage.

As usual, we can start by setting up headings

Old assembly line
1. Does the old assembly line meet the criteria for an "asset held for sale"?
2. Accounting treatment

We can then apply the usual steps for financial reporting tasks:

- State the rules as concisely as possible without over-simplifying

Old assembly line
1. Does the old assembly line meet the criteria for an "asset held for sale"?
To be reclassified as an asset held for sale, an asset needs to be available for immediate sale in its present condition and its sale must be highly probable.
A sale is highly probable when: management are committed to sell the asset; there is an active programme to find a buyer; the asset is marketed at a reasonable price; the sale is expected to take place within 12 months; and it is unlikely that the plan to sell the asset will change.
2. Accounting treatment
[*Don't know yet, so no point adding anything here*]

- Apply the rules to the facts in the scenario

Old assembly line

1. Does the old assembly line meet the criteria for an "asset held for sale"?

To be reclassified as an asset held for sale, an asset needs to be available for immediate sale in its present condition and its sale must be highly probable.

A sale is highly probable when: management are committed to sell the asset; there is an active programme to find a buyer; the asset is marketed at a reasonable price; the sale is expected to take place within 12 months; and it is unlikely that the plan to sell the asset will change.

The old assembly line will cease to be used on 31 October 2020 but will not be available for immediate sale in its present condition until it has been dismantled, which will happen in November.

From 1 December 2020 the assembly line will be advertised for sale and therefore from that date it could be said that there is a management plan to sell the asset and that a buyer is being sought, presumably at a reasonable price.

In addition, we expect the old assembly line to sell quite easily and therefore this would be within 12-month period specified in the accounting standard.

Therefore, once it has been dismantled the old assembly line asset will be reclassified as an asset held for sale and depreciation will stop.

2. Accounting treatment

At 31 December 2020 it is unlikely that the asset will have been sold and therefore, it will be recorded in the statement of financial position as an asset held for sale.

This will be at the lower of its carrying amount at the date that is reclassified as held for sale (which is after it has been dismantled and so will be E$35,000 less any depreciation) and fair value less costs to sell (E$50,000 less $4,500).

It would appear that this asset would be carried at its carrying amount as this is lower than the fair value less costs to sell.

Marking grids

Trait	Level	Descriptor	Marks
Asset held for sale	**Level**	**Descriptor**	**Marks**
		No rewardable material	0
	Level 1	Demonstrates some understanding of the recognition criteria of IFRS 5 in respect of assets held for sale but there is little attempt to apply these to the scenario. The impact of the reclassification to asset held for sale in the financial statements is only partially explained and lacks clarity.	1-2
	Level 2	Demonstrates reasonable understanding of the recognition criteria of IFRS 5 in respect of assets held for sale and attempts to apply these to the scenario. The impact of the reclassification to asset held for sale in the financial statements is explained, but the explanation may not be complete or may lack some clarity.	3-4
	Level 3	Demonstrates full understanding of the recognition criteria of IFRS 5 in respect of assets held for sale and applies these to the scenario. The impact of the reclassification as an asset held for sale in the financial statements is comprehensively and clearly explained.	5-6

Examiner's comments

This was reasonably answered by many candidates. To achieve a level 3 score candidates were expected to not just list the IFRS5 criteria for recognition of an asset held for sale, but to explain within the context of the scenario given if these had been satisfied. In addition, for a level 3 score candidates were expected to also explain and apply the valuation rule and the need to stop depreciation. Reasons why candidates did not score at level 3 included: a lack of knowledge of IFRS5; a lack of application of the criteria to the scenario; confusion regarding the valuation rule and confusion about how the E$4,500 selling fees affected the valuation.

7 Core Activity E: Decision making

7.1 Introduction

The May/August 2020 sittings examined the following tasks relating to Core Activity E (Decision making):

- Variant 1
  - – Multi-product B/E chart
  - – Relevant costs – make or buy decision
- Variant 2
  - – Relevant costs – minimum price decision
  - – Decision making with uncertainty
- Variant 3
  - – Linear programming
  - – Decision making with uncertainty
- Variant 4
  - – Decision making with risk
  - – Relevant costs – replacement decision
- Variant 5 – Decision tree
- Variant 6
  - – Using expected values to choose between suppliers
  - – Linear programming

Core Activity E generally causes the most problems for students. This is partly due to the wide range of methodologies that might be called upon, but mainly because it is not enough simply to learn the steps in a method. Case study tasks usually ask you both to apply and explain a model, so it is vital that you understand what you are doing.

The tasks that caused the most difficulties for students related to the distinction between risk (variant 4) and uncertainty (variant 3), multi-product break even (variant 1), and linear programming (variant 6). These are discussed below.

7.2 Variant 4 – section 1 – decision making with risk

Scenario

- The directors have carried out a review of operations following a decline in sales and an increase in production costs. As a result, it was agreed to consider investing in a new promotional campaign to boost sales. Three such campaigns are being considered.
- Students were given a schedule detailing possible impacts on profit, together with associated probabilities for each campaign, along with the standard deviation and co-efficient of variation for each campaign.
- Note: here we have possible outcomes with probabilities, so are dealing with *risk* rather than *uncertainty.*

Task

Students were asked to produce a briefing paper explaining:

(1) What the expected values, standard deviations and co-efficient of variations on Sophie's schedule mean and how different attitudes to risk will affect the decision about which promotional campaign to choose.

(2) Any limitations of basing our decision about which campaign to choose solely on the information in the schedule.

The question specified 48% of 45 minutes = 21.6 minutes or 12 marks for the task. The marking grid split this as 7 marks for the first subtask and 5 for the second.

Suggested answer approach/structure

Once you are clear on the requirements, the next step is to set up headings in the answer box as suggested by the question.

Promotional Campaign Decision
1. What the different measures mean
• expected values
• standard deviations
• co-efficient of variation
2. How risk attitudes will affect the decision
3. Limitations of using just the information in the schedule

Taking each of these in turn:

1. What the different measures mean

- Start with technical knowledge:

> The expected value for each campaign is the weighted average of all outcomes, weighted by the probabilities associated with each outcome.
>
> The standard deviation for each campaign is a measure of the variations of the outcomes from the expected value and is therefore a measure of volatility.
>
> The co-efficient of variation for each campaign is its standard deviation divided by its expected value. This gives the relative size of the risk when compared to the expected return and so enables comparison between the campaigns in respect of risk.

- Then relate the concepts to the information in the scenario:

> The expected value for each campaign is the weighted average of all outcomes, weighted by the probabilities associated with each outcome.
>
> **The schedule shows that Campaign 2 has the highest expected value and Campaign 3 the lowest.**
>
> The standard deviation for each campaign is a measure of the variations of the outcomes from the expected value and is therefore a measure of volatility.
>
> **Based on the estimates Campaign 3 has the greatest volatility of possible outcomes and is therefore potentially the riskiest.**
>
> The co-efficient of variation for each campaign is its standard deviation divided by its expected value. This gives the relative size of the risk when compared to the expected return and so enables comparison between the campaigns in respect of risk.
>
> **The schedule shows that Campaign 1 has the lowest risk per E$1 of expected value.**

2. How risk attitudes will affect the decision

- The next step would be to start with technical knowledge but, to do so, you need to stop and plan. Is the examiner asks you about 'risk attitudes' there are three that they will expect you to consider: risk seeking, risk neutral and risk averse:

> A risk seeker is a decision-maker who is interested in the best outcome no matter how small the likelihood that it will occur.
>
> A risk neutral decision maker will consider all possible outcomes and will choose the campaign that maximises the expected value.
>
> A risk averse decision-maker will choose the campaign which given the same level of return has the lowest level of risk. Such a decision-maker will choose the lowest coefficient of variation because this is a measure of risk for each E$1 of expected return.

- We can then see which campaign each type of investor will choose:

A risk seeker is a decision-maker who is interested in the best outcome no matter how small the likelihood that it will occur.

Campaign 3 has the highest of all of the nine possible outcomes of E$1,900,000 and a risk seeking decision-maker would therefore choose this campaign, despite the fact that there is only a 20% chance of this occurring.

A risk neutral decision maker will consider all possible outcomes and will choose the campaign that maximises the expected value.

Thus, a risk neutral decision-maker would select Campaign 2. This type of decision-maker would ignore both standard deviation and coefficient of variation.

A risk averse decision-maker will choose the campaign which given the same level of return has the lowest level of risk. Such a decision-maker will choose the lowest coefficient of variation because this is a measure of risk for each E$1 of expected return.

Such a decision-maker would therefore choose Campaign 1.

3. Limitations

- As before, the next step would be to start with technical knowledge but, again, it is worth planning an approach. Limitations could relate to the estimates used or to reliance of the specific statistics calculated:

Estimates used

The expected values, standard deviations and coefficients of variation are all based on Anthea Mansell's estimates of the impact of each campaign in terms of generating additional profit. Although Anthea is clearly an experienced marketeer and will know the Eastland market well, these estimates could be wrong, and this could affect the decision.

In addition, the probabilities are estimated. It could be that the chance of a very good reaction is higher than 20% and this would give more weighting to this outcome for each campaign which, again, might change the decision.

Statistics used

Expected value is not the most likely result, it is the long run average outcome if the same event was to be repeated over and over. This is a one-off decision and hence the expected value is not representative.

In addition, the co-efficient of variation assumes a linear relationship between risk and return and that decision-makers will be willing to risk more when the return is higher. This is seldom the case as a decision-maker's attitude towards losing changes as the value risked changes.

Marking grids

Trait			
The decision	**Level**	**Descriptor**	**Marks**
		No rewardable material	0
	Level 1	Explains with technical accuracy at least one of the measures. Demonstrates some understanding of how different risk attitudes affect the decision but there is little or no attempt to apply this to the information.	1-2
	Level 2	Explains with technical accuracy at least two of the measures. Demonstrates reasonable understanding of how different risk attitudes affect the decision and attempts to apply this to the information with some accuracy.	3-5
	Level 3	Explains with technical accuracy all three measures. Demonstrates good understanding of how different risk attitudes affect the decision and applies this to the information mostly correctly.	6-7
Trait			
Limitations	**Level**	**Descriptor**	**Marks**
		No rewardable material	0
	Level 1	Explains at least one limitation, although the explanation may lack clarity and / or depth.	1-2
	Level 2	Explains at least two limitations, although the explanation may lack clarity or depth.	3-4
	Level 3	Explains at least three limitations in mostly a clear and comprehensive manner.	5

Examiner's comments

Whilst most candidates were able to explain expected value and standard deviation, lower performing candidates did not know the meaning of the coefficient of variation. Good answers to this part of the question made use of the data to improve the clarity of their explanations. Candidates were mostly able to identify the campaigns that would be chosen given a risk seeking, risk averse and risk neutral attitude. However, some candidates tried to use maximax, maximin and minimax regret to answer this part of the question rather than referring to the measures they had been given. A level 3 answer to this task demonstrated good technical understanding of the risk measures and then used them to recommend which campaign would be chosen under each campaign and why. Risk and uncertainty are tested in several ways within the case study and it is important that candidates answer the task set. The task clearly signposted the three measures of risk as the basis of decision making. Most candidates were able to score at least a level 2 in relation to the limitations of using the data to make decisions. However, candidates are reminded to ensure points are sufficiently well developed.

7.3 Variant 3 – section 2 – decision making with uncertainty

Scenario

- Sales demand has increased significantly. As a result the directors are considering outsourcing some of the production of plastic parts. A potential supplier has been found but they are insisting that we guarantee in advance the quantity that we will buy from them.
- However, there is still uncertainty over sales demand so the directors have to choose between placing a low, medium or high order with the supplier.
- Students were given a pay-off table and a regret table showing incremental contribution for each order level under three different demand projections.
- Note: here we have possible outcomes but no probabilities, so are dealing with *uncertainty* rather than *risk,* and will thus discuss optimistic /pessimistic approaches as part of this.

Task

Students were asked to produce notes explaining:

(1) The figures shown in the payoff table and how the maximax, maximin, and minimax regret decision criteria would be applied to select the order level.

(2) Please also state the order level that would be chosen under each criterion.

The question specified 48% of 45 minutes = 21.6 minutes or 12 marks for the task. The marking grid split these 3:9.

Suggested answer approach/structure

Once you are clear on the requirements, the next step is to set up headings in the answer box as suggested by the question.

> <u>Determining the order level for plastic parts</u>
>
> 1. Explanation of figures in the pay-off table
> 2. Decision criteria
>   - maximax,
>   - maximin
>   - minimax regret

<u>1 Explanation of figures in the pay-off table</u>

- Start with technical knowledge – explain what a pay-off table shows but keep this part brief. Comments could include:

> Table 1 illustrates the impact on contribution of nine different combinations of order level and increased sales demand for the next 6 months period.

- Then start to explain the figures using the actual figures and scenario given. Note that the requirement is to explain the figures, not just describe them, so you need to add value.

  One way would be to look at where the figures come from, what elements they are comprised of or how they have been calculated, noting that this depends on whether the order level equals demand, there is a shortfall or if there is a surplus.

> Table 1 illustrates the impact on contribution of nine different combinations of order level and increased sales demand for the next 6 months period.
>
> **If we choose an order level equal to the level of increased demand, then we will earn incremental contribution at that level. We will earn incremental contribution of E$2,973,000 for 10%, E$4,459,000 for 15% and E$5,945,000 for 20%.**
>
> **If we choose an order level which is lower than the additional demand, we will earn the incremental contribution associated with the order level but there will be a lost opportunity as we have failed to fulfil the increased demand.**
>
> **If we choose an order level greater than the level of demand, we will earn the incremental contribution associated with the level of demand less the cost of recycling the excess plastic parts.**

2 Explanation of Maximax, Maximin and Minimax Regret

- Start with technical knowledge.

  Note that you have to explain how the criteria are applied, so as well as outlining the basic approach, try to explain underlying assumptions and link to attitudes to decision making:

> *Maximax criterion:*
>
> The maximax criterion is where the decision maker takes an optimistic approach.
>
> In this approach, the alternative that maximises the maximum pay-off achievable under each alternative will be selected.
>
> *Maximin criterion:*
>
> Under the maximin criteria we would select the alternative that maximises the minimum pay-off achievable under each alternative.
>
> This is where a pessimistic approach is taken.
>
> *Minimax regret criterion:*
>
> Under this criterion the alternative that minimises the maximum regret under each alternative is selected.
>
> This is generally used where we want to minimise the effect of making a bad decision. 'Regret' refers to the opportunity loss from having made the wrong decision. This is also where a pessimistic approach is taken to the decision.

- As before we can then apply these to the figures given in the table.

Maximax criterion:

The maximax criterion is where the decision maker takes an optimistic approach. In this approach, the alternative that maximises the maximum pay-off achievable under each alternative will be selected.

We would therefore choose a high order level which has the maximum payoff of E$5,945,000.

Maximin criterion:

Under the maximin criteria we would select the alternative that maximises the minimum pay-off achievable under each alternative. This is where a pessimistic approach is taken.

We would therefore choose a low order level as this gives the maximum of the minimum payoffs of E$2,973,000.

Minimax regret criterion:

Under this criterion the alternative that minimises the maximum regret under each alternative is selected.

This is generally used where we want to minimise the effect of making a bad decision. 'Regret' refers to the opportunity loss from having made the wrong decision. This is also where a pessimistic approach is taken to the decision.

In this case the maximum regret would be E$2,972,000 at a low order level, E$1,486,000 at a medium order level and E$414,000 at a high order level. Therefore, if we want to minimise the maximum regret, we would choose a high order level.

- Note: the first part of the question only asked you to explain the figures in the pay-off table but not the regret table, so you may have wondered whether you should explain the latter when discussing the minimax regret criterion. If so, you could include an extra paragraph as follows:

Minimax regret criterion:

Under this criterion the alternative that minimises the maximum regret under each alternative is selected. This is generally used where we want to minimise the effect of making a bad decision. 'Regret' refers to the opportunity loss from having made the wrong decision. This is also where a pessimistic approach is taken to the decision.

The regret matrix shows the regret depending on sales demand and the order level which we had chosen. For example, if the sales demand increase turned out to be at the low level, we would have no regret if we had chosen a low order level. The regret for each of the other order levels would be the difference between a contribution of E$2,973,000 and the contribution from each of the other order levels. Having calculated the regret for each different level of demand, we can then establish the maximum regret for each order level.

In this case the maximum regret would be E$2,972,000 at a low order level, E$1,486,000 at a medium order level and E$414,000 at a high order level. Therefore, if we want to minimise the maximum regret, we would choose a high order level.

Marking grids

Trait			
Payoff table	**Level**	**Descriptor**	**Marks**
		No rewardable material	0
	Level 1	Provides a weak explanation of the figures in the payoff table.	1
	Level 2	Provides a reasonable explanation of the figures in the payoff table.	2
	Level 3	Provides a good explanation of the figures in the payoff table.	3
Trait			
Criteria	**Level**	**Descriptor**	**Marks**
		No rewardable material	0
	Level 1	Demonstrates a weak technical understanding of the decision criteria and how they are applied. The explanation given may lack clarity and / or the order quantities identified are incorrect.	1-3
	Level 2	Demonstrates a reasonable technical understanding of the decision criteria and how they are applied. There may be some inaccuracies in the explanation and / or one or more of the order quantities identified are incorrect.	4-6
	Level 3	Demonstrates a good technical understanding of the decision criteria and how they are applied. The explanation given is mostly clear and the correct order quantities are identified for at least two of the criteria.	7-9

Examiner's comments

The first part of this task to explain the payoff table was ignored by most candidates. Those who did attempt to explain the payoff table often described the figures rather than explaining them and therefore failed to achieve more than a level 1 here. Future candidates must understand the difference between a description and an explanation; an explanation adds value to the description.

Most candidates provided level 2 and level 3 answers when explaining and applying the decision criteria, although it was interesting to notice, how many believed that these were somehow based on probabilities.

7.4 Variant 1 – section 1 – break even analysis including a graph

Scenario

- The company has decided to bring out a new range of e-bikes. Given this the Senior Management Team has requested an analysis of the break-even position for the new range.
- Students were given a multi-product break even chart with supporting tables of information.

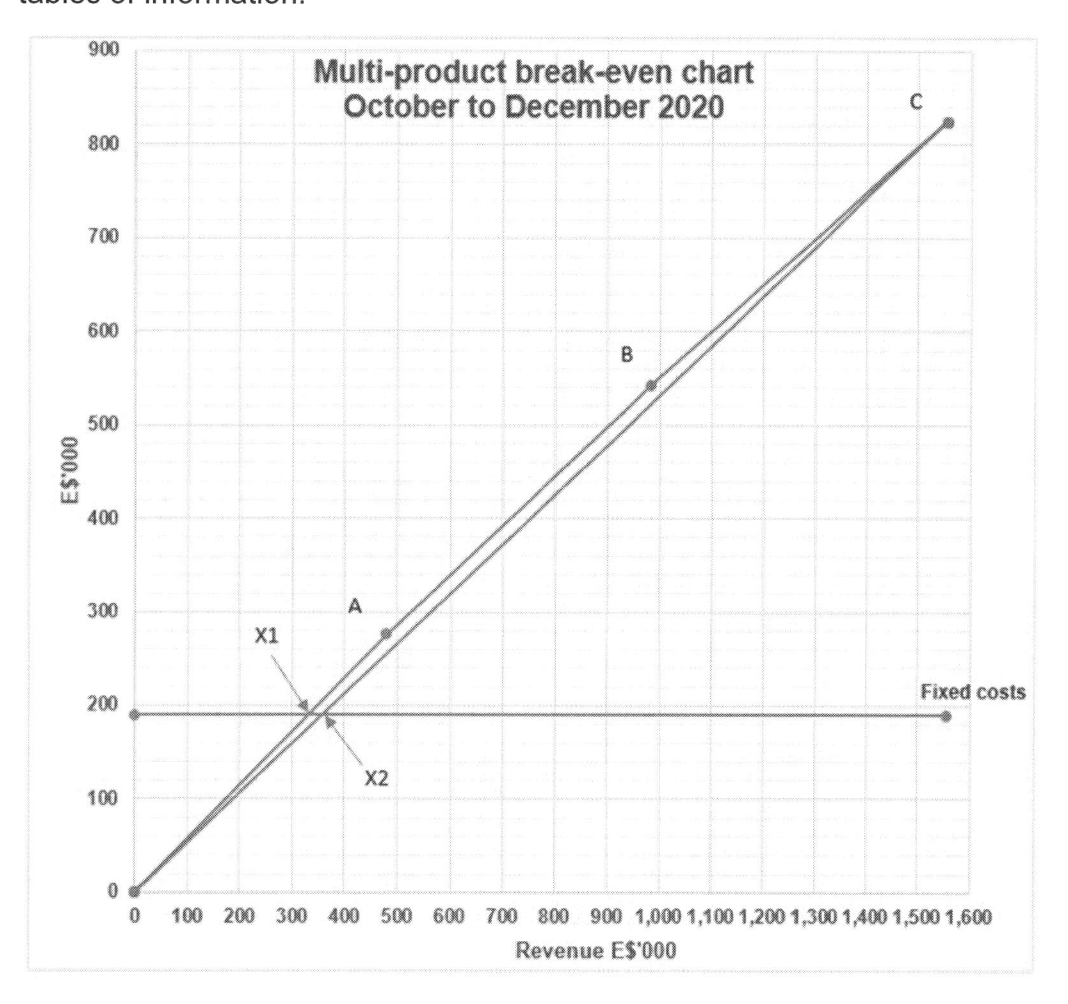

Task

Students were then asked to produce a report explaining:

(1) The multi-product break-even chart and the benefits and

(2) limitations of the break-even analysis for the new range of e-bikes.

The question specified 52% of 45 minutes = 23.4 minutes or 13 marks for the task. The marking grid split this 5:8.

Suggested answer approach/structure

Once you are clear on the requirements, the next step is to set up headings in the answer box as suggested by the question.

Multi-product break even chart 1. Explanation of the chart 2. Benefits and limitations

1. Explanation of the chart

- Based on your technical knowledge you should be able to understand what each point and line represents. As well as explaining this, you would need to apply your comments to ChargeIT by incorporating actual figures and details from the chart given in the scenario:

> The horizontal line is the fixed cost line which does not change at different activity levels within the relevant range.
>
> The straight line 0C represents the weighted average contribution line at different sales levels assuming that the expected sales mix remains constant.
>
> Point X2 is the breakeven point on the weighted average contribution line. Based on the average contribution to sales ratio we can see that in order to break even we would need to achieve sales revenue of approximately E$350,000.
>
> The other line which connects points 0, A, B and C represents the relationship between contribution and sales on the assumption that we sell the products in order of the contribution to sales ratio.
>
> For example, the line from Point 0 to Point A represents the contribution from the sale of the Urban bike which has the highest contribution to sales ratio.
>
> Point X1 is the break-even point on this line. As you can see the break-even point is lower (and therefore reached sooner) on this line than on the weighted average contribution line.

2. Benefits and limitations

- Start with technical knowledge. Comments could include:

> *Benefits*
>
> The chart is useful because it gives us an idea of the sales level required to cover our fixed costs.
>
> By knowing the break-even position, it helps to understand the margin of safety that we have from the forecast or budgeted figures. The margin of safety is the amount by which revenue can fall from the expected revenue before a loss is made. The margin of safety is usually measured as a percentage.

> *Limitations*
>
> It is likely that we will not be able to sell the products in the order of their respective contribution to sales ratios. Therefore, plotting the line 0ABC is unlikely to reflect the true situation.
>
> Equally, it is unlikely that we will sell our products at a constant sales mix. The true break-even is probably going to lie somewhere between the two lines.
>
> The weighted average contribution line assumes that the products will be sold in a certain mix however there is a risk that the weighted average contribution to sales ratio will be lower and therefore the break-even point will be higher if we sell in a different mix.

- Then try to illustrate or apply ideas to the specific chart and figures. Comments could include:

> *Benefits*
>
> The chart is useful because it gives us an idea of the sales level required to cover our fixed costs. By knowing the break-even position, it helps to understand the margin of safety that we have from the forecast or budgeted figures. The margin of safety is the amount by which revenue can fall from the expected revenue before a loss is made. The margin of safety is usually measured as a percentage.
>
> **The chart shows us that the expected revenue is approximately E$1.55 million and therefore we have a margin of safety of approximately E$1.2 million before we would make a loss. Whilst this is a new market for us and the estimates may be over optimistic, this represents a significant margin of safety.**
>
> *Limitations*
>
> It is likely that we will not be able to sell the products in the order of their respective contribution to sales ratios. Therefore, plotting the line 0ABC is unlikely to reflect the true situation.
>
> Equally, it is unlikely that we will sell our products at a constant sales mix. The true break-even is probably going to lie somewhere between the two lines.
>
> The weighted average contribution line assumes that the products will be sold in a certain mix however there is a risk that the weighted average contribution to sales ratio will be lower and therefore the break-even point will be higher if we sell in a different mix.
>
> **For example, if we sell a higher proportion of the mountain bike which has the lowest contribution to sales ratio then the weighted average contribution to sales ratio will be lower.**

- Finally revisit the requirement to see if there is an angle you have missed or a wider perspective that could be added. In this question a discussion of "limitations" could be expanded to also discuss the figures used, how they have been derived and any assumptions made:

Limitations

The figures used are estimates only and assume a linear relationship over the whole range of production. The analysis also assumes that we can define costs as fixed or variable. In reality all costs are variable in the long term and in the short term many costs that we think of as variable are fixed, for example, labour costs.

Additionally, the fixed costs included in the chart represent only the specific fixed costs associated with the new product range. We would however expect our products to also contribute to the general fixed costs. If the new product range was allocated a share of general fixed overhead costs, the break-even point would increase and the margin of safety would fall.

Marking grids

Trait			
Chart	**Level**	**Descriptor**	**Marks**
		No rewardable material	0
	Level 1	Identifies correctly some of the lines and points on the chart.	1-2
	Level 2	Identifies correctly most of the lines and points on the chart.	3-4
	Level 3	Identifies correctly all of the lines and points on the chart.	5
Trait			
Benefit & Limitations	**Level**	**Descriptor**	**Marks**
		No rewardable material	0
	Level 1	Identifies at least one benefit of the analysis and at least one limitation but the explanation lacks clarity.	1-3
	Level 2	Identifies more than one benefit of the analysis and at least two limitations and gives a reasonable explanation of these.	4-6
	Level 3	Identifies the main benefits of the analysis and more than two limitations and gives a good explanation of these.	7-8

Examiner's comments

Most candidates were able to explain the chart and identify the various lines and points, with many scoring at level 3. The part of the task relating to the benefits and limitations of break-even analysis was not particularly well-answered. Most candidates gave a very brief answer here, which therefore limited their ability to score much above a low level 2.

7.5 Variant 6 – section 4 – linear programming including a graph

Scenario

- A fire has destroyed one of the small raw materials warehouses, resulting in a short term shortage of two types of raw materials (grey plastic pellets and bought-in component FF), both of which are required for production of products P56 and R18.
- A linear programming graph has been produced to help plan production, along with supporting notes.

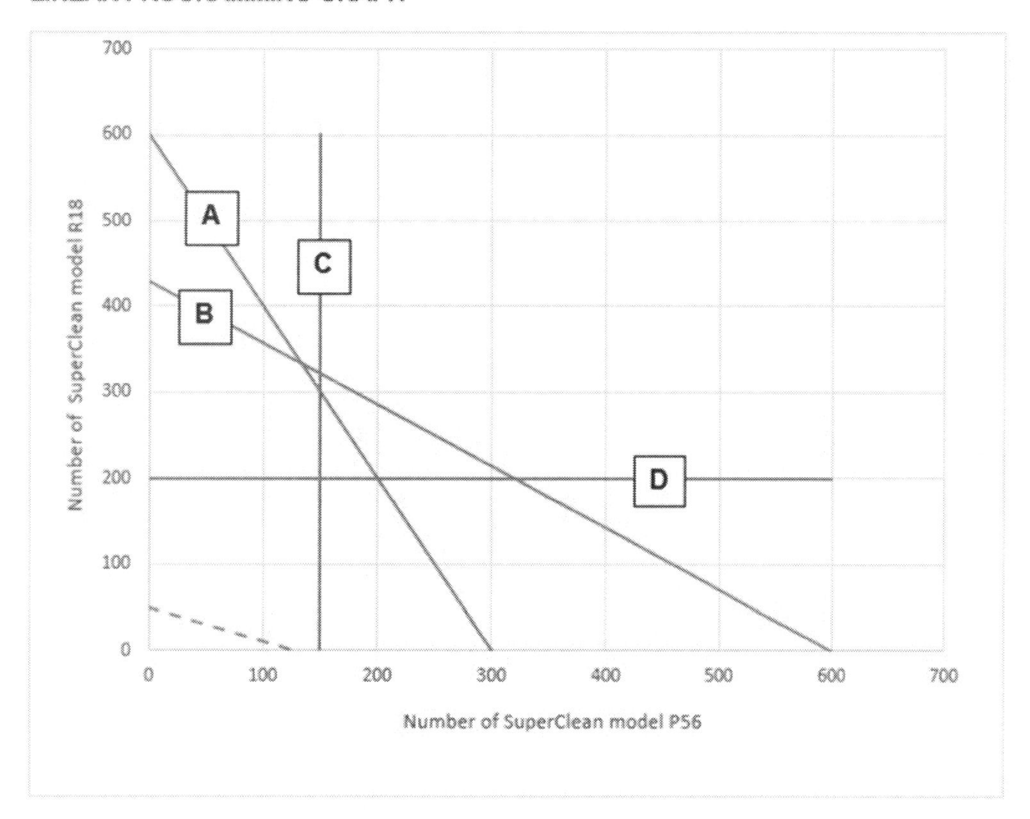

Task

Students were then asked to produce a briefing note explaining:

(1) Where the feasible region is on the linear programming graph and what the optimal production plan for the next two weeks is.

(2) How we could use the graph to determine the maximum quantity we should order and the maximum price we should pay for additional grey plastic pellets from the alternative supplier.

The question specified 56% of 45 minutes = 25.2 minutes or 14 marks for the overall task. The marking grid split this 7:7.

Suggested answer approach/structure

Note: This would have been very tricky had you forgotten basic technical knowledge concerning linear programming, especially with the second part on shadow prices!

Once you are clear on the requirements, the next step is to set up headings in the answer box as suggested by the question.

Linear programming graph
1. Feasible region and optimal production plan
2. Purchasing additional grey plastic pellets

Taking each of these in turn:

1. Feasible region and optimal production plan

- Linear programming has a well-defined series of steps:

  (1) identify/explain constraints,

  (2) identify/explain the feasible region,

  (3) identify/explain the objective function/iso-contribution line,

  (4) identify the optimal solution and interpret.

  The first task only asks for steps 2 and 4 but you need to walk through each step to get to the end.

  Note that the requirement asks you to explain the process, rather than just describe it, emphasising the point that to do well in Core Activity E you need to understand the steps in a particular method, not just learn them.

  Unlike other tasks, there are very few generic technical points you can put down here. Instead you need to walk through the steps applying (and explaining) them as you go:

Introduction The feasible region is the area of the graph which includes all of the possible combinations of SuperClean model P56 and SuperClean model R18 that can be produced given the raw material constraints and the two minimum production levels. *Constraint lines* Lines A and B on the graph represent the different combinations of production of SuperClean model P56 and SuperClean model R18 which utilise all of the available grey plastic pellets and FF components respectively. These lines therefore represent the maximum that can be produced and form a boundary for the feasible region which will be to the left of these lines. Given the constraints, it is impossible to produce above the line. Lines C and D on the graph represent the committed orders for each model.

Line C is for model P56 and shows that minimum production needs to be 150 units.

Line D is for model R18 and shows that minimum production needs to be 200 units.

The feasible region will be to the right of line C and above line D.

Feasible region

The feasible region is the small triangular area of the graph which starts at the point where lines C and D intersect and is contained by line A.

Iso-contribution line and optimal solution

The optimal production plan can be found by moving the iso-contribution line (the dotted line which represents the relative contributions of each SuperClean model) until it reaches the furthest point from the origin that is still within the feasible region: this is where lines A and C intersect.

Therefore, the optimal production plan for the next two weeks is to produce approximately 150 of model P56 and approximately 300 of model R18 over the next 2 weeks.

Note: it is acceptable to use the graph to give a rough idea of the optimal solution. There is no need to solve simultaneous equations here to get a more exact figure.

2. Purchasing additional grey plastic pellets

- The maximum price we will pay for a resource = normal price + shadow price.
- Determining shadow prices also follows a well-defined series of steps:
  (1) Confirm whether the resource in question is a binding constraint. If not, then the shadow price is zero.
  (2) If we do have a binding constraint, then change the constraint equation to incorporate one extra unit of that resource. This effectively moves the constraint line out.
  (3) This moves the optimal solution outwards. Calculate the new product mix for this solution.
  (4) Determine the new value of the objective function (usually contribution) and compare this to the original optimal value. The difference will give the shadow price.
  (5) This process can be repeated until a different constraint becomes binding, so there is a limit on how many extra units of a resource would be wanted.

However, you need to ensure that you answer the question. The task specifically asks about how to use the graph and therefore it was expected that students explained moving the iso-line. It was not a general question about how to determine the shadow price or the maximum to pay and therefore there was no need to talk about simultaneous equations, say.

- Given this, we can develop our answer as follows:

Confirm whether the resource in question is a binding constraint.

We need to consider if it is worth purchasing more grey plastic pellets at a premium price to allow us to satisfy more of the uncommitted orders for the next 2 weeks.

The optimal point is where lines A and C intersect which means that grey plastic pellets are a binding constraint and FF components are a non-binding constraint. Therefore, it would potentially be worthwhile buying more grey plastic pellets.

The maximum price that we would be prepared to pay will be the normal price per kilogram plus its shadow price, where the shadow price is the increase in contribution from obtaining an additional kilogram of grey plastic pellets.

Move the constraint line outwards and recalculate optimal solution

Assuming that purchasing more grey plastic pellets is worthwhile in terms of its shadow price, as we purchase each additional kilogram, line A on the graph will move away from the origin and the size of the feasible region increases.

This changes the optimal solution and given that we cannot obtain more of component FF gives us two new potential solutions: where lines B and C intersect or where lines B and D intersect.

If we move the iso-contribution line away from the origin, we can see that contribution will be maximised where lines B and C intersect (because this is the furthest point that the line will reach in this new feasible area).

Determine the shadow price

At this point line A would only have moved a small amount and the new optimum production plan would therefore be 150 P56s and approximately 320 R18's. Therefore, we need to purchase enough grey plastic pellets to make an additional 20 R18s.

The maximum price that we would pay for these additional pellets would be normal price per kilogram plus the additional contribution earned from the additional 20 R18s.

Marking grids

Trait	Level	Descriptor	Marks
The LP graph		No rewardable material	0
	Level 1	Explains with some accuracy where the feasible region of the graph is, but explanation lacks clarity. The optimal solution might not have been stated, but if it has, it is likely to have been incorrectly identified based on the explanation of the feasible region	1-2
	Level 2	Explains with reasonable accuracy where the feasible region on the graph is and identifies the optimal solution based on this explanation (that is, not necessarily the correct solution, but consistent with their explanation of the feasible region).	3-5
	Level 3	Explains accurately where the feasible region on the graph is and identifies the correct optimal solution.	6-7
Trait	**Level**	**Descriptor**	**Marks**
Grey pellets		No rewardable material	0
	Level 1	Demonstrates some understanding of binding constraints and shadow price but fails to apply this to the scenario.	1-2
	Level 2	Demonstrates reasonable understanding of binding constraints and shadow price. Is unlikely to identify the new optimal point but will make an attempt to use the graph to determine how much to buy and how much to pay.	3-5
	Level 3	Demonstrates good understanding of binding constraints and shadow price. Will correctly identify the new optimal point and explain this in the context of how much to buy and at what price.	6-7

Examiner's comments

A wide range of answers were provided for this task with a significant minority of candidates getting a "no rewardable material" mark. Other candidates were able to identify the correct feasible region but failed to explain how this was arrived at. Other candidates simply guessed at an optimal production plan.

Also, very few candidates could make a valid attempt at determining the maximum price to pay for additional grey pellets. There was a recognition by some candidates that this involved a shadow price, but even these could not always explain this term. For example, some thought the shadow price was the price that should be paid rather than being the increase in contribution.

Only a few of candidates explained how the graph could be used to determine the maximum to order, although some did recognise that it was only worth ordering up until the point that component FF was used up. Few candidates scored well here.

8 Core Activity F: Working Capital

8.1 Introduction

The May/August 2020 sittings examined the following tasks relating to Core Activity F (Working Capital):

- Variant 1 – Avoiding a cash deficit.
- Variant 2 – Review of supplier's working capital.
- Variant 3 – Short term investment.
- Variant 4 – Management of inventory
- Variant 5 – EOQ
- Variant 6 – Receivables management.

On the whole, most students were reasonably good at working capital tasks, and no specific tasks caused major problems. Given this we have not discussed any tasks in greater detail for this core activity.

9 Final tips

Finally, as part of the examiner's report, the examiner has given the following general advice for candidates:

How to achieve a level 3 answer

To achieve a level 3 in most traits, it was expected that a candidate would

- Demonstrate good technical understanding of the topic being tested
- Give clear and comprehensive explanation
- Apply this technical understanding to the business and the particular scenario within the task.

Reasons why a student may only score a level 1

If a candidate scored only at a level 1 on a trait, it is likely that they did one or all of the following:

- Demonstrated some technical understanding, but with gaps in knowledge.
- Explained issues too briefly or with a lack of clarity.
- Failed to relate their answer to the task scenario and the specifics of the business concerned.

The need for application to the scenario

- It must be stressed that demonstrating good technical understanding is not enough on its own to pass. Candidates need to demonstrate technical understanding in the context of the scenario and the particulars of the issue being addressed.
- Information given to candidates as part of the task is there for a reason and should be, as far as possible, incorporated into answers, along with relevant information from the pre-seen.
- Application to the scenario is key to achieving high level 2 and level 3 scores

The need for technical knowledge

- Clearly where there are gaps in knowledge, application is not possible and therefore the importance of candidates ensuring that their knowledge base is complete needs to be stressed.

The importance of explaining answers

- One other area worthy of mention is candidates' ability to explain.
- At the operational level many of the tasks require explanation and to achieve high level 2 and level 3, it is expected that this will be clear and comprehensive. It should also be an explanation rather a description.

Chapter

7

February 2020 exam session by core activity

Chapter learning objectives

- To understand the core activities and assessment outcomes required for the case study exam.

1 Core Activities

As stated in chapter 1, the blueprint defines the following core activities:

	Core Activity	Weighting
A	Prepare costing information for different purposes to meet the needs of management.	12–18%
B	Prepare budget information and assess its use for planning and control purposes.	17–25%
C	Analyse performance using financial and non-financial information.	17–25%
D	Apply relevant financial reporting standards and corporate governance, ethical and tax principles.	12–18%
E	Prepare information to support short-term decision-making.	17–25%
F	Prepare information to manage working capital.	7–13%

As also stated in chapter 1, **all** core activities will be assessed in each variant of the examination in line with the above weightings.

These core activities are linked to associated assessment outcomes expressed in terms of 'I Can' statements that speak directly to the skills and competencies that drive the employability of successful learners. While every core activity is examined in each variant, a selection of assessment outcomes is covered.

In the rest of this chapter we will look at how these were examined in the three variants of the February 2020 real exam. In this chapter exam tasks have been separated out and then grouped by core activity, thus enabling the following:

- It will help you appreciate the range of possible tasks within each core activity
- You can revise and practice one core activity at a time, making it easier to identify gaps in knowledge that need addressing.

You are encouraged to attempt the tasks as part of your preparation.

2 February 2020 real exam – summary of pre-seen scenario

The pre-seen information concerns a company called Lottie Graphite that manufactures high-quality pencils in Gawland in Western Europe.

Business Model

The company makes three products – graphite pencils, coloured pencils and PEXECO pencils. Founded in 1902, the company now has a globally recognised brand with all products acknowledged as being of premium quality.

While product developments in the industry have been rare, the company has tried to take full advantage of new technologies, especially in production. With the exception of packaging, almost every aspect of manufacturing is now automated with production flow managed by robotics.

Many other aspects of business are also kept "in-house" – the company has sales offices in 20 countries, operates its own warehouses in strategic locations and maintains its own transport fleet, although local couriers are used for some website sales.

The last main product development was five years ago and it could be argued that the Board have lacked ambition, that the company has stagnated to a degree and is in need of new growth areas.

Industry trends

Sales growth in the pencil industry has been slow but steady over recent years. However, within this, higher growth opportunities exist in certain regions. New products and markets are needed to achieve higher growth.

Financial performance

Revenue grew by 1.3% from 2018 to 2019, resulting in an increase of 5.0% in operating profit and an increase in gross profit margins from 44.2% to 44.6%.

In terms of working capital and liquidity, cash decreased by G$1.7 million, due partly to a net investment of G$7.5 million in non-current assets and a dividend payment of G$6.1 million. Going forwards, if Lottie Graphite intends to invest more in new products then it may not be able to achieve a similar level of dividends unless long term debt is raised.

The other concern is that the overall investment in working capital increased by G$1.8 million. Within this, inventory days went up to 101 days, which seems unnecessarily excessive.

Ownership and governance

The company is still owned by the original founder's family. As such there has been little drive or need to ensure it complies with governance best practice.

The future

Three new areas for growth are highlighted:

- To develop and sell cosmetics pencils
- To develop and sell a stylus pencil to be used on laptops
- Expansion into the neighbouring country of Feland.

3 Core Activity A – Costing

Core activity A tasks will be worth, in total, between 12 and 18% of the paper.

The February 2020 exam had the following Core Activity A tasks:

Variant	Total marks	Task	Marks	Details
1	15	2(b)	10	Compare the effect on profit of using marginal costing compared to absorption costing
		2(c)	5	Explain throughput accounting
2	13	2(b)	13	Explain digital costing and its benefits
3	13	1(a)	13	Costing of a digital cost object

3.1 Exam variant 1 – tasks 2(b) and 2(c)

[Context]

The decision has been made to expand into Feland.

[Task]

Julie Welk, Head of Finance sends you the following email:

From: **Julie Welk, Head of Finance**

To: **Finance Officer**

Subject: **Different costing methods**

In the light of the expected increase in demand from the expansion into Feland, Jack Berlin, Production Director has asked whether our costing systems are fit for purpose. We sent Jack a copy of the summary management accounts for weeks 1 and 2 for graphite pencil production (see below). These include a version using marginal costing principles as well as the usual absorption costing version. This has caused him to ask a lot of questions. He wants to know why marginal costing gives a higher profit than absorption costing in both weeks, even though the revenues are the same. He is also asking why we use absorption costing as he has heard that it has many weaknesses.

Please draft an explanation of:

- The reasons for the differences between the marginal and absorption profits shown in the two profit statements, for each of weeks 1 & 2.
- Whether marginal costing will always show a higher profit than absorption costing.
- The benefits of using absorption costing to our business.

Finally, Jack has heard of throughput accounting and wonders if it would be of any value to our business especially as we expect an increase in demand.

Please draft an explanation of:

- The principles of throughput accounting and its potential benefit to our business. Use examples in our business to illustrate where possible.

(sub-task (b) = 40%)

REFERENCE MATERIALS:

Table 2: Profit Statements for weeks 1 and 2 using absorption and marginal costing

	Week 1		**Week 2**	
Number of batches produced	3,800		3,900	
Number of batches sold	3,900		4,100	
Absorption Costing	G$000	G$000	G$000	G$000
Sales		2,145		2,255
Cost of sales				
Opening inventory	1,812		1,782	
Production cost	1,148		1,178	
Closing inventory	(1,782)		(1,722)	
		(1,178)		(1,238)
(Under) over absorption		(9)		1
Gross profit		**958**		**1,018**
Marginal Costing	G$000	G$000	G$000	G$000
Sales		2,145		2,255
Cost of sales				
Opening inventory	1,078		1,060	
Production cost	683		701	
Closing inventory	(1,060)		(1,024)	
		(701)		(737)
Contribution		**1,444**		**1,518**
Fixed production overhead		(474)		(476)
Profit		**970**		**1,042**

Notes:

1 Budgeted fixed production overhead was G$477,000 and budgeted production was 3,900 batches for each of the two weeks.

2 Other than fixed production overhead, all other costs and selling prices were as standard.

Exercise 1

Write the draft content for the sections of the report as requested by Julie Welks.

3.2 Exam variant 2 – task 2(b)

[Context]

Sales of the PEXECO pencil are higher than expected. The directors have decided to invest in a new, highly digitised production line for PEXECO production.

[Task]

Julie Welk, Head of Finance sends you the following email:

From: **Julie Welk, Head of Finance**

To: **Finance Officer**

Subject: **PEXECO assets and digital costing**

Mia Schmied, Managing Director, has just sent me an email asking for some information about a couple of things.

[...]

Secondly, Mia has been talking to an old friend of hers who is a director of a large manufacturing company. Apparently, his company has recently installed highly digitised and integrated production machinery and purchasing systems like we are now installing for PEXECO and they have been able to utilise these systems through digital costing to improve their costing information. Mia has asked me to look into this.

I would like you to prepare content for a briefing paper to Mia Schmied, in which you explain:

- How our current costing system works, how digital costing might change this and the benefits of doing this for our business.

(sub-task (b) = 52%)

Julie Welk

Exercise 2

Write the briefing paper to Mia Schmied as requested by Julie Welk.

3.3 Exam variant 3 – task 1(a)

[Context]

The new S-Pencil (a digital stylus) has been developed. In addition, the associated app has also been developed. Initial development of the app was carried out by a third-party specialist tech company called FirstApps at a cost of G$250,000. The S-Pencil will be launched onto the market in two months' time when the app has been fully tested by FirstApps.

[Task]

You receive the following email from Cameron Scott, Finance Manager:

From: **Cameron Scott, Finance Manager**

To: **Finance Officer**

Subject: **S-Pencil budget and costings**

I have been talking to Ben Thakar, Sales and Marketing director and Mia Schmied, Managing Director about the budget for the new S-Pencil.

Ben has told me that he still hasn't decided on the S-Pencil's selling price. This is because he wants to make sure that the price gives us a decent profit margin as well as covering the manufacturing costs of the pencil and the cost of developing and operating the app. The basic app, for which FirstApps will charge us a small royalty fee, will allow the user to use the stylus on their mobile, tablet or laptop screen and will be included free of charge to the customer with each S-Pencil purchased. However, within the app there are options for users to buy additional content such as drawing and colouring tools. We've got a good idea of what the costs are to manufacture the S-Pencil, but it will be quite difficult to establish a cost per app. I've told Ben I'll send him a briefing paper on what these difficulties are together with some ideas of what future costs we will incur in respect of the app.

I need you to write content for a briefing paper that I need to send to each director which explains:

- The difficulties associated with establishing a cost per app for the S-Pencil and the types of cost still to be incurred for the app.

(sub-task (a) = 52%)

Cameron Scott

Exercise 3

Write the content for the briefing papers as requested by Cameron Scott.

4 Core Activity B – Budgeting

Core activity B tasks will be worth, in total, between 17 and 25% of the paper.

The February 2020 exam had the following Core Activity B tasks:

Variant	Total marks	Task	Marks	Details
1	25	1(a)	9	Explain the advantages and disadvantages of participatory budgeting
		1(b)	10	Explain time series information
		1(c)	6	Explain the limitations of time series analysis for predicting future demand
2	17	3(a)	9	Explain what-if analysis
		3(c)	8	Explain the application of activity-based budgeting
3	18	1(b)	12	Time series analysis
		4(c)	6	Beyond budgeting

4.1 Exam variant 1 – Tasks 1(a, b and c)

[Context/Trigger]

The decision has been made to begin selling pencils in Feland, a large country that has only recently allowed foreign trade. This will involve setting up a new sales office and distribution centre in Feland. Key personnel are already located in Feland; establishing a workforce, customer base and supply network.

[Task]

You receive the following email from Julie Welk, Head of Finance:

From: **Julie Welk, Head of Finance**

To: **Finance Officer**

Subject: **Budgeting and forecasting for Feland**

Although we have several experienced managers who are already working in Feland: making contracts, visiting potential customers and suppliers, seeking out suitable locations for our offices and so on, we have yet to set any formal budgets.

The managers on location, while not all senior, are likely to be budget holders in various roles in Feland for at least two years following the start-up of operations and we intend to include a bonus element in their remuneration packages that will be related to the achievement of budget targets.

It has been suggested that the budgets for the operations in Feland should be produced using a participative approach to budget setting, as opposed to our usual method. I have agreed to put together a briefing paper for the senior manager responsible for this new market explaining the implications of this.

Please prepare content for the briefing paper, which:

- Explains the advantages and disadvantages to Lottie Graphite of using a participative approach to budget setting in these circumstances. Please also explain whether you think participative budgeting would be an appropriate method for setting the budgets for the operations in Feland.

(sub-task (a) = 36%)

As a starting point for the budgets, I have prepared time series based on our sales in Neland, a country similar to Feland in size and cultural traits (see below). The trend was calculated using linear regression analysis based on the last three years' sales. The results are shown in table 2. The seasonal variations were calculated on an additive basis, but I'm not sure if this is appropriate. I would like you to prepare a briefing paper that explains:

- What tables 1, 2 and 3 of the attached schedule tell us about the demand for pencils in Neland and whether the calculation of seasonal variations on an additive basis is appropriate.

(sub-task (b) = 40%)

- The limitations of this analysis for use in predicting future demand for pencils in Feland.

(sub-task (c) = 24%)

REFERENCE MATERIALS:

Table 1: TIME SERIES ANALYSIS OF NELAND SALES

Year	Quarter	Sales Volume Pencils (000)	Trend Pencils (000)	Seasonal variation pencils (000)
2017	1	1,899	2,108	–209
	2	3,768	2,216	1,552
	3	1,400	2,324	–924
	4	1,941	2,432	–491
2018	1	2,286	2,540	–254
	2	4,504	2,648	1,856
	3	1,657	2,756	–1,099
	4	2,296	2,864	–568
2019	1	2,679	2,972	–293
	2	5,236	3,080	2,156
	3	1,920	3,188	–1,268
	4	2,633	3,296	–663

REFERENCE MATERIALS (Continued):

Table 2: LINEAR REGRESSION EQUATION

Y = a + bX

Where

Y = Trend (000 pencils)

a = 2,000

b = 108

X = the quarter number (where quarter 1 2017 = 1, quarter 2 2017 = 2 etc)

Table 3: SEASONAL VARIATIONS

Quarter	1	2	3	4
Average seasonal variation (000)	–235	1,872	–1,080	–557

Notes:

- The time series is based on our sales in Neland, a country of a similar size and cultural traits to Feland.
- Lottie Graphite have traded successfully in Neland for over a decade. It has a young population and its economy is developing rapidly.
- A peculiar feature of Neland is that its academic year for schools and universities begins in May. In Feland the academic year begins in September.

Exercise 4

Write your response to Julie Welk.

4.2 Exam variant 2 – Tasks 3(a and c)

[Summary of context]

Sales of the PEXECO pencil are higher than expected. The directors have decided to invest in a new, highly digitised production line for PEXECO production.

[Task]

Julie Welk, Head of Finance, calls you into her office and says:

The directors have been looking at the draft budget for the new PEXECO production facility for the four-month period September to December 2020. Ben Thakar, Sales and Marketing Director, believes that there is real scope to increase the volume of PEXECO sales by decreasing selling prices.

He is optimistic about this and believes that if selling prices were reduced by 5%, sales volumes would increase by 15%, and if selling prices were reduced by 10%, sales volumes would increase by 30%.

Mia Schmied, Managing Director, is far less confident that sales will increase as much as Ben believes She has requested that we perform sensitivity analysis and also consider expected values. I prefer 'what-if' to sensitivity analysis and have produced profit estimates based on Ben's assumptions. I think there is likely to be an increase in fixed costs when volumes increase by more than 20%, so my profit estimates also include the effect of this. I have also estimated probabilities so that I could calculate expected values.

There has been some discussion amongst the directors about the fixed production overheads included in the budget for the new production facility. Whilst some overhead expenditures, such as depreciation, have been easy to predict, other overheads, such as machinery maintenance are more difficult. Within the new facility it is planned that each piece of machinery will have a routine service three times a year to ensure that it is in optimal condition. In addition, maintenance employees will be required to make repairs as and when the need arises. Diane Rechnung, Finance Director, has suggested the use of activity-based budgeting as a different approach for establishing some of the overhead expenditure budget. She has asked me to look into this.

I have included the 'what-if' analysis in a schedule I will give to you shortly. I would like you to prepare a briefing paper for the senior management team which explains:

- The revised profit figures shown in table 1 of my schedule and why 'what-if' analysis is more appropriate than sensitivity analysis in this situation.

  (sub-task (a) = 36%)

- How the budget for the maintenance employee cost in the new production facility could be established using an activity-based budgeting approach.

  (sub-task (c) = 32%)

REFERENCE MATERIALS:

'WHAT-IF ANALYSIS ON THE PEXECO BUDGET FOR THE FOUR MONTHS SEPTEMBER TO DECEMBER 2020

Table 1

	Original budget G$000	Assumption A Revised budget G$000	Assumption A % change	Assumption B Revised budget G$000	Assumption B % change
Revenue	4,860	5,310	+9%	5,686	+17%
Variable costs	(1,347)	(1,550)	+15%	(1,751)	+30%
Contribution	**3,513**	**3,760**	**+7%**	**3,935**	**+12%**
Fixed costs	(1,120)	(1,120)	0%	(1,176)	+5%
Profit	**2,393**	**2,640**	**+10%**	**2,759**	**+15%**

Notes:

- Assumption A is that a 5% reduction in average selling price will lead to a 15% increase in volumes sold.
- Assumption B is that a 10% reduction in average selling price will lead to a 30% increase in volumes sold and a 5% increase in fixed costs.
- The % change under each assumption is from the original budget.

Exercise 5

Write the briefing paper requested by Julie Welk.

4.3 Exam variant 3 – task 1(b)

[Context]

The S-Pencil (a digital stylus with an inner electromagnetic resonance core and PEXECO outer shell) has now been developed. In addition, the associated app has also been developed. Initial development of the app was carried out by a third-party specialist tech company called FirstApps at a cost of G$250,000.

The S-Pencil will be launched onto the market in two months' time when the app has been fully tested by FirstApps.

[Task]

You receive the following email from Cameron Scott, Finance Manager:

From: **Cameron Scott, Finance Manager**

To: **Finance Officer**

Subject: **S-Pencil budget and costings**

I have been talking to Ben Thakar, Sales and Marketing director and Mia Schmied, Managing Director about the budget for the new S-Pencil.

[…]

Mia told me that, whilst Ben is highly confident that the S-Pencil will be a success, she is unsure what the likely sales volumes will be. She has suggested that we look at past sales of our HB Graphite and PEXECO pencils to see if this will help us forecast sales volumes for the S-Pencil. As it happens, one of your colleagues had recently drawn up a schedule of time series information for these two products (see attached) and I would now like you to prepare an explanation of the data in the schedule and its usefulness for forecasting S-Pencil sales which I can then send to Mia.

I need you to write content for a briefing paper that I need to send to each director which explains:

- What the attached time series information means and how useful it is to enable us to predict sales volume for our new S-Pencil.

(sub-task (b) = 48%)

Cameron Scott

REFERENCE MATERIALS: TIME SERIES INFORMATION

These results are based on quarterly sales volumes for our HB Graphite and PEXECO pencils during 2017, 2018 and 2019.

Trend

	HB Graphite Pencil	PEXECO Pencil
Regression line	Y = 30,000,000 – 168,000Q	Y = 5,000,000 + 210,000Q

Seasonality (based on the multiplicative model)

	HB Graphite Pencil	PEXECO Pencil
January to March	plus 10%	plus 20%
April to June	minus 20%	minus 25%
July to September	plus 15%	plus 10%
October to December	minus 5%	minus 5%

Key:

Q = the quarter number (where Q =1 is the first quarter of 2017).

Exercise 6

Write the content for the briefing papers as requested by Cameron Scott.

4.4 Exam variant 3 – task 4(c)

[Context]

The S-Pencil has now been successfully launched and the PEXECO production facility expanded to accommodate the extra production required.

[Task]

You receive the following email from Julie Welk, Head of Finance:

From: **Julie Welk, Head of Finance**

To: **Finance Officer**

Subject: **S Pencil app and Beyond Budgeting**

The directors are having a meeting tomorrow. Mia Schmied, Managing Director, has asked me to produce a briefing paper ahead of the meeting to address three of the agenda items and I would like your assistance.

[...]

Thirdly, Mia recently attended a conference where there was a session on 'beyond budgeting'. She had to miss the session because of a clash with another session she wanted to attend, but, is curious to know what it is about. She has asked for some information on this.

I would like you to prepare content for the briefing paper, which:

- Explains what beyond budgeting is and how we might apply it.

(sub-task (c) = 24%)

Exercise 7

Write the briefing paper requested by Julie Welk.

5 Core Activity C – Analysing Performance

Core activity C tasks will be worth, in total, between 17 and 25% of the paper.

The February 2020 exam had the following Core Activity C tasks:

Variant	Total marks	Task	Marks	Details
1	17	4(a)	11	Interpret sales price mix and quantity variances
		4(b)	6	Justify appropriate KPIs
2	20	1(a)	12	Explain raw material and fixed production overhead variances
		4(b)	8	Identify and explain KPIs
3	20	3(a)	13	Sales variances
		4(b)	7	KPIs

5.1 Exam variant 1 – tasks 4(a & b)

[Context]

The decision was made to begin selling pencils in Feland, a large country that has only recently allowed foreign trade. This involved setting up a new sales office and distribution centre in Feland. It is now February 2021.

[Task]

You open the following email from Julie Welk, Head of Finance:

From: **Julie Welk, Head of Finance**

To: **Finance Officer**

Subject: **Feland sales and receivables**

I have just received the monthly variances and supporting data (see attached schedule) from Cameron Scott, Finance Manager. We need a commentary adding for the Feland management team meeting tomorrow. I know that you have been working on sales variances this month, so would like you to do this.

As Feland is a new market it is vital that we focus on sales growth. To do this we need to develop relationships with potential new customers and win business. The sales team in Feland is not authorised to offer discounts on the list price and at present the only bonus paid to sales staff is based on them achieving the monthly quantity sales budget. The value of the bonus paid is a set amount and does not change regardless of how much actual sales quantity exceeds the budgeted quantity. This has led to concerns that the processing of sales orders is delayed deliberately for months where the budgeted quantity has been achieved.

There is also a suspicion that the sales team are focussing on selling the lower priced products when they visit customers, in order to increase the sales quantity. Both of these actions may reduce profit.

I am not sure that sales variances alone are a good indication of the sales team's performance and think we should introduce some key performance indicators (KPIs) to measure the performance of the sales team.

I am going to present at the Feland management meeting and would like your help with sections of my report. Please email me:

- An explanation of how each of the three sales variances in the attached schedule have been calculated and what they mean. Please also comment on what may have caused these variances and how useful they are for measuring the performance of the sales team in January.

  (sub-task (a) = 44%)

- Three KPIs that we can use to measure the performance of the sales team. Please explain and justify each KPI.

  (sub-task (b) = 24%)

REFERENCE MATERIALS:

SALES VARIANCES FOR FELAND FOR JANUARY 2021

	G$	
Sales price variance	4,620	Adverse
Sales profit quantity variance	512	Favourable
Sales profit mix variance	9,616	Favourable

Supporting information used for the monthly management accounts and variance calculations

Product	Actual selling price (G$)	Budgeted selling price (G$)	Actual profit (G$)	Standard profit (G$)
Graphite	548	548	307	248
PEXECO	512	554	294	336
Regular coloured	500	500	221	221
Artist coloured	840	840	504	504

Product	Budgeted sales (pencils)	Actual quantity of pencils sold in budgeted mix	Actual quantity of pencils sold
Graphite	466,000	467,335	467,000
PEXECO	58,000	58,166	110,000
Regular coloured	156,000	156,447	92,000
Artist coloured	18,000	18,052	31,000
Total	**698,000**	**700,000**	**700,000**

Notes:

- All prices and profits are stated per thousand pencils.
- A promotion for PEXECO pencils was initiated by Head Office in mid-January.
- A new competitor started selling regular coloured pencils in Feland in January 2021 and undercut Lottie Graphite's selling price by more than 20%.
- All selling price and profit figures are averages within the product ranges.
- The mix variance was calculated using the individual units method.

Exercise 8

Write the briefing paper for the directors as requested by Julie Welk.

5.2 Exam variant 2 – task 1(a)

[Context]

Sales of the PEXECO range of pencils are higher than budgeted and the PEXECO production facility is working at near to full capacity.

[Task]

Cameron Scott, Finance Manager calls you into his office and says:

'I am in the process of preparing the variance report for the PEXECO production facility and yesterday had a meeting with Cho Amanja, Head of PEXECO production. Cho informed me that a few things affected production costs in February.

At the start of the month our supplier unexpectedly increased the price of the resin used to make the composite for PEXECO pencils. In addition, in order to meet the increasing level of demand for PEXECO pencils, external specialist engineers were contracted in, at additional cost, to increase the speed that the production line was operating at. Initially this worked quite well, but as a result of a number of new employees being taken on the rate of production ended up being slower than it should have been because of their unfamiliarity with the process. There was also a higher than anticipated level of machine break-down, which meant that we had to hire in additional machinery. In addition, the quality of wood used in the PEXECO composite was poor in the month, which resulted in having to use more resin within the mix.

[...]

I need you to help me complete the narrative for the variance report. Here is a schedule which shows the variances that I need you to comment on.

To summarise, I would like you to prepare content for briefing papers which explains:

- What each of the six variances on my schedule means and gives reasons for each variance.

(sub-task (a) = 48%)

REFERENCE MATERIALS:

PEXECO: Resin Raw Material and Fixed Production Overhead Variances for February 2020

Resin Raw Material

Variance	**G$**
Price	15,660 A
Usage	15,618 A

Fixed Production Overhead

Variance	**G$**
Expenditure	15,873 A
Efficiency	7,984 A
Capacity	3,735 F
Total	**20,122 A**

Notes:

- A = adverse and F = favourable.
- The material usage variance is based on good production.

Exercise 9

Write your response to Cameron Scott.

5.3 Exam variant 2 – task 4(b)

[Context]

It is now March 2021.

[Task]

You receive the following email from An Mutty, Finance Manager

From:	**An Mutty, Finance Manager**
To:	**Finance Officer**
Subject:	**Supplier Issues**

There have been a few issues with suppliers recently, not least, Jacksters, our supplier of graphite. There have been delays in delivery and some of the raw materials that we've received have been of such poor quality that we have had to return them. In addition, some suppliers are not easy to get hold of when things go wrong. I've been asked to make some suggestions about KPIs that we could establish to monitor the performance of our suppliers.

I would like you to send me:

- Suggestions for three key performance indicators (KPIs) that we can establish to monitor the performance of our suppliers. Please include a justification of why each KPI that you suggest is appropriate.

(sub-task (b) = 32%)

Exercise 10

Write your response to An Mutty.

5.4 Exam variant 3 – task 3(a)

[Context]

The S-Pencil (a digital stylus) has been developed and launched.

[Task]

Julie Welk, Head of Finance calls you into her office and says:

'I've just been talking to Ben Thakar, Sales and Marketing Director, about the S-Pencil. In the first few months after the launch sales volumes were a little lower than budgeted. As a result of this, three months ago two things happened: Firstly, Ben authorised a special promotional price for the S-Pencil on our website for sales direct to the public and, secondly, he tasked his sales teams to secure new retail customer and gave them authority to offer small discounts and extended credit terms to any new retail customers.

Ben has asked me to look in detail at the impact of his actions three months ago on our actual profit compared to budget.

I have so far created a schedule which shows sales variances for the S-Pencil for the last three months. I would like you to prepare commentary to go with this schedule which explains:

- What the sales price, mix and quantity variances mean and the reasons for their occurrence. Please also comment on whether you think Ben's two actions have been successful, with reference to each of the customer groups.

(sub-task (a) = 52%)

REFERENCE MATERIALS:

SALES VARIANCES FOR THE S-PENCIL FOR THE LAST 3 MONTHS

Variance	Large Retailers G$	Small retailers G$	Website G$	Total G$
Sales price	0	135,000 A	84,000 A	219,000 A
Sales mix	256,500 A	247,438 F	143,437 F	134,375 F
Sales quantity	121,500 F	76,313 F	47,812 F	245,625 F

Notes:

1 A = adverse and F = favourable.

2 These variances are for our sales to large retailers, small retailers and directly to consumers through our website.

3 The sales mix and quantity variances are calculated using the individual units method and budgeted gross profit. The budgeted gross profits are as follows:

	Large Retailers G$	Small retailers G$	Website G$
Budgeted gross profit	6.75	9.25	12.75

4 During the period there was a change in the profile of S-Pencil customers (Large retailers: small retailers) from 3:64 three months ago to 3:100 now.

Exercise 11

Write the commentary requested by Julie Welk.

5.5 Exam variant 3 – task 4(b)

[Context]

The S-Pencil (a digital stylus) has been developed and launched, along with a supporting app.

[Task]

You receive the following email from Julie Welk, Head of Finance

From: **Julie Welk, Head of Finance**

To: **Finance Officer**

Subject: **S-Pencil app and beyond budgeting**

The directors are having a meeting tomorrow. Mia Schmied, Managing Director, has asked me to produce a briefing paper ahead of the meeting to address three of the agenda items and I would like your assistance.

Firstly, the contract for the provision of IT administrative services for the S-Pencil app is to be renewed. Rather than just renew the contract with the existing supplier, Mia is keen to consider alternative providers to see if we can achieve a better deal financially. Three providers have been identified, all of which have different pricing structures. It is not altogether clear which is the best option financially because we don't know at this stage how many users there will be. […]

Secondly, each of the three providers are offering to manage app updates, user profiles, app content and in app add-on purchases. In addition, each provider will manage the promotion of add-on in app purchases as well. The directors would like to use more key performance indicators (KPIs) across the business and have asked for ideas of suitable KPIs for suppliers and in particular the new provider of IT administrative services for the S-Pencil app.

[…]

I would like you to prepare content for the briefing paper, which:

- Suggests and justifies three KPIs that we could introduce to measure the performance of the IT administrative services provider for our S-Pencil app.

(sub-task (b) = 28%)

Exercise 12

Write the briefing paper requested by Julie Welk.

6 Core Activity D – Financial Reporting

Core activity D tasks will be worth, in total, between 12 and 18% of the paper.

The February 2020 exam had the following Core Activity D tasks:

Variant	Total marks	Task	Marks	Details
1	17	2(a)	10	Explain the accounting treatment of IFRS16
		3(b)	7	Inventory valuation IAS 2
2	18	2(a)	12	Apply the rules in IFRS 5 and IAS 16 in respect of asset disposals and additional expenditure
		4(a)	6	Apply IAS 10
3	14	2(b)	8	Purchase of plant and equipment
		2(c)	6	Disposal of property, including taxation aspects

6.1 Exam variant 1 – task 2(a)

[Context]

The decision has been made to expand into Feland.

[Task]

You arrive at work and open the following email from Julie Welk, Head of Finance:

From: **Julie Welk, Head of Finance**

To: **Finance Officer**

Subject: **Leased equipment**

A number of issues have arisen this week and I need your help writing sections of a report that I have to present at a senior management meeting.

Firstly, I need to explain to senior management how to account for a new baking machine due for delivery later this month. I have included the details for this in table 1 of the schedule attached to this email.

Please draft an explanation of:

- How the leased equipment in table 1 of the attached schedule will be recorded within the financial statements for the year ended 31 December 2020 and subsequent years.

(sub-task (a) = 40%)

REFERENCE MATERIALS:

Table 1: Leased equipment

Item leased	Notes
Baking machine	• The machine will be leased for a period of four years beginning on the 1 of May 2020. • The useful economic life of the asset is expected to be six years. • There will be four equal payments of G$100,000 payable annually, with the first payment due on the 30 of April 2021. • If we borrowed money from the bank to buy this asset outright we would be charged an interest rate of 5%. • Expenses totalling G$3,000 have been incurred in obtaining the lease.

Exercise 13

Write the draft content for the sections of the report as requested by Julie Welks.

6.2 Exam variant 1 – task 3(b)

[Task]

It is now January 2021. Julie Welk, Head of Finance calls you into her office and says:

"Earlier this week we discovered that some pencils had been embossed with the wrong information. As the embossing includes the barcode that we use for to record inventory levels we investigated all our graphite pencil inventories. This investigation incurred significant overtime expense and revealed embossing errors in three grades of pencil: 9H, 4H and 8B. Large quantities of these were in fact HB pencils that had been mislabelled as 9H, 4H and 8B.

We completed the year-end inventory count last week and, because this was based on the barcode information, the graphite pencil inventory value is now wrong. Usually we would destroy these pencils but, Barney San, Head of Finishing and Packaging, has developed a process for removing the embossing, which means we can sell them at a reduced price.

We have a buyer willing to pay G$300 per thousand for approximately 60% of the incorrectly embossed pencils and the remainder can be donated to an educational charity.

Please draft a briefing paper that explains:

- How the financial statements for the year ended 31 December 2020 will be affected by the incorrectly embossed graphite pencils. Please make reference to the appropriate financial reporting standards."

(sub-task (b) = 28%)

Exercise 14

Write the briefing paper as requested by Julie Welks.

6.3 Exam variant 2 – task 2(b)

[Context]

It is now July 2020. Three months ago the Directors decided, because of increasing demand for PEXECO pencils (especially from corporate customers) to invest in a highly digitised production line for PEXECO in a new facility, two kilometres from the main production facility. The new PEXECO production facility will be operational from 1 September 2020.

[Task]

Julie Welk, Head of Finance sends you the following email:

From: **Julie Welk, Head of Finance**

To: **Finance Officer**

Subject: **PEXECO assets and digital costing**

Mia Schmied, Managing Director, has just sent me an email asking for some information about a couple of things.

Firstly, along with Cho Amanja, Head of PEXECO, she has been going through the non-current assets register for the old PEXECO production facility to establish which assets will be transferred and which will be sold. She has so far identified three assets where three is a definite plan of action: two to be sold externally and one which will be reconditioned and then retained within the business (see attached schedule). She would like to know how these disposals and the expenditure incurred on the reconditioning will be treated in the financial statements.

[...]

I would like you to prepare content for a briefing paper to Mia Schmied, in which you explain:

- Whether the two asset disposals identified in the attachment will need to be reclassified as assets held for sale and the impact of these disposals on the financial statements for the year ended 31 December 2020. Please also explain how the additional expenditure reconditioning the third asset will be treated in the same financial statements.

(sub-task (a) = 48%)

REFERENCE MATERIALS:

NON-CURRENT ASSETS IN THE OLD PEXECO PRODUCTION FACILITY

Assets to be sold

Asset	Carrying amount at 1 January 2020 G$	Current monthly depreciation charge G$	Plan of action
Packing equipment	70,000	2,500	This asset will be sold for G$75,000 as soon as it is no longer needed in the old PEXECO production facility. A buyer for this asset has already been found and is likely to take the equipment in very early September 2020.
Production conveyor line	210,000	5,000	As soon as production finishes in the old PEXECO facility on 31 August 2020 the production conveyor line will be carefully dismantled so that it can be sold. Cho believes that a buyer can be found for this but anticipates that it could take up to 12 months to find the right buyer. Cho expects that the sale will happen in 2021 and expects to sell the conveyor line for G$130,000. It will cost G$8,000 to dismantle.

Assets to be reconditioned

Asset	Carrying amount at 1 January 2020 G$	Current monthly depreciation charge G$	Plan of action
Mixing machinery	82,000	4,000	The mixing machinery is to be reconditioned and transferred to the main production facility. Reconditioning the machinery will increase its capacity, extend its useful economic life by 4 years and will cost G$72,000. Moving the machinery to its new home will incur additional expenditure of G$6,000.

Exercise 15

Write the briefing paper to Mia Schmied as requested by Julie Welk.

6.4 Exam variant 2 – task 4(a)

[Context]

It is now March 2021.

[Task]

You receive the following email from An Mutty, Finance Manager

From: **An Mutty, Finance Manager**

To: **Finance Officer**

Subject: **Supplier Issues**

I need to finalise the financial statements for the year ended 31 December 2020. The following two things happened in 2021 that will affect these financial statements and I would like you to let me know how you think these should be treated.

1 On 10 January 2021 there was a small fire in the PEXECO production facility which damaged inventory and a fork lift truck.

2 On 10 February 2021 one of our suppliers, Jacksters, paid us G$25,000 in settlement of a legal case that we had taken out against them in December 2020.

I would like you to send me:

- An explanation of how the two events identified above will affect the financial statements for the year ended 31 December 2020.

(sub-task (a) = 24%)

Exercise 16

Write your response to An Mutty.

6.5 Exam variant 3 – tasks 2(b and c)

[Context]

It is now 1 September 2020. The S-Pencil (a digital stylus) was successfully developed and launched in the market and PEXACVO production facility was expanded to accommodate the extra production required.

[Task]

You receive the following email from Julie Welk, Head of Finance

From:	**Julie Welk, Head of Finance**
To:	**Finance Officer**
Subject:	**Expansion of PEXECO production facility**

I am due to have a meeting with the directors later today and need your assistance with a briefing paper that I need to prepare for the meeting.

[…]

Secondly, we have spent money on expanding the PEXECO production facility to enable the production of the S-Pencil. Part of this expenditure is on new baking equipment which cost G$160,000 to purchase and G$5,000 to install and test. We also spent G$2,000 installing additional ventilation on site to meet safety requirements. The lining of the baking equipment will need to be replaced every three years, although the equipment itself should be operational for 15 years. I need to let the directors know how this will affect our financial statements for the year ended 31 December 2020.

Thirdly, to partly fund the production facility expansion, we sold a warehouse building on 31 May 2020 for G$600,000. We purchased the building years ago for G$350,000 and at its date of disposal it had a carrying amount of G$140,000. I need to let the directors know how this will affect both our financial statements for the year ended 31 December 2020 and the tax charge for the year.

I would like you to prepare content for a briefing paper, which explains:

- How the expenditure associated with the new baking equipment will be initially recorded in our statement of financial position and how we should depreciate the asset.

  (sub-task (b) = 32%)

- How the disposal of the warehouse building will affect both the tax change for the year and our financial statements for the year ended 31 December 2020.

  (sub-task (c) = 24%)

Exercise 17

Write the briefing paper requested by Julie Welk.

7 Core Activity E – Decision Making

Core activity E tasks will be worth, in total, between 17 and 25% of the paper.

The February 2020 exam had the following Core Activity E tasks:

Variant	Total marks	Task	Marks	Details
1	17	3(a)	10	Short-term decision making using limiting factor analysis
		3(c)	7	Short-term decision making using EV and probability distribution
2	21	1(b)	9	Apply decision criteria under conditions of uncertainty
		1(c)	4	Explain non-financial factors for a decision
		3(b)	8	Explain EV and attitudes to decision making
3	23	2(a)	11	Multi-product break-even
		4(a)	12	Short term decision making

7.1 Exam variant 1 – task 3(a and c)

[Task]

It is now January 2021. Julie Welk, Head of Finance calls you into her office and says:

"Earlier this week we discovered that some pencils had been embossed with the wrong information. As the embossing includes the barcode that we use for to record inventory levels we investigated all our graphite pencil inventories. This investigation incurred significant overtime expense and revealed embossing errors in three grades of pencil: 9H, 4H and 8B. Large quantities of these were in fact HB pencils that had been mislabelled as 9H, 4H and 8B.

This means that we will not have enough of 9H, 4H and 8B pencils in inventory to fulfil this week's orders and we do not have enough production capacity to meet the shortfall. We cannot make all we need because we are short of packing labour. However, there are some priority orders that must be met. I have here a schedule (appendix 1) that prioritises the production of these grades of pencils in order to maximise contribution. I also want to use the schedule to determine if it is worth offering a G$14 an hour overtime premium to make up the production capacity shortfall. I need you to add commentary to the schedule for a meeting I have later today.

Please draft a briefing paper that explains:

- The principles behind the production schedule (appendix 1) and how it has been used to determine the number of batches that should be made for each of the three types of pencil grade.

Please also explain whether, from a financial perspective, it is worth offering members of the packing department the G$14 overtime premium.

(sub-task (a) = 40%)

We are now deliberating whether or not to check the barcoding on the coloured pencils inventory to prevent shipping incorrectly labelled pencils. I have produced two tables (appendix 2), using probabilities based on previous barcode errors and an estimate of rectification costs, to help us reach a decision. Please also send me an explanation of:

- What the expected values as shown on appendix 2 mean, and the limitations of using this information to decide whether to investigate the coloured pencil inventory."

(sub-task (c) = 32%)

REFERENCE MATERIALS:

Appendix 1 – Production schedule and workings

Type of pencil	**9H**	**4H**	**8B**	
Batches needed for priority orders	20	25	40	
Batches needed for maximum demand	50	200	45	
Average contribution per batch	G$505.56	G$411.73	G$499.10	
Packing labour needed per batch (minutes)	35	28	40	
Contribution per packing labour minute	G$14.44	G$14.70	G$12.48	
Ranking	**2**	**1**	**3**	
Production schedule				**Packing labour available (minutes)**
				8,950
Packing time needed to make priority orders (minutes)	(35 × 20) = 700	(28 × 25) = 700	(40 × 40) = 1,600	5,950
Packing time allocated after making priority orders (minutes)	(35 × 30) = 1,050	(28 × 175) = 4,900	0	0
Total batches to be made	**50**	**200**	**40**	

REFERENCE MATERIALS (continued):

Appendix 2 – Rectification cost of barcode errors if we check or do not check coloured pencils inventories

Check

Predicted outcome	Cost G$	Probability	Expected value G$
No errors found	0	0.25	0
Moderate level of errors found	1,000	0.60	600
High level of errors found	16,000	0.15	2,400
Expected value			**3,000**

Note: the cost of checking (not included above) will be G$73,000

Do not check

Predicted outcome	Cost G$	Probability	Expected value G$
No errors present	0	0.25	0
Moderate level of errors present	50,000	0.60	30,000
High level of errors present	300,000	0.15	45,000
Expected value			**75,000**

Exercise 18

Write the briefing paper as requested by Julie Welks.

7.2 Exam variant 2 – task 1(b and c)

[Context]

Sales of the PEXECO range of pencils are higher than budgeted and the PEXECO production facility is working at near to full capacity.

[Task]

Cameron Scott, Finance Manager calls you into his office and says:

'I am in the process of preparing the variance report for the PEXECO production facility and yesterday had a meeting with Cho Amanja, Head of PEXECO production. Cho informed me that a few things affected production costs in February.

At the start of the month our supplier unexpectedly increased the price of the resin used to make the composite for PEXECO pencils. Cho has been looking for an alternative source of resin and has been offered an opportunity to buy resin from a new supplier under a six month supply contract.

The resin would need to be purchased at the start of the contract in one of three quantities, each at a different price per kilogramme (all of which are lower than the current supplier's price). Because resin deteriorates, any resin not used at the end of six months would need to be disposed of at a cost to us. Any additional resin needed would be purchased from our usual supplier at their increased price. Since our meeting, Cho has sent me the financial information about this six-month supply contract opportunity. There is uncertainty regarding how much resin we'll need for production and so I've used Cho's information to create pay-off and regret tables based on total cost of resin supply for the period.

I need you to help me report back to Cho about the one-off resin purchase opportunity. To summarise, I would like you to prepare content for briefing papers which explains:

- Three decision criteria that we could use, given the uncertainty over production levels, and how each of these could help us decide, based on cost, which resin quantity to purchase. Please state the quantity we would purchase under each of these decision criteria.
  (sub-task (b) = 36%)
- Two non-financial factors we should consider before contracting with the new supplier.
  (sub-task (c) = 16%)

REFERENCE MATERIALS:

Pay-off and regret tables

Payoff table (G$)

		Options	
Production level	Quantity 1	Quantity 2	Quantity 3
Low	804,800	926,400	1,108,800
Medium	926,000	914,400	1,096,800
High	1,136,000	1,080,000	1,084,800

Note: The table shows the total cost of resin supply at different production levels for the six-month period of the contract for each of the resin quantities that the new supplier is offering.

Regret table (G$)

		Options	
Production level	Quantity 1	Quantity 2	Quantity 3
Low	0	121,600	304,000
Medium	11,600	0	182,400
High	56,000	0	4,800

Exercise 19

Write your response to Cameron Scott.

7.3 Exam variant 2 – Tasks 3(b)

[Summary of context]

Sales of the PEXECO pencil are higher than expected. The directors have decided to invest in a new, highly digitised production line for PEXECO production.

[Task]

Julie Welk, Head of Finance, calls you into her office and says:

The directors have been looking at the draft budget for the new PEXECO production facility for the four-month period September to December 2020. Ben Thakar, Sales and Marketing Director, believes that there is real scope to increase the volume of PEXECO sales by decreasing selling prices.

He is optimistic about this and believes that if selling prices were reduced by 5%, sales volumes would increase by 15%, and if selling prices were reduced by 10%, sales volumes would increase by 30%.

Mia Schmied, Managing Director, is far less confident that sales will increase as much as Ben believes She has requested that we perform sensitivity analysis and also consider expected values. I prefer 'what-if' to sensitivity analysis and have produced profit estimates based on Ben's assumptions. I think there is likely to be an increase in fixed costs when volumes increase by more than 20%, so my profit estimates also include the effect of this. I have also estimated probabilities so that I could calculate expected values.

I would like you to prepare a briefing paper for the senior management team which explains:

- The figures shown in table 2 and table 3 and how our attitude to risk will affect our decision about which reduction in selling price would potentially give us the best result.

(sub-task (b) = 32%)

REFERENCE MATERIALS:

IMPACT OF CHANGING SELLING PRICES USING EXPECTED VALUES

Table 2: If decrease average selling prices by 5%

Change in sales volume	Probability	Budgeted profit G$000	Expected value G$000
No change	0.2	2,150	430
+7.5%	0.5	2,395	1,198
+15%	0.3	2,640	792
			2,420

REFERENCE MATERIALS (Continued):

IMPACT OF CHANGING SELLING PRICES USING EXPECTED VALUES

Table 3: If decrease average selling prices by 10%

Change in sales volume	Probability	Budgeted profit G$000	Expected value G$000
No change	0.1	1,907	191
+15%	0.8	2,361	1,889
+30%	0.1	2,759	276
			2,356

Exercise 20

Write the briefing paper requested by Julie Welk.

7.4 Exam variant 3 – tasks 2(a)

[Context]

It is now 1 September 2020. The S-Pencil (a digital stylus) was successfully developed and launched in the market and PEXECO production facility was expanded to accommodate the extra production required.

[Task]

You receive the following email from Julie Welk, Head of Finance

From: **Julie Welk, Head of Finance**

To: **Finance Officer**

Subject: **Break-even and expansion of PEXECO production facility**

I am due to have a meeting with the directors later today and need your assistance with a briefing paper that I need to prepare for the meeting.

Firstly, we have revised our budget to reflect sales and variable costs for the S-Pencil, recent changes in selling prices for all other products, changes in expected sales volumes and changes to fixed cost. Mia Schmied, Managing Director, has asked for an analysis of our breakeven position based on the revised budget compared to the original budget for next month. I have therefore drawn up a profit-volume chart that I would like you to write some commentary for (see attached).

I would like you to prepare content for a briefing paper, which explains:

- Line A on the profit-volume chart and the information that this gives us based on the original budget. Please also explain how the revised budget, represented by line B, changes your analysis.

(sub-task (a) = 44%)

REFERENCE MATERIALS:

PROFIT-VOLUME CHART FOR NEXT MONTH: ORIGINAL BUDGET VS REVISED BUDGET

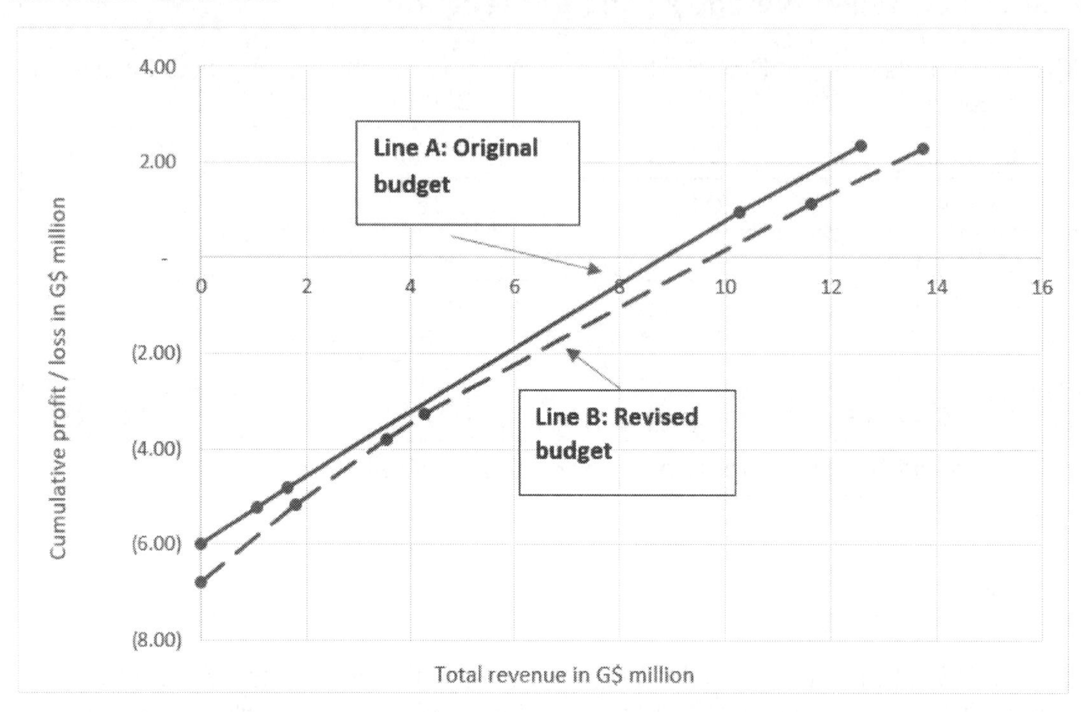

Other information

- The c/s ratios used in the above chart are as follows:

	Original budget	Revised budget
Graphite	0.67	0.60
PEXECO	0.73	0.78
S-Pencil	n/a	0.90
Regular coloured	0.60	0.55
Artist coloured	0.72	0.75
Weighted average	**0.66**	**0.66**

- The original budget was revised to reflect the new S-Pencil as well as new selling prices and expected sales volumes for all existing products. Budgeted variable costs are in line with the original budget, although budgeted fixed costs have been increased to reflect expansion of the PEXECO facility.

Exercise 21
Write the briefing paper requested by Julie Welk.

7.5 Exam variant 3 – task 4(a)

[Context]

The S-Pencil (a digital stylus) has been developed and launched, along with a supporting app.

[Task]

You receive the following email from Julie Welk, Head of Finance

From: **Julie Welk, Head of Finance**

To: **Finance Officer**

Subject: **S-Pencil app and beyond budgeting**

The directors are having a meeting tomorrow. Mia Schmied, Managing Director, has asked me to produce a briefing paper ahead of the meeting to address three of the agenda items and I would like your assistance.

Firstly, the contract for the provision of IT administrative services for the S-Pencil app is to be renewed. Rather than just renew the contract with the existing supplier, Mia is keen to consider alternative providers to see if we can achieve a better deal financially. Three providers have been identified, all of which have different pricing structures. It is not altogether clear which is the best option financially because we don't know at this stage how many users there will be. One of your colleagues has prepared a payoff table at different volumes and calculated coefficients of variation based on my probability assessment.

[...]

I would like you to prepare content for the briefing paper, which:

- Explains how we could decide which provider of IT administrative services to use under different attitudes to risk using the data in the attached schedule and identifies what the decisions would be using each attitude. Please also explain the limitations of this analysis for selecting the IT administrative services provider.

(sub-task (a) = 48%)

REFERENCE MATERIALS:

COST OF POTENTIAL SUPPLY OF IT ADMINISTRATIVE SERVICES

Payoff table and expected values

Number of users	Probability	Provider A G$	Provider B G$	Provider C $
900,000	0.2	1,650	1,530	1,370
1,000,000	0.5	1,800	1,700	1,500
1,200,000	0.3	1,620	2,040	2,000
Expected value		**1,716**	**1,768**	**1,624**

Coefficients of variation

	Provider A	Provider B	Provider C
Coefficient of variation	0.049	0.107	0.155

Exercise 22

Write the briefing paper requested by Julie Welk.

8 Core Activity F – Working Capital

Core activity F tasks will be worth, in total, between 7 and 13% of the paper.

The February 2020 exam had the following Core Activity F tasks:

Variant	Total marks	Task	Marks	Details
1	8	4(c)	8	Explain how to improve receivables management
2	11	4(c)	11	Interpret working capital ratios
3	12	3(b)	12	Receivables management

8.1 Exam variant 1 – task 4(c)

[Context]

The decision was made to begin selling pencils in Feland, a large country that has only recently allowed foreign trade. This involved setting up a new sales office and distribution centre in Feland. It is now February 2021.

[Task]

You open the following email from Julie Welk, Head of Finance:

From: **Julie Welk, Head of Finance**

To: **Finance Officer**

Subject: **Feland sales and receivables**

As Feland is a new market it is vital that we focus on sales growth. To do this we need to develop relationships with potential new customers and win business.

Unfortunately, the customers in Feland are not paying on time. Receivables days are averaging 65 days when all credit terms are 30 days. We have a credit control function in Feland staffed by local people, which we intend to keep. However, so far customers have ignored email requests for on-time payment.

I am going to present at the Feland management meeting and would like your help with sections of my report. Please email me:

- An explanation of how to improve the receivables days of the Feland customers.

(sub-task (c) = 32%)

Exercise 23

Write the briefing paper for the directors as requested by Julie Welk.

8.2 Exam variant 2 – task 4(c)

[Task]

You receive the following email from An Mutty, Finance Manager

From: **An Mutty, Finance Manager**

To: **Finance Officer**

Subject: **Supplier Issues**

There have been a few issues with suppliers recently, not least, Jacksters, our supplier of graphite. There have been delays in delivery and some of the raw materials that we've received have been of such poor quality that we have had to return them.

I've been asked to look at some financial information relating to a potential new supplier of graphite called BGF Graphite. So far, I've prepared the attached schedule which shows its working capital days and information about revenue and cash balance and I'd like you to prepare a commentary to go with it.

I would like you to send me:

- An explanation of BGF Graphite's working capital position based on the information in the attached schedule. Please also explain any risks associated with this position that might affect our decision to use them as a supplier.

(sub-task (b) = 32%)

REFERENCE MATERIALS:

FINANCIAL INFORMATION ABOUT BGF GRAPHITE

	2020 Industry Average	2020 BGF Graphite	2019 BGF Graphite	2018 BGF Graphite
Operating cycle	**Days**	**Days**	**Days**	**Days**
Inventory days	32	18	31	30
Trade receivable days	39	62	51	35
Trade payable days	(45)	(86)	(63)	(38)
	J$000	**J$000**	**J$000**	**J$000**
Revenue	18,268	4,250	2,416	1,234
Cash/(overdraft)	1,490	(630)	56	825

Other information:

- BGF Graphite has standard credit terms for both payables and receivables of 30 days.

Exercise 24
Write your response to An Mutty.

8.3 Exam variant 3 – task 3(a)

[Context]

The S-Pencil (a digital stylus) has been developed and launched.

[Task]

Julie Welk, Head of Finance calls you into her office and says:

'I've just been talking to Ben Thakar, Sales and Marketing Director, about the S-Pencil. In the first few months after the launch sales volumes were a little lower than budgeted. As a result of this, three months ago two things happened: Firstly, Ben authorised a special promotional price for the S-Pencil on our website for sales direct to the public and, secondly, he tasked his sales teams to secure new retail customer and gave them authority to offer small discounts and extended credit terms to any new retail customers.

Ben has asked me to look in detail at the impact of his actions three months ago on the recoverability of our retail customer receivables. I have so far created a schedule which shows the aged receivables information for the S-Pencil customer. I would like you to prepare commentary to go with this schedule which explains:

- How the profile of aged receivables has changed over the last three months, reasons for these changes and the potential implication of these changes. Please also include two measures that we could take to manage these implications'.

(sub-task (b) = 48%)

REFERENCE MATERIALS:

AGED RECEIVABLES COMPARISON: S-PENCIL CUSTOMERS

3 months ago

Type of customer	Number of customers	Total amount due G$000	Due within payment terms G$000	Up to 30 days overdue G$000	Over 60 days overdue G$000
Large retailers	3	711	612	78	21
Small retailers	64	367	320	42	5

REFERENCE MATERIALS (Continued):

AGED RECEIVABLES COMPARISON: S-PENCIL CUSTOMERS

Now

Type of customer	Number of customers	Total amount due G$000	Due within payment terms G$000	Up to 30 days overdue G$000	Over 60 days overdue G$000
Large retailers	3	665	498	108	59
Small retailers	100	697	510	97	90

Notes:

- Standard terms for credit customers is 30 days.
- The three large retailer customers are the same customers.

Exercise 25

Write the commentary requested by Julie Welk.

9 Summary

Next steps:

(1) You can begin to revisit and revise technical material from your previous studies according to the core activities and assessment outcomes given in this chapter. However we suggest you continue to do this alongside working through the rest of this book so you can also learn how you may need to apply the knowledge.

(2) Remember that you are very unlikely to have to perform calculations in the case study exam. However you may need to explain or interpret calculations and so an appreciation of how they are prepared is still relevant and useful.

10 Solutions to chapter exercises

Exercise 1

Absorption costing versus marginal costing

Differences in the profit statements:

Both statements are compiled using the same data: the units produced and sold, the number of units in opening inventory and the total variable and fixed costs. The difference between the two methods is the way in which the fixed overhead is treated. In the absorption costing statement, an element of fixed overhead is included in the cost of each unit whereas the marginal costing statement shows the fixed overhead as a weekly cost (G$474,000 in week one and G$476,000 in week 2). The opening inventory, production cost and closing inventory values are all higher in the absorption costing statement than in the marginal costing statement because they contain this fixed cost element.

In both weeks the inventory level is decreasing, and this means that less fixed overhead is being carried forward in closing finished goods inventory valuation than is being brought forward in opening finished goods inventory. This results in a higher cost of sales and a lower profit than under marginal costing.

Marginal costing will not always give us a higher profit figure than absorption costing, for the same reasons given above. In times where inventory levels are rising, marginal costing profit will be lower and when inventory levels are static, both methods will produce the same profit.

Benefits of using absorption costing in our business:

The fixed production overheads at Lottie Graphite are budgeted to be G$31,840,000 which is approximately 38% of total production cost. This is a significant value and if we did not absorb this overhead into our product cost, we would run the risk of not measuring and controlling our product costs. Presently we use fixed overhead variances to monitor and control costs. In addition, understanding the full product cost is an important aspect of pricing.

Although absorption costing is a crude method of calculating each product's share of fixed overhead, it is largely appropriate to our business. As over 90% of our products (by sales revenue) are wooden pencils, they all pass through the same raw material and finishing departments. Given that graphite and coloured pencils vary little in production methodology, it is debatable whether the cost of using a more sophisticated method of overhead costing would be worthwhile in our business.

Absorption costing conforms to the matching concept. As described above, the adjustment to closing inventory ensures that cost of sales are matched to the sales value when the pencils are sold.

This stabilises our figures and avoids extreme profits and losses being reported. Given we have an element of seasonality in our business this is particularly important as there are likely to be periods where our inventory levels fluctuate significantly.

IAS 2 requires that conversion costs are included in inventory valuation. This includes fixed production overhead so long as it is allocated on a systematic and consistent basis. Our use of absorption costing, rather than marginal costing, ensures that the financial statements conform to accounting standards.

Marking guide:

Trait	Level	Descriptor	Marks
Differences MC & AC		No rewardable material	0
	1	Demonstrates some technical understanding of the difference between profit under marginal costing and absorption costing. Limited use of figures within the reference material. No application of the benefits of absorption costing to Lottie Graphite.	1–3
	2	Demonstrates reasonable technical understanding of the difference between profit under marginal costing and absorption costing. Uses the figures within the reference material but may omit some elements. Some limited application of the benefits of absorption costing to Lottie Graphite.	4–7
	3	Demonstrates good technical understanding of the difference between profit under marginal costing and absorption costing. Utilises fully the figures in the reference material and applies the benefits of absorption costing to Lottie Graphite.	8–10

The principles of throughput accounting and its potential benefit to our business

The aim of throughput accounting is to maximise throughput contribution (sales revenue less direct materials), while at the same time reducing operational expense and investment. Operating expense is the cost incurred to convert the raw material into the finished pencil. Operating expense usually comprises of labour and production overhead. Investment is the monetary value invested in inventory and non-current assets, in other words the money tied up in assets in order that Lottie Graphite can make the throughput.

As we are expecting demand to increase, we might eventually find that some of our production processes cause delay to the throughput.

A process that delays throughput is a bottleneck and throughput accounting would give us the information to identify the bottleneck and improve performance. We could benefit from using throughput accounting in the following ways:

The product mix can be optimised by maximising the throughput contribution per hour of bottleneck resource. This is calculated in the same way as limiting factor analysis, where the bottleneck is the limiting factor. Therefore, we benefit by maximising our short-term profits by using throughput accounting to determine the optimal production plans.

Management's focus will be set to alleviating the pressure on a bottleneck as this will reduce delays in the production process that reduces the throughput. This may mean finding ways to ensure that the bottleneck is fully utilised. For example, if the bottleneck was the baking process, we would make sure that the blast furnace was operated 24 hours a day, filled to capacity every bake and loaded and unload as quickly as possible. Alternatively, there may be the need to invest in a new blast furnace.

Any process that occurs prior to the bottleneck will also be examined. For example, if raw pencil were the bottleneck it would be pointless producing more spindles than could be processed as this would increase inventory cost. Therefore, management will reduce activity in the processes that occur before the bottleneck which in turn will usually reduce costs.

Marking guide:

Trait	Level	Descriptor	Marks
Throughput accounting		No rewardable material	0
	1	Explains some of the characteristics of throughput accounting but there is no application to Lottie Graphite.	1–2
	2	Explains the concept of throughput accounting with reasonable technical accuracy. There is an attempt to use the company to explain the benefits.	3–4
	3	Explains BOTH the concept of throughput accounting and the benefits that Lottie Graphite can expect to gain, using examples of the business processes to illustrate.	5

Examiner's comments

The second element of this task asked for an explanation of the reasons why absorption cost and marginal cost profits were different based on given data, whether marginal costing always gave a lower profit and the benefits of using absorption costing for the business.

Most candidates could explain the principles that caused the difference in profit reasonably well. However, it was disappointing that so few candidates could give a good explanation of the benefits of absorption costing to the business. The fact that the company used absorption costing was clearly highlighted in the pre-seen and therefore it was hoped that candidates would ensure that they were prepared for a question on this part of the syllabus.

The third element of this task asked for an explanation of the principles of throughput accounting and its potential benefit to the business. This was quite well answered as most candidates could explain the basic principles of throughput accounting and made a good attempt to apply these to the production processes at Lottie Graphite.

Exercise 2

Digital costing

Current costing system

Currently we use a standard costing system. We have standard cost cards in which we set expectations, or in other words, standards, for all of the inputs that go into making 1,000 of each type of pencil that we produce. For example, we set the standard that 1,000 HB graphite pencils will require 1.5 kilogrammes of graphite at a cost of G$4.00 per kilogramme. The standard cost card also includes a share of variable and fixed production overheads based on the expected level of expenditure and the number of machine hours required to make the 1,000 pencils. These standard cost cards are currently only updated once a year and are used to assist in setting our budget, valuing inventory and to allow reporting by exception where actual performance is not in line with the standard (this is highlighted through variance reporting).

How this could be changed through a digital costing system

A digital costing system is dynamic and involves linking our internal digital systems (for example, our digital production machinery, purchasing and sales systems) with those of our suppliers, customers and the market. In a digital costing system, data is gathered from all of these sources and from the internet in real time to give up-to-date costing information which reflects current information.

For example, our production systems could give us up-to-date information about time in production, purchasing and supplier systems would give us current input prices for say graphite. Linking this to information on the internet would also allow us to compare prices with alternative suppliers. Purpose built digital costing systems can be developed which allow all of this to happen. However, it must be noted that we would still use standard costing as our costing method. All that would be different is that these standards would be up-to-date.

Marking guide:

Trait	Level	Descriptor	Marks
Current and digital?		No rewardable material	0
	1	Demonstrates some understanding of the current standard costing system. Little or no reference made to digital costing.	1–2
	2	Demonstrates a reasonable understanding of the current standard costing systems. Some understanding of the features of digital costing.	3–4
	3	Demonstrates a clear understanding of the current standard costing system. Reasonable understanding of the features of digital costing system and how this might change the current standard costing system.	5–6

The benefits of doing this for our business

Sourcing supplies and suppliers could be improved because we will be able to identify the best price or the best lead times. Some digital costing systems can even make intelligent suggestions for supply options through the use of artificial intelligence.

Standards can be regularly updated. Currently standards are only changed once a year and therefore can potentially be out of date quite quickly where prices are changing. Furthermore, these standards are used to calculate variances which are in turn used to hold our procurement and production operations accountable for performance. By using digital costing, information used to set standards are always appropriate for the time (that is, reflect ruling market prices and current operating conditions). Knowing these standards, managers will be aware of the current environment and should act accordingly in terms of purchasing and operating decisions. As a result of the standards being real time there should be no planning variances and any operational variances will arise because the manager is not acting in accordance with the current environment. Instead of holding a procurement manager responsible for a large graphite price variance based on an out of date standard, the performance of this manager can be assessed against the current standard and through detailed information about how the cost of graphite per kilogramme is being controlled over time.

In addition, it will allow us to better understand the factors or activities that are driving cost. This is particularly important for overhead costs (which for us is a significant proportion of total production cost). The system will give us information that allows us to see where cost is being incurred and therefore where focus should be directed in managing cost. Digital costing also gives us better information to allow us to use dynamic pricing of our products so that we can change prices as soon as costings change or the market changes.

Marking guide:

Trait	Level	Descriptor	Marks
Benefits of digital costing		No rewardable material	0
	1	Explains at least one benefit associated with digital costing but the explanation lacks clarity, or the benefits are general rather than specific to costing.	1–2
	2	Explains more than one benefit associated with digital costing with reasonable clarity of explanation. Some of the benefits may be general rather than specific to costing.	3–5
	3	Explains a range of benefits associated with digital costing in a clear and comprehensive manner.	6–7

Examiner's comments

The second element of this task asked for an explanation of how the current costing system works, how digital costing might change this and the benefits of doing this for the business. This tested core activity A and was very poorly answered. Many candidates did not seem to understand what the question was about and made some very general points about the benefits of improved systems.

Most candidates explained the current system in terms of an absorption costing system and sometimes then explained the weakness of a traditional absorption costing system. Few candidates explained how standards were set and could then link this to a digital costing system. Some candidates confused digital costing systems with the costing of digital products which resulted in an answer that was completely irrelevant. Other candidates thought that a digital costing system was similar to an activity-based costing system.

Exercise 3

Costing of the digital app

Difficulties of establishing a cost per app for the S-Pencil

The S-Pencil app is a digital product without physical form. There are significant indirect costs associated with developing the app (including FirstApps contractual development fee of G$250,000), but once developed, the app can be reproduced without incurring additional direct production cost because there are no raw materials and negligible labour is involved. Each time we sell an S-Pencil (with the app included for free), we will incur a royalty fee, but this is the only direct cost that can be associated with the app.

To establish a cost per app we will need to firstly establish any direct costs, which in this case will simply be the royalty fee per app. We then need to establish how much of the indirect costs associated with the app, which include development and future support costs (see below), relates to a single app. To do this we will need to determine the total indirect cost associated with the app and divide this by the number of S-Pencils that we expect to sell over the app's lifetime. However, there are two main issues with this.

- Firstly, the indirect costs associated with the app can be spread over a number of periods and hence it can be difficult to establish up-front what these costs are. The cost associated with design and development is G$250,000, but other costs such as testing and operating the app will be spread into the future. Given that this is the first time that we have operated an app, these will be especially difficult to estimate.
- Secondly, it is difficult to determine the lifespan of our app. If the S-Pencil is not successful or other products come onto the market which supersede it, then the app may have a short-life. On the other hand, it could operate for years. Alternatively, it might need to be redeveloped if different types of technology emerge in the future.

Marking guide:

Trait	Level	Descriptor	Marks
Difficulties		No rewardable material	0
	1	Explains at least one difficulty of measuring the cost per S-Pencil for the app, but this explanation may lack clarity. The explanation makes little or no reference to the scenario.	1–2
	2	Explains more than one difficulty associated with measuring the cost per S-Pencil for the app, but this explanation may lack some clarity. The explanation makes some reference to the scenario.	3–5
	3	Explains with clarity a range of difficulties of measuring the cost per S-Pencil for the app. The explanation makes good reference to the scenario.	6–7

Types of cost still to be incurred

Infrastructure services: The infrastructure required for operating our app will include the platform and servers which support the hosting of the app, data storage and data delivery. In addition, our app will include the facility to make payments for additional content. The more complicated the platform and what we want the app to do, the higher the cost will be.

IT support services: Operating our app will require ongoing technical IT support services. Firstly, in the form of testing the app and dealing with any bugs that are present (which is what FirstApps is about to do). After launch, there will be on-going IT support required regarding the maintenance and monitoring of servers, data storage and image data.

Administrative services: Our app is designed so that users can purchase additional drawing and colouring tools. This content will need to be managed through an administrative dashboard, which will also manage functionality, app updates and user profiles.

Royalties: For every app that is actioned by S-Pencil users, FirstApps will charge a small royalty fee which as noted above will be a direct cost.

Marking guide:

Trait	Level	Descriptor	Marks
Types of cost		No rewardable material	0
	1	Explains at least one future cost associated with the app. The explanation may demonstrate little understanding of the digital aspects such as infrastructure and IT support. An answer at this level may just explain testing and royalty costs.	1–2
	2	Explains at least two future costs associated with the app. The explanation demonstrates some understanding of the digital aspects such as infrastructure and IT support.	3–4
	3	Explains at least three future costs associated with the app. The explanation clearly demonstrates understanding of the digital aspects such as infrastructure and IT support.	5–6

Examiner's comments

The first element of this task asked for explanation of the difficulties associated with establishing a cost per app for the S-Pencil and the types of cost still to be incurred for the app. Most candidates appeared well prepared for this type of task (especially in respect of the future costs) and given that this is a new area in the P1 syllabus, this was very pleasing to see. Stronger candidates separated their answers into two clear parts and could clearly identify the costing issues and future costs. Indeed, many candidates scored at level 3 in respect of the future costs part of their answers. Weaker candidates confused these two criteria and tried to answer them together. Other weaker candidates, failed to realise that the subject of the task was the app, choosing to explain costings for the tangible S-Pencil product instead.

Exercise 4

The advantages and disadvantages of using participative budgeting for the operations in Feland

Participation refers to the extent that managers are able to influence the figures that are incorporated into their budgets or targets. A budget where the manager participates is referred to as a bottom-up budget whereas a non-participatory approach is referred to as top-down budget. A bottom up approach may prove more beneficial for a number of reasons.

If the sales forecast is wrong this will lead to poor budgeting. This is because the sales forecast is the first step in the budgetary process and all functional budgets are based on it. Therefore, it makes sense that the sales budget is compiled by those managers that are established in Feland because these managers will have a much greater understanding of the likely customer demand and buying behaviour. Similarly, those managers who have been establishing the best site for the distribution centre will already understand staff and transport costs better than the more senior managers in Gawland.

As the managers are already earmarked as responsible for their own areas, participation in the budget setting process is likely to ensure a strong buy-in or ownership of the budget; they are more likely to work to succeed with their own budget than one they view as poorly conceived or unrealistic. Thus, participation in the budget setting process is likely to motivate.

There are drawbacks to participative budget setting: it can take longer than a top-down approach because the managers may not have the skills to build a budget or the time to coordinate with other managers to ensure that all aspects of the budget are considered properly. Lower level managers often lack the strategic vision that senior managers have and thus budgets can lack a clear purpose and direction.

A final point is that often performance against budget is linked to performance reviews and financial reward. Therefore, there may be a tendency to build slack into the budget as a margin for error and managers may deliberately underestimate revenues and overestimate costs to give themselves targets that can be easily achieved. This problem is exacerbated by our intention to include a bonus related to the achievement of budget targets in manager's remuneration packages. Thus, the budgets set by lower level managers may be less accurate.

In the circumstances I think the best approach would be to allow the budget holders (with the help of the accounting department as required) to prepare the first draft of the budgets for the Feland operation, that is to say to take a participative approach. This would allow us to benefit from local knowledge and get the budget holders to buy in to the budget.

Budget holders could then present their budgets to senior managers where their assumptions and performance levels could be challenged. At the end of this process we can produce an "agreed" budget.

Marking guide:

Trait	Level	Descriptor	Marks
Participatory budgets		No rewardable material	0
	1	Explains a limited number of points without application to the context of the scenario.	1–3
	2	Explains a reasonable number of points that include both advantages and disadvantages. Some limited application to the context of the preseen and/or scenario. May not contain consideration of whether participative is an appropriate approach.	4–6
	3	Explains fully both the disadvantages and advantages and applies the detail provided in the preseen and scenario to illustrate the points made in context. Contains a clear consideration of whether participative is an appropriate approach.	7–9

Time series analysis

Explanation of Tables 1, 2 and 3: Table 1 shows us the volume of pencil sales in Neland. Sales are growing but there is a lot of seasonal variation with quarter 2 always having the highest sales of the year, and quarter 3 the lowest. Quarter 2 coincides with the start of the academic year in Neland and the high sales are possibly explained by schools, universities and students building up their supplies of pencils.

Lower sales in later quarters could similarly be due to them not needing further supplies.

The trend represents the long-term movement in sales through the period and excludes the impact of seasonality on sales. We can see that the trend reveals a rapid growth in sales during the period. Seasonal variation represents the difference between trend and actual sales volume. This confirms that sales are above trend in quarter 2 and below trend in other quarters particularly quarter 3.

In Table 2 the regression equation models the behaviour of the trend:

- a = 2,000 tells us that in quarter 0 (the last quarter of 2016) the trend value is 2,000,000 pencils.
- b = 108 tells us that in each subsequent quarter the trend value of sales increased by 108,000 pencils.

Table 3 shows the average seasonal variation for each quarter and confirms that there is a strong seasonal element in sales.

Over the three years quarter 2 sales are on average 1.872 million pencils higher than the trend whereas quarter 3 sales are on average 1.080 million pencils below trend.

Average seasonal variation has been analysed on an additive basis – that is it is stated as an absolute number of pencils. This is not appropriate when the trend in sales is rising rapidly. Table 1 shows that as the trend increases so does the absolute size of the seasonal variation. For example, quarter 1 is 209,000 units below trend in 2017, falling to 254,000 in 2018 and 293,000 in 2019. Using an average of these three figures would give inaccurate results if used to forecast future sales.

In these circumstances it would be better to measure seasonal variation in a multiplicative way to show that seasonal variation increases in proportion to sales.

Marking guide:

Trait	Level	Descriptor	Marks
Time series		No rewardable material	0
	1	Demonstrates limited understanding of what the time series information shows. No or poor explanation of the appropriateness of the additive model.	1–3
	2	Demonstrates reasonable understanding of what the time series information shows. No or limited comments about the multiplicative or additive seasonal variation methods.	4–7
	3	Demonstrates good understanding of what the time series information shows. Demonstrates a good understanding of the multiplicative and additive seasonal variation in context.	8–10

The limitations of using this information to predict future demand for pencils in Feland

Firstly, the time series information has been gathered from a different country, albeit one of a similar size and with similar cultural traits. This mean that several factors that affect demand for pencils could be completely different in Feland to Neland. For example, the competitive environment may be completely different in Feland which may mean lower or higher demand for our pencils. Similarly, if the spike in sales during quarter 2 is due to the start of the school year it is probable that the spike in sales in Feland would be in quarter 3. Therefore, basing Feland forecasts on Neland trend and seasonal variation could lead to inaccurate budgets.

Secondly, Neland is a rapidly developing country with a young population where we have traded successfully for over a decade. Growth in the trend of sales is rapid but consistent.

We are only just about to start trading in Feland and are unlikely to experience the same trend in sales as in Neland. This means that we can expect lower sales in the first year or two following launch than we would hope to achieve once established.

Thirdly the data we have used is historic and it is possible that future sales will not resemble past sales. Assuming that past trends in sales growth will continue in the future may well be wrong. Time series analysis does not consider the underlying drivers of pencil sales. The age structure of the population, the income per head in the country, the literacy rate are all likely to drive sales in the long run. If any of these change then the trend in sales will change.

Marking guide:

Trait	Level	Descriptor	Marks
Limitations		No rewardable material	0
	1	Limitations are limited to a text-book list, which may be correct but either not applied or applied badly to the scenario context.	1–2
	2	At least one well applied and correctly explained limitation of the data is included although there may also be text-book limitations that are less well applied.	3–4
	3	The limitations of the data are correctly identified in the context of the scenario.	5–6

Examiner's comments

The first element of this task asked for an explanation of the advantages and disadvantages of participative budgeting in the context of setting up an operation and selling pencils in a new country. Most answers did contain a range of advantages and disadvantages indicating that candidates had good technical knowledge. However, many candidates failed to score at level 2 or higher because they presented a textbook list that was not applied to the context of the case scenario. For example, answers asserted that an advantage of the approach to setting budgets was that the managers setting the budget would have a better operational knowledge but failed to explain that as Feland was a new market with no trading record, that this would be vital knowledge when setting a budget for the first time. Similarly, answers stated that there was a danger of budgetary slack being introduced but failed to explain that this was a particular problem as bonuses were linked to the achievement of the budget for the managers in this new location.

The second element of this task asked for an explanation of given time series information (consisting of three tables) and the limitations of using this analysis to predict future demand for pencils in Feland. In order to score at a level 3, candidates were expected to comment on all three tables as well as the limitations.

Unfortunately, many candidates chose to only explain one or two of the tables, although most did make a good attempt at explaining the limitations.

Exercise 5

What – If Analysis

The revised profit figures in the analysis

Table 1 shows what would happen to each of the figures in the PEXECO budget under different 'what-if' assumptions.

The assumption A column shows what would happen to profit if we assume that a 5% reduction in selling price leads to a 15% increase in volumes sold. The assumption B column uses the assumption of a higher selling price reduction and therefore a higher increase in sales volumes as well as a 5% increase in fixed costs. Table 1 indicates that under assumption A, sales revenue would increase by 9% and under assumption B by 17%: these changes are affected by both the increase in volume and the reduction in selling price. Variable costs would increase under both assumptions by the same proportion as volumes. Fixed costs would only increase at the higher increase in volume because it is recognised that there will be an increase if volumes increase by more than 20%.

The percentage increase in budgeted profit under each assumption is bigger than the percentage increase in contribution. For assumption A fixed costs stay the same and given that volumes have increased this means that fixed cost per unit has decreased. The effect is more complex for assumption B because the increase in volume also leads to an increase in fixed costs, although given that these only increase by 5% this is not enough to outweigh the positive affect of the increased volumes on fixed cost per unit. Overall, the analysis shows that reducing selling prices by 10% would have the largest positive impact on budgeted profit.

Why 'what-if' analysis is more appropriate than sensitivity analysis in this situation

Sensitivity analysis involves changing one variable at a time and seeing how this change will affect budgeted profit. Such an approach is limited because it ignores the inter-dependence of the variables. For example, a reduction in selling price is likely to lead to an increase in volumes. An increase in volume might then lead to a step increase in fixed costs (as expected when volumes increase by more than 20% in our case) or could result in bulk purchase discounts for raw material inputs or additional overtime (affecting variable costs). 'What-if' analysis allows more than one variable to be changed at a time and allows us to model all of these potential inter-relationships.

Our 'what if' analysis is relatively simple in that we are changing only three variables (selling price, volumes sold and fixed costs) but it could be extended to include other impacts such as volume related changes to variable costs.

Marking guide:

Trait	Level	Descriptor	Marks
What-if analysis		No rewardable material	0
	1	Demonstrates some understanding of what-if analysis and gives a limited explanation of the figures in Table 1. Explanation of why what-if analysis is more appropriate may be limited or generic rather than linked to the scenario.	1–3
	2	Demonstrates reasonable understanding of what-if analysis and gives a reasonable explanation of the figures in Table 1. Explanation of why what-if analysis is more appropriate may be generic rather than linked to the scenario.	4–6
	3	Demonstrates comprehensive understanding of what-if analysis and gives a detailed and accurate explanation of the figures in Table 1. Explains why what-if analysis is more appropriate with good reference to the scenario.	7–9

Activity based budgeting for maintenance employee costs

The first step when using activity based budgeting is to establish the activities that drive the cost that is being budgeted. For machinery maintenance these will be routine services and repairs. The next step is to calculate the number of routine services and the number of repairs expected in the period. For routine services this is relatively straightforward because by nature a routine service means that it happens at regular intervals. In our case our plan is to routinely service each piece of equipment three times a year to ensure its best performance.

For repairs, it is a little more complex because repairs could be required for all sorts of reasons. In addition, this is a new production facility with new machinery and so, certainly initially, we might expect the number of repairs to be minimal.

Once the level of activity is quantified, the total time required to meet this level of activity needs to be calculated. We should be able to easily establish how long a routine service will take for each type of machine. The total hours for routine services will be calculated as the sum of the time per service multiplied by three for each type of machine in the facility. For repairs, establishing total hours required is a little more difficult because each repair is different and will require a different amount of time.

However, although this is a new production facility, it is using much the same machinery as our main production facility and the old PEXECO production facility. Therefore, we can estimate time taken based on previous experience, assuming that we have kept this information.

The final step is to work out the total number of hours required for machinery maintenance to determine how many employees are required to achieve this. We should bear in mind though that an employee will not work 52 weeks a year, because of holidays and training. We also need to make sure that adequate set up time between activities is included and to allow for unforeseen issues such as a major machine break down. The total budgeted cost for the machinery maintenance employee cost will be the number of employees multiplied by the annual wage or salary, including national insurance and pension costs.

Marking guide:

Trait	Level	Descriptor	Marks
Application of ABB		No rewardable material	0
	1	Demonstrates some understanding of an activity-based budgeting approach. There may be an attempt to apply this to explain how to establish the budget but this explanation is poor. Little or no reference is made to the scenario.	1–3
	2	Demonstrates reasonable understanding of an activity-based budgeting approach and makes a reasonable attempt to apply this to explain how to establish the budget. Explanation makes reference to the scenario.	4–6
	3	Demonstrates clear understanding of activity-based budgeting and applies this to explain how to establish the budget. Explanation is clearly linked to the scenario and recognises that this is a new production facility.	7–8

Examiner's comments

The first element of this task asked for an explanation of the effect of changing assumptions on budgeted profit and why "what if" analysis was more appropriate than sensitivity analysis in the situation. Few candidates scored highly here, with many only achieving level 1. The explanations of the revised profit figures were generally very limited with many candidates merely restating the figures in the table. Better answers discussed the impact of cost behaviour on the revised figures. Most candidates understood the difference between what-if analysis and sensitivity analysis but failed to relate this to the specific scenario.

The third element of this task asked for explanation of how the budget for maintenance employee cost in the new production facility could be established using an activity-based budgeting approach. Many candidates could explain the steps involved in activity-based costing in general terms, however this scored few marks because the task was about creating a budget for maintenance staff costs using activity-based budgeting. Most candidates failed to consider the information given in the scenario about the number of services and of those that did, few then considered the need for estimates of time taken for each type of service and the number of services required each period. Those few candidates that explained the process of building up the budget for the cost pool (rather than establishing a cost driver rate for product costing) scored at level 3. However, the vast majority of candidates scored at level 1.

Exercise 6

Time series information

The trend

The regression trend line represents the trend in the sales volumes for HB Graphite and HB PEXECO pencils over the past three years. The trend is the average position over time with seasonal variations smoothed out.

The first number in each equation represents the number of each type of pencil sold in the first quarter of 2017: 30 million HB Graphite pencils were sold and 5 million HB PEXECO pencils. The second part of each equation represents the trend in sales units since this starting point. For HB Graphite pencils that means that for each successive quarter the trend is for the volume sold to fall by 168,000: a fall because this is taken away from the starting position. For HB PEXECO pencils the other hand the trend is for the volume sold to increase by 210,000 in each successive quarter.

The trend lines show that based on the last three years of data, there is a downward trend in sales of Graphite pencils and an upward trend in the corresponding time periods for the PEXECO pencil. This is to be expected given that our PEXECO pencil carries out exactly the same function as our graphite pencil and that they are substitutes for each other. The fact that the decrease in volumes for Graphite is more than compensated for by the increase in volumes for PEXECO indicates that certainly for the HB pencil we are not losing market share in what is a relatively stable market.

Seasonality

The second part of the analysis looks at how seasonality affects the trend.

For example, looking at HB Graphite pencils we can see that in the period April to June sales were on average 20% lower than the trend, but in the following month were 15% higher than the trend.

Both types of pencils have similar seasonality profiles. Many of our customers are organisations such as local authorities and large businesses which are likely to buy in bulk once or twice a year, quite often when budgets have been released: this could be affecting seasonality. In addition, our large stationary retail customers cater to students and school children and therefore are likely to stock up before school and college years start.

Marking guide:

Trait	Level	Descriptor	Marks
Trend and SV		No rewardable material	0
	1	Explains the trend and seasonal variation data with some technical accuracy. Reasons for and implications of the trend and seasonal variations may be missing.	1–2
	2	Explains the trend and seasonal variation data technically accurately for the most part. Reasons for and implications of the trend and seasonal variations are given, but these might not be always relevant to the scenario and the products.	3–5
	3	Explains the trend and seasonal variation data with technical accuracy. Reasons for and implications of the trend and seasonal variations are given which are relevant to the scenario and the products.	6–7

Usefulness of this information for predicting S-Pencil sales volumes

The S-Pencil is a different type of product to our normal HB pencils because it is a stylus to be used on a screen rather than on paper. There are some similarities with the products in that the S-Pencil will feel like a PEXECO pencil and will have the same look and branding as our Graphite pencils.

However, the market for stylus type pencils is likely to be quite different to normal writing pencils in that a stylus will be a relatively expensive one-off purchase, whilst normal writing pencils are not. In addition, stylus pencils are a relatively new innovation compared to the normal writing pencil. There will also possibly be a greater seasonal affect for stylus type pencils, given that that this type of product would make a good gift at Christmas. Taking all of these factors into account, this time series analysis is not really that useful for forecasting S- Pencil sales volumes.

Marking guide:

Trait	Level	Descriptor	Marks
Usefulness		No rewardable material	0
	1	Demonstrates some understanding of the usefulness of using time series data to forecast sales in a general sense, but there is little reference to the S-Pencil product.	1–2
	2	Demonstrates reasonable understanding of the usefulness of using this time series data to forecast sales for the S-Pencil with some consideration of the nature of this particular product and its market compared to normal graphite pencils.	3–4
	3	Demonstrates understanding of the usefulness of using this time series data to forecast sales for the S-Pencil with detailed consideration of the nature of this particular product and its market compared to normal graphite pencils.	5

Examiner's comments

The second element of this task asked for explanation of what given time series information on the PEXECO and HB graphite pencils meant and how useful it would be to predict sales volumes for the S-Pencil. The first part of this was not as well answered as might have been expected given that this type of task has been set many times before. Many candidates approached this poorly, with few candidates able to expand further than explaining the seasonal variations in a general sense (often explanations of the trend were inaccurate). Some candidates were able to apply the scenario to explain why there were peaks and troughs in the seasons, but only a small proportion considered further the implications these fluctuations would have on Lottie Graphite. As a result, most candidates could only score at level 1 or 2 for this part. The second part of this was better answered. The majority of candidates were able to understand that the S-Pencil would have a different market, and would likely be a one-off purchase, so therefore, the previous data could not predict the future sales. Weaker candidates did not apply the scenario to their solution and just discussed the positive factors about using time series data in general.

Exercise 7

What is beyond budgeting and how might we apply it

Currently we take a traditional approach to budgeting in that we set our standards on an annual basis and create the budget using a top-down approach from these standards. We report variations against budget in the form of variance reporting which means that our control system is very backward looking rather than forward looking.

Beyond budgeting is an approach to budgeting which seeks to address some of the limitations of traditional budgeting such as it being backward looking and rigid. Under such an approach, rolling forecasts on a monthly or quarterly basis, are used as an alternative to the annual budget. These rolling budgets will use the latest information each time (for example, latest prices for graphite, cedar and all out other inputs as well as latest sales and production forecasts). This means that are budgets will be more up-to-date and should result in better resource allocation and allow us to adapt to changes more quickly. Also, the budgets are more forward looking.

Additionally, under a beyond budgeting approach, instead of just evaluating performance against budget targets (through variance reporting) the focus is on a wide range of performance measures or key performance indicators (KPIs), such as customer returns and production times. We already do this to a limited extent and using this approach would expand this throughout the business. We should look at external targets set by our competitors when setting these targets. For example, if our main competitor promised next day delivery then we should be setting similar targets.

Beyond budgeting also involves participation across the business. At the moment we take a central approach to budgeting where the annual budget is set by the directors and the Finance Department each year, with little input from the rest of the business. Under a beyond budgeting approach this would change as the people within the business with the detailed knowledge would be involved in creating the rolling budgets.

Marking guide:

Trait	Level	Descriptor	Marks
Beyond Budgeting		No rewardable material	0
	1	Explains at least one of the key principles of beyond budgeting (rolling budgets, expanded performance measures and participation) and how this can be applied. The answer may lack clarity and is unlikely to make reference to Lottie Graphite.	1–2
	2	Explains at least two of the key principles of beyond budgeting (rolling budgets, expanded performance measures and participation) and how this can be applied. The answer makes some reference to Lottie Graphite.	3–4

	3	Explains clearly at least two of the key principles of beyond budgeting (rolling budgets, expanded performance measures and participation) and how this can be applied. The answer makes good reference to Lottie Graphite.	5–6

Examiner's comments

The third element of this task asked for explanation of what beyond budgeting is and how it might be applied. This was once again well answered.

Most candidates demonstrated a good understanding of beyond budgeting and how it would be useful for Lottie Graphite to adopt rather than its current incremental budgeting processes. Clearly candidates were prepared for this and many scored at level 3 here.

Exercise 8

Sales variances

Sales price variance G$4,620 Adverse: This variance calculates the effect on profit due to selling at a different price to standard. The variance is calculated by multiplying the actual number of units sold by the difference between the standard selling price and the actual selling price. In January this was an adverse variance as PEXECO pencils were on a promotion from the middle of the month and were being sold at below list price. The likely effect of this promotion is that a higher volume of PEXECO pencils were sold than expected.

The sales price variance cannot be used to assess the performance of the sales team because they do not have the authority to change the sales price. The only product that was priced differently to the list price was the discounted PEXECO pencils and this was a Head Office initiative. During January the overall sales performance might have been improved if the sales team had been able to match the new competitor's price for regular coloured pencils.

Sales profit quantity variance G$512 Favourable: This variance calculates the effect on profit of selling a different total quantity, in standard mix, to the budget. The variance is calculated by multiplying the standard weighted average profit by the difference between actual sales and budgeted sales. In January we have sold 2,000 (700,000 - 698,000) more pencils than budgeted and therefore the variance is favourable.

Sales quantity is the basis of the sales team's bonus and as sales quantity is the one aspect that members of the team have some control over, it is a reasonable if basic performance measure.

It must be recognised that the sales volume increases due to the PEXECO promotion and the sales volume reduction due to the actions of a competitor are outside the control of the sales team and therefore, are not good indicators of performance. However, it is possible that the excellent sales volume of the artists pencils are a result of good performance by the sales team.

Sales profit mix variance G$9,616 Favourable: This variance calculates the effect on profit of the actual sales volumes of the different products being sold in a different proportion to the budgeted proportion. For each product the difference between the actual quantity sold and the budgeted mix for the actual quantity sold is multiplied by the standard profit. In January the variance is favourable because we have sold more of the two products with the highest standard profit and less of the product with the lowest standard profit. Most of this additional profit is due to the PEXECO pencil promotion. The lower proportion of sales of the regular coloured pencils would indicate that the concern that the sales team are focusing on selling the lower value products, is unfounded.

The sales team can improve this variance by selling more of the more profitable products and they may have done this with the artists coloured pencils. However, in January the reduction of the relatively low profit items and increase in the relatively high PEXECO was not due to the sales team's actions and is therefore not a reflection of their performance.

Marking guide:

Trait	Level	Descriptor	Marks
Variances		No rewardable material	0
	1	Explains one or two of the variances with technical accuracy. Reasons given for the variances might be missing or not linked to the correct variance. No or limited application to sales team performance.	1–4
	2	Explains at least two of the variances with technical accuracy with reasonable explanation of what these variances mean. Reasons given for the variances might not be drawn from the information presented or maybe missing in some cases. No or limited application to sales team performance.	5–8
	3	Explains each of the three variances with technical accuracy with good explanation of what these variances means in terms of the sales team's performance in January. Reasons given clearly relate to the specific variance and are drawn from the information presented in the task.	9–11

Three key performance indicators (KPI) for the Feland sales team

Number of visits to potential customer per month. As growth and winning new customers is a specific objective in the Feland market we need to measure the sales team's input, the effort that they expand in winning the new business. Over time this KPI will tell a story as the proportion of visits to new customers reduce and the "maintenance" and repeat business to existing customers increase.

The percentage of visits to potential new customers that result in a sales order. This KPI measures the effectiveness of the sales team's techniques. The higher the percentage of visits resulting in a sale, the more we can deduce that the sales team are correctly interpreting and addressing customer needs.

Average value of sales each week. There is a suspicion that sales orders are being deliberately delayed and not passed for despatch/ invoicing in a timely manner. The consequence of this, if it is true, is that customers will be waiting longer for their orders than necessary. This could mean that we lose customers and future orders. Monitoring the value of sales in the pipeline each week will help managers to identify abnormal swells in outstanding orders. If the first or final weeks in a month shows a spike or slump, this might indicate that the sales team are manipulating the sales quantities processed and action can be taken to stop this. However, this is a useful indicator even if the sales team are not regulating the speed of orders submitted, as it is a leading indicator. Weekly sales orders, sales in the pipeline indicate future sales and measure sales growth which is linked to the Feland sales goals.

Marking guide:

Trait	Level	Descriptor	Marks
KPIs		No rewardable material	0
	1	Identifies at least two KPIs although these may lack a timescale or quantification. Offers some justification but this may not be linked to the sales objectives of the Feland business as set in the scenario.	1–2
	2	Identifies three KPIs although these may lack good quantification and/or time. Some justification linked to the sales, and to some extent the objectives, of the Feland business detailed in the scenario.	3–5
	3	Identifies and justifies three KPIs that are quantified and/or time assigned. All three KPIs are relevant to the detail given in the scenario and linked to the objectives of sales growth/new business and/or address the concern re the withholding of sales orders.	5–6

Examiner's comments

The first element of this task asked for an explanation of how sales price, mix and quantity variances were calculated, what they meant and reasons for the variances. The task also asked for an explanation of the usefulness of these variances for measuring the performance of the sales teams in the month. This tested core activity C. Sales variances, including the subdivision of the volume profit variance into quantity and mix should be an area that candidates are comfortable explaining and interpreting given the large number of previous questions they could use as practice. However, this appeared to be far from the case. Few candidates achieved a level 3 mark because they failed to address all parts of the task: the calculation, meaning, reasons for and appropriateness of these variances as a performance measure for the sales team. It was disappointing to note how many candidates failed to use the case information to explain the reasons for the variances preferring instead to use generic possible causes. As always, candidates need to apply technical understanding to the facts presented in the case to gain high marks. They also need to understand the difference between a sales profit volume variance and a sales profit quantity variance.

The second element of this task asked for an explanation and justification of three KPIs that could be used to measure the performance of the sales team. This tested core activity C. Future candidates should be aware that when asked for KPIs appropriate to a situation, generic answers will not score above a level 1.

In this case the KPIs were required to assess the performance of the sales team and therefore "cost of production", "cost per mileage of distribution" and "quality rejection rates" did not apply to their activities. Also, KPIs that actually contradict the facts presented in the case, such as "discounts on list price offered to customers", are not considered valid. Answers must be applied to the context of the case.

Exercise 9

PEXECO production facility variances

Resin: raw material variances

The price variance for resin is adverse which means that we paid more per kilogramme for resin than standard for the actual quantity purchased. This is a direct result of the price increase from the resin supplier.

The usage variance for resin is also adverse which means that we used more resin that we should have compared to standard for the PEXECO pencils that were produced in the month.

This adverse variance will have arisen because the quality of the wood cut-offs used to create the composite in February meant that there needed to be a greater proportion of resin in the composite mix. Therefore, each pencil will have required more resin than standard.

Marking guide:

Trait	Level	Descriptor	Marks
Raw materials		No rewardable material	0
	1	Explains the raw material variances with some technical accuracy but with limited explanation of how these variances have arisen.	1
	2	Explains the raw material variances with reasonable technical accuracy. There are reasonable explanations of the reasons why these variances have occurred. Reasons given might not relate to the correct variance or might not be drawn from the information presented in the task.	2–3
	3	Explains the raw material variances with technical accuracy. There are good explanations of the reasons why these variances have occurred. Reasons given clearly relate to the specific variance and are drawn for the information presented in the task.	4

Fixed production overhead variances

The total fixed production overhead is adverse which means that we have under-absorbed overheads for the month. The reasons for this are related to the three following variances.

The fixed overhead expenditure variance is the difference between actual fixed overhead incurred in February and the budgeted overheads. The variance is adverse which means that we incurred a higher level of overhead than we had budgeted for the month. One rea son for this is that external engineers were called in to increase the speed of the production machinery and this presumably would not have been foreseen at the time the budget was set. Also, as a result of some machinery breaking down, we had to hire additional equipment, the cost of which would not have been included in the budget.

The efficiency variance looks at the efficiency of the chosen absorption bases which in our case is machine hours. It compares the actual hours used with the hours that we thought we would need to produce the actual output based on the standard. This difference in hours is then valued at the overhead absorption rate. The variance is adverse which means that overall we used more machine hours to produce the pencils than compared to standard. In other words, the machinery was not as efficient as it should have been.

Overall it would appear that despite the engineer's attempts to speed up production, the machinery worked more slowly than it should have. It's possible that this was due in part to the new direct employees not operating the machinery properly.

The capacity variance is the difference between the originally budgeted machine hours and the actual machine hours for the month, multiplied by the standard absorption rate. The variance is favourable which means that we got more hours out of our machinery compared to the original budget. This is because the capacity of the production line has increased overall as a result of the engineer's work.

Marking guide:

Trait	Level	Descriptor	Marks
Fixed production overhead		No rewardable material	0
	1	Explains the fixed production overhead variances with some technical accuracy but with limited explanation of how these variances have arisen.	1–3
	2	Explains the fixed production overhead variances with reasonable technical accuracy. There are some explanations given of the reasons why these variances have occurred. Reasons given might not relate to the correct variance or might not be drawn from the information presented in the task.	4–6
	3	Explains the fixed production overhead variances with technical accuracy. There are a number of explanations given of the reasons why these variances have occurred. Reasons given clearly relate to the specific variance and are drawn for the information presented in the task.	7–8

Examiner's comments

The first element of this task asked for an explanation of the meaning of raw material and fixed production overhead variances and reasons for each variance. This tested core activity C.

Most candidates understood how the raw material variances were calculated and the reasons why they may have arisen and therefore scored at level 2 or 3. However, as a point for the future, candidates need to be more precise in their explanation of variances to clearly demonstrate their technical understanding. For example, some candidates did not make it clear that the material price variance was in respect of the actual material purchased or that the standard usage was for the actual level of output. The fixed overhead variances were less well explained, and most candidates were not able to clearly demonstrate technical understanding of the variances. As a result, many struggled to get above a level 1 for this trait. Many candidates failed to recognise that the overhead absorption rate was based on machine hours and when discussing the efficiency variance referred to labour hours rather than machine hours. Understanding of the capacity variance was very weak.

Exercise 10

KPI measures

Three measures which would be used as KPIs to assess the performance of our individual suppliers are as follows:

Number of late deliveries

Many of our suppliers are based in other countries (some even on the other side of the world) and therefore it is inevitable that there will be a period of time between ordering and receiving raw materials (in other words, lead time). However, it is important for our production planning and to ensure that we don't end up holding excessive inventory levels that our suppliers keep to these lead times. Therefore, a useful performance measure would be to keep track of the number of late deliveries (as measured against expected lead time) for each supplier.

Percentage of returns due to poor quality

The quality of our raw materials is central to the quality of all of the pencils that we produce. We should therefore be making sure that the quality of all raw materials received is as expected and return any that fail this inspection. Regular tracking of the percentage of returns against total deliveries by supplier will allow us to assess which suppliers are failing in terms of delivering poor quality raw materials.

Number of supplier queries taking more than two days to resolve

One of the issues with Jacksters was that it was very difficult for our procurement employees to talk to someone. Therefore, another performance measure for all of our suppliers could be linked to how quickly and efficiently they deal with queries. We need to have suppliers which we can work collaboratively with.

Marking guide:

Trait	Level	Descriptor	Marks
Identify and explain KPIs		No rewardable material	0
	1	Identifies one or two KPIs which are relevant for measuring the performance of suppliers but the measure might not be clearly stated and/or the justification is either missing or not clear.	1–3
	2	Identifies two or three KPIs which are relevant for measuring the performance of suppliers but the measure might not be clearly stated and/or justification lacks some clarity.	4–6
	3	Identifies three KPIs which are appropriate for measuring the performance of suppliers which are well justified.	7–8

Examiner's comments

The second element of this task asked for suggestions for three KPIs to monitor the performance of suppliers. This was generally well answered with a significant minority of candidates scoring a high level 2 or level 3. The tested core activity C. The majority of candidates described three relevant issues relating to suppliers that an entity would want to monitor and could explain why these were important for the business. In many cases however, the actual description of the KPI was not given. For example, many mentioned that quality was an issue and went on to describe why it was important to monitor quality. However clear explanations about how quality would be measured were often missing.

Exercise 11

Sales variances

Sales price variances

For large retailer customers there is no variance, which means that actual and budgeted sales prices were the same. Given that there are only three customers that have remained the same throughout the period, this is not surprising: prices will have been negotiated and agreed with these customers up front. There are however adverse variances for small retailers (which represents 100 customers at the end of the period) and for website customers, meaning that average selling prices for these groups were lower than we expected. The variance for website customers can be directly linked to the decision by Ben Thakar to authorise a special promotion during the period. The variance for small retailers will be due to the sales teams negotiating with new customers and offering discounts.

Marking guide:

Trait	Level	Descriptor	Marks
Sales price variance		No rewardable material	0
	1	Demonstrates some understanding of the sales price variances but is unlikely to provide any reasons or the reasons are not valid.	1
	2	Demonstrates reasonable understanding of the sales price variances and provides at least one reason for the variance which is linked to the scenario.	2
	3	Demonstrates good understanding of the sales price variances and provides reasons for the variance which are linked to the scenario.	3

Sales mix variances

This variance is adverse for the large retailers and means that for our total sales, a lower proportion was to large retailers than we had expected. For both small retailer and website customers the opposite is true: the favourable variances mean that we sold proportionately more to these customers than expected. Overall the variance is favourable which means that we sold proportionately more to the customers with the higher profit margins (website and small retailer customers) and proportionately less to the customers with the lower profit margin (large retailers). There are two main reasons why the mix of sales to customers has changed. Firstly, there was a specific sales promotion targeted at website customers, which will have boosted sales volumes for this type of customer. Secondly, the sales teams have been more successful than we anticipated securing small retailer customers, although there has been no change in the number of large retail customers.

Sales quantity variances

This variance is best considered in total and indicates that gross profit is increased by G$245,625 for the three-month period as a result of selling more S-Pencils in standard mix than we expected to. One reason for this is that we have increased the customer base for small retailers and the website as a result of the specific promotion and the sales teams' efforts as already explained above.

Marking guide:

Trait	Level	Descriptor	Marks
Sales mix and quantity variances		No rewardable material	0
	1	Demonstrates some technical understanding of the mix and quantity variances but is unlikely to provide any reasons or the reasons are not valid.	1–2
	2	Demonstrates reasonable technical understanding of the sales mix and quantity variances and provides at least one reason for the variances which is linked to the scenario.	3–4
	3	Demonstrates good understanding of the sales mix and quantity variances and provides reasons for the variance which are linked to the scenario.	5–6

Overall impact

Overall, Ben's authorised price promotion and the activities of the sales teams will have increased actual profit for the three months compared to that budgeted.

The reduction in profit from sales price discounts given is more than compensated for by both the increase in volumes sold and the change in the mix towards customers that generate a higher gross profit per pencil. This increase in sales volume, however, is not universal for all customer types: there is an adverse volume variance for large retailers (because the adverse mix variance is bigger than the favourable quantity variance) and indicates that sales volumes were lower to these customers. Given that there has been no change to the individual large retailer customers in the period, this reduction in volume is slightly concerning. It would be interesting to look at an analysis by customer to see if this relates to just one customer or all three.

Marking guide:

Trait	Level	Descriptor	Marks
Overall		No rewardable material	0
	1	Explains that overall there is a positive impact on profit but does not link this to the different types of variances.	1
	2	Explains that overall the negative impact of the discounts given is outweighed by both the change in mix and the increase in volume. The explanation may lack some clarity.	2–3
	3	Explains clearly and comprehensively overall the negative impact of the discounts given is outweighed by both the change in mix and the increase in volume. Identifies that overall the volume variance for large retailer customers is adverse and the implications of this.	4

Examiner's comments

The first element of this task asked for explanation of what sales price, mix and quantity variances meant and the reasons for their occurrence. It also asked for explanation of whether two actions undertaken by the Sales & Marketing Director had been successful in relation to two customer groups. This tested core activity C and was surprisingly poorly answered. Few candidates were able to accurately explain the variances beyond the price variance.

Most candidates demonstrated a clear lack of technical understanding in respect of the sales mix and quantity variances, which is disappointing given that this has been tested many times before. Some candidates ignored the second part of this about the success of the actions taken and therefore did not score well here.

Exercise 12

KPIs

Number of user complaints: The IT app administration service provider will be managing the administration of the app that allows the S-Pencil to function. If app updates are not managed properly or the functionality of the app fails, the users of our S-Pencil will not be happy and complain. The level of complaints is therefore a good indicator of how well the provider is administering the app.

Percentage of user complaints dealt with within a target time: Where there are complaints it is important that they are dealt with quickly and efficiently. A target can be set about how quickly we expect queries to be dealt with and the provider's performance measured against this. The higher this percentage is greater our confidence that the provider to appropriately dealing with our customers.

Percentage of users that make in-app purchases: Part of the administration of the app will include promoting in-app purchases. Clearly the greater the number of in-app purchases the greater our revenue. We would want as many of our users to make in-app purchases as possible and therefore this measure would indicate how successful the provider was in achieving this.

Marking guide:

Trait	Level	Descriptor	Marks
KPIs		No rewardable material	0
	1	Identifies one or two KPIs which are relevant for measuring the performance of the IT services supplier, but the explanation is either missing or not clear.	1–2
	2	Identifies two or three KPIs which are relevant for measuring the performance of the IT services supplier, but the explanation lacks some clarity.	3–5
	3	Identifies three KPIs which are wholly appropriate for measuring the performance of the IT services supplier which are well explained.	6–7

Examiner's comments

The second element of this task asked for suggestions and justifications for three KPIs to measure the performance of the IT administrative services provider for the S-Pencil app. This was answered well by many candidates who had clearly thought about the nature of what the IT administrative services provider would be doing. Weaker candidates, however, did not use the scenario and looked at KPIs for the app itself rather than for the provider of administrative services.

Exercise 13

Accounting treatment of leased equipment

As the baking machine is leased, we must apply IFRS16: Leases. Leased assets give rise to both a right-of use asset and a lease liability.

The right-of use-asset represents the value of our right to use the baking machine for the four years of the lease and the lease liability reflects our obligation to pay the future lease payments.

The value that will be credited to the lease liability is the present value of the four lease payments, discounted at 5%. We should use a discount rate implicit in the lease agreement, but as this is not evident, we can use 5% as this is our incremental borrowing rate. The value that will be debited to the right-of use-asset will be the present value of the four lease payments discounted at 5% plus the G$3,000 direct costs to obtain the lease. The G$3,000 direct costs to obtain the lease will be credited to cash or payables.

As we are not due to make a lease payment until 30 April 2021, in the financial statements for the year-ended 31 December 2020 we will simply charge the profit or loss account with eight months of the interest charge and add the same amount in the statement of financial position to the lease liability.

In subsequent years each of the four G$100,000 lease payments will be deducted from the lease liability and the interest payable, accrued at 5%, will be added to the lease liability. Thus, at the end of each year the lease liability will reduce by the amount paid less the interest incurred. The right-of-use asset will be depreciated over the shorter of the lease term or the useful economic life of the asset. In our case the four-year lease is the shorter of the two, and eight-months depreciation will be charged for the year.

IFRS 16 allows two exceptions to the above treatment: where the lease is either short-life (where the lease term is less than 12 months) or low value. Although there is not absolute definition of “low value”, our baking machine is unlikely to fall into this category.

Marking guide:

Trait	Level	Descriptor	Marks
IFRS 16		No rewardable material	0
	1	Demonstrates some technical understanding of the principles of initial and subsequent recognition of the right of use asset and lease liability. The explanation lacks clarity and is unlikely to identify the need to pro rata for 2020.	1–3
	2	Demonstrates reasonable technical understanding of the principles of initial and subsequent recognition of the right of use asset and lease liability. The explanation might not be clear and is unlikely to identify the need to pro rata for 2020.	4–7

	3	Demonstrates good technical understanding of the principles of initial and subsequent recognition of the right of use asset and lease liability. The explanation is clear and probably identifies the need to pro rata for 2020.	8–10

Examiner's comments

The first element of this task asked for an explanation of how leased equipment should be recorded in the financial statements for the year ending 31 December 2020 and subsequent years. This tested core activity D. Candidates either scored very well or very badly because they either knew the correct treatment of leases or did not. Some candidates stated that this was probably an operational lease. In accordance with the new financial reporting standard on leasing, IFRS 16, operational leases are no longer relevant when considering how a lessee records a lease. Only a minority of candidates did well here and clearly this is a technical area that future candidates would be advised to revise.

Exercise 14

Inventory valuation in the financial statements for the year ended 31 December 2020

The fundamental principle of IAS2: Inventories, is that inventory should be stated at the lower of cost and net realisable value (NRV). If we were going to dispose of all the incorrectly labelled pencils the NRV would have been zero and this is still the case for the 40% of pencils that are being donated to the educational charity. These pencils should now be excluded from the finished goods inventory valuation. This will have the effect of lowering our finished goods inventory, which will increase our cost of sales and reduce our profit for the year ended 31 December 2020.

The remaining 60% of inventory can be salvaged and therefore we need to consider the NRV in more detail to establish whether or not it is less than cost. As the buyer of the pencils is offering only G$300 per thousand, the NRV is likely to be below our cost of production as the average full production cost for a graphite pencil is over G$300.

NRV is the estimated selling price in the normal course of business, less the estimated cost of completion and the estimated cost necessary to make the sale. The cost of Barney San's procedures for erasing the embossing needs to be deducted from the selling price, as does any anticipated packaging or selling costs. This write down to NRV will be recognised as an expense in the year ended 31 December 2020 as this is the period in which the inventory was impaired.

The effect will be to reduce the value of the inventory in the statement of financial position and to reduce the profit for the period.

Marking guide:

Trait	Level	Descriptor	Marks
IAS 2		No rewardable material	0
	1	Explains some of the principles of IAS 2 but does not apply to the two different parts of the inventory (the 60% and 40%).	1–2
	2	Explains most of the principles of IAS 2, with a reasonable definition of NRV. Applies the rules to the two parts of the inventory under review fairly well. May not mention that there will be a reduction in profit for the period.	3–5
	3	Explains IAS 2 principles clearly and applies them well to the two different parts of inventory. Clearly explains the effect on inventory and debates the lower of cost V NRV in the context of the information in the case. Clearly explains the effect on profit for the period.	6–7

Examiner's comments

The second element of this task asked for an explanation of how the financial statements would be affected by an issue regarding inventory that had been incorrectly labelled. This tested core activity D. Candidates did not appear to appreciate that IAS 2 would be an appropriate standard and when it was used, it was explained in a scattergun and incomplete manner. Only a very few candidates achieved a level 3 because they could explain the principles of IAS 2 and the effect on the financial statements in the context of the case. Excellent answers considered that the net realisable value of the inventory was likely to be below the cost because they knew the average cost of a batch of graphite pencils as detailed in the pre-seen.

Exercise 15

Accounting treatment of PEXECO non-current assets

Assets held for sale

To be reclassified as an asset held for sale, an asset needs to be available for immediate sale in its present condition and its sale must be highly probable. A sale is highly probable when: management are committed to sell the asset; there is an active programme to find a buyer; the asset is marketed at a reasonable price; the sale is expected to take place within 12 months; and it is unlikely that the plan to sell the asset will change.

The packing equipment will become 'available for immediate sale in its present condition' on 1 September 2020 which is when we will no longer need it for production. There is already a buyer for the asset which has presumably agreed the price of G$75,000 and therefore the sale is highly probable at a reasonable price. Therefore, strictly speaking, the packing equipment becomes an asset held for sale on 1 September 2020 and depreciation should cease. However, given that it is expected to be sold in early September we would simply record this as an asset disposal. Therefore, assuming that it is sold in very early September 2020, the asset will be derecognised on that date and a profit on disposal calculated as the difference between its sales price of G$75,000 and it's carrying amount (G$70,000 less G$2,500 × 8 (representing depreciation to the point it becomes available for sale)).

The production conveyor line will cease to be used on 31 August 2020 but will not be available for immediate sale in its present condition until it has been dismantled. It would appear that there is a management plan to sell the asset and that a buyer is being sought, presumably at a reasonable price. In addition, the sale is expected to happen within 12 months. Therefore, once it has been dismantled the production conveyor line asset will be reclassified as an asset held for sale and depreciation will stop. At 31 December 2020 it is unlikely that the asset will have been sold and therefore, it will be recorded in the statement of financial position as an asset held for sale within current assets. It will be recorded at the lower of its carrying amount at the date that is reclassified as held for sale (which is after it has been dismantled) and fair value less costs to sell (which is G$130,000 less the costs of dismantling of G$8,000). If fair value less costs to sell are lower than carrying amount the difference is written off to profit or loss.

Marking guide:

Trait	Level	Descriptor	Marks
Assets held for sale		No rewardable material	0
	1	Demonstrates some understanding of the recognition criteria of IFRS 5 in respect of assets held for sale but they are incorrectly applied to the asset disposals. The impact of the disposals on the financial statements is only partially or incorrectly explained.	1–3
	2	Demonstrates reasonable understanding of the recognition criteria of IFRS 5 in respect of assets held for sale and attempts to apply these to the asset disposals. The impact of the disposals on the financial statements is explained but explanation lacks some detail or accuracy.	4–6
	3	Demonstrates full understanding of the recognition criteria of IFRS 5 in respect of assets held for sale and applies these correctly to the asset disposals. The impact of the disposals on the financial statements is comprehensively explained.	7–8

Additional expenditure on the mixing machinery

IAS 16: Property, plant and equipment, normally requires expenditure on an asset already recognised to be charged to profit or loss as incurred. However, if that expenditure is expected to increase the future economic benefit of the asset in excess of the originally assessed level of performance, then it can be added to the carrying value of the asset.

In our case, the mixing equipment is to be reconditioned, the effect of which is to increase its capacity and to extend its useful economic life by four years compared to our original assessment. Therefore, the future economic benefit that will be derived from this asset is increased and hence this subsequent expenditure on the asset can be capitalised.

In addition, we can also capitalise the additional expenditure of G$6,000 for moving the equipment as this is directly attributable to getting it ready for its intended use. The new carrying amount for the mixing machinery asset will be depreciated over its newly assessed remaining economic life.

Marking guide:

Trait	Level	Descriptor	Marks
Additional expenditure		No rewardable material	0
	1	Explains the recognition rule for capitalisation of subsequent expenditure in IAS16 with no application to the scenario.	1
	2	Explains how the subsequent expenditure on the asset can be capitalised in accordance with IAS 16 but explanation lacks clarity. The costs of dismantling might not be mentioned.	2–3
	3	Explains fully how the subsequent expenditure on the asset can be capitalised in accordance with IAS 16 and that the cost of dismantling can also be included as this is directly attributable.	4

Examiner's comments

The first element of this task asked for an explanation of how two asset disposals and expenditure incurred on reconditioning a third asset should be treated in the financial statements. Most candidates were able to demonstrate a good knowledge of the recognition criteria in IFRS 5: Assets held for sale, although some descriptions of these criteria were incomplete. The application of these recognition criteria to the specific scenario was less well answered. Many candidates did not seem to appreciate that the question required the position at 31 December 2020 (which is when the financial statements would need to be prepared) and therefore discussed whether the assets could be classified now as held for sale. This meant that the production conveyor was often described as not being sold within

12 months and so should not be held for sale. The packing equipment was better dealt with as most candidates noted that it would be sold soon, although candidates forgot to depreciate up to the point of reclassification/sale and so described a gain of G$75,000 – G$70,000. The accounting treatment was described well with most candidates understanding that depreciation stops once the asset is classified as held for sale, although the description of where in the financial statements to present the assets held for sale was often inaccurate. The treatment of the additional expenditure on the mixing machinery was generally well answered, although it was not always clearly explained why the G$6,000 "moving" costs were added to the capital cost. Candidates need to be more precise in their answers if they want to score at level 3.

Exercise 16

Impact of legal case and fire on Financial Statements

Because the financial statements for the year ended 31 December 2020 are still to be finalised it is possible to make adjustments for events happening after the reporting period as long as these are adjusting events in accordance with IAS 10: Events after the reporting period.

Fire

The small fire which occurred in the PEXECO production facility happened on 10 January 2021 which is after the end of the reporting period. This is a non-adjusting event because the fire is independent of any condition existing at the reporting date.

Any impairment as a result of the damage caused will be charged to profit or loss in the year ending 31 December 2021 rather than 2020. This impairment is unlikely to be significant enough to disclose in the financial statements for the year ended 31 December 2020.

Settlement of legal case

The settlement of the legal case against Jacksters on 10 February 2021 represents an adjusting event. It is adjusting because the settlement of the case is an event which gives evidence of a condition that existed at the reporting date of 31 December 2020. The case was initially taken out in December 2020 and therefore was outstanding at the reporting date.

Because this is an adjusting event, the G$25,000 received from Jacksters should be credited to profit or loss for the year ended 31 December 2020.

Marking guide:

Trait	Level	Descriptor	Marks
Application of IAS 10		No rewardable material	0
	1	Explains correctly how at least one of the events will affect the financial statements for the year ended 31 December 2020. Explanation of why the events are adjusting/ non-adjusting is either missing or poor.	1–2
	2	Explains correctly how at least one of the events will affect the financial statements for the year ended 31 December 2020. The reasons why the events are adjusting/non-adjusting are explained, although the explanation might lack some clarity.	3–4
	3	Explains mostly accurately how BOTH of the events will affect the financial statements for the year ended 31 December 2020. The reasons why the events are adjusting/non-adjusting are comprehensively explained.	5–6

Examiner's comments

The first element of this task asked for explanation of how two events after the reporting period would affect the financial statements for the year ended 31 December 2020. This tested core activity D. Most candidates clearly explained how to determine an adjusting and a non-adjusting event and applied the definitions correctly to the scenario. Unfortunately, how these events affected the financial statements was not so well explained, especially the adjusting event, which was often thought to relate to an irrecoverable debt rather than a dispute with a supplier.

Exercise 17

Expenditure on new baking equipment

Initial measurement

The baking equipment will be recognised as a tangible non-current asset in accordance with IAS 16: Property, plant and equipment, because it is probable that future economic benefit will flow into our business and because the asset can be reliably measured. The amount that the asset is initially recorded at will be its purchase price (G$160,000) plus any expenditure which is directly attributable to getting the asset ready for its intended use. The directly attributable costs are the costs of installation and testing of G$5,000 because both of these are required to get the asset ready for its intended use.

The G$2,000 spent on additional ventilation will also be included in the cost of the asset because this expenditure is required to ensure that the site of the baking equipment is safe. Presumably the equipment cannot be used without this ventilation and therefore this expenditure is also directly attributable to getting the baking machinery ready for its intended use.

Marking guide:

Trait	Level	Descriptor	Marks
Initial recognition		No rewardable material	0
	1	Explains the recognition rules of IAS 16 but does not apply this to the scenario.	1
	2	Explains the recognition rules of IAS 16 and applies these to explain recognition of the baking equipment as a non-current asset and/or how each type of expenditure will affect the amount capitalised. There may be a lack of clarity in the explanation.	2–3
	3	Explains the recognition rules of IAS 16 and applies these to clearly explain recognition of the baking equipment as a non-current asset and how each type of expenditure will affect the amount capitalised.	4

Depreciation

The asset will need to be depreciated from the date that the baking equipment is available for use (even if it isn't being used from that date) over its useful economic life. Where an asset has elements to it which have different useful economic lives, IAS 16 states that the initial carrying amount of the asset should be split into its separate elements and depreciated separately. In this instance the baking equipment itself has a useful economic life of 15 years, however the lining only has a useful life of three years (because it then needs to be replaced). Therefore, we need to establish how much of the total cost of the baking equipment relates to the lining and treat this as separate asset depreciated over three years. The remaining cost will be depreciated over 15 years.

Marking guide:

Trait	Level	Descriptor	Marks
Depreciation		No rewardable material	0
	1	Explains the principle of depreciating over the UEL of an asset but does not apply this to the scenario.	1
	2	Explains the principle of depreciation and attempts to apply this to the scenario. Explanation of splitting of the asset into component parts may be missing.	2–3
	3	Explains the principle of depreciation and applies this to the scenario to clearly and fully explain the splitting of the asset into component parts.	4

Disposal of warehouse property

Impact on our tax charge

The sale of our warehouse property will give rise to a capital gain which will be chargeable to tax at the corporate tax rate of 30%. The amount of the capital gain will be the proceeds of sale (G$600,000) less the property's original cost of G$350,000 less the indexation allowance available for the period from the date of purchase of the property until the date of sale of 31 May 2020. This indexation allowance will be calculated as the indexation percentage relevant to the time period multiplied by G$350,000.

Marking guide:

Trait	Level	Descriptor	Marks
Tax impact		No rewardable material	0
	1	Demonstrates some understanding that this gives rise to a capital gain. Little else is explained.	1
	2	Demonstrates reasonable understanding that this gives rise to a capital gain and explains how this will be calculated and/or taxed.	2
	3	Demonstrates good understanding that this gives rise to a capital gain and explains how this will be calculated and taxed.	3

Impact on our financial statements

In terms of accounting treatment, we will depreciate the property up until the date of disposal and calculate a profit on disposal of G$600,000 less G$140,000 (which is the property's carrying amount at the disposal date). The asset will be derecognised in the statement of financial position and the profit on disposal will be recognised in the statement of profit or loss. In addition, the statement of cash flow will show the G$600,000 as proceeds from the sale of property, plant and equipment.

Marking guide:

Trait	Level	Descriptor	Marks
Accounting impact		No rewardable material	0
	1	Demonstrates some understanding that this gives rise to a profit on disposal. Little else is explained.	1
	2	Demonstrates reasonable understanding that this gives rise to a profit on disposal and explains how this will be calculated and reflected in the financial statements, although not all impacts may be noted.	2
	3	Demonstrates good understanding that this gives rise to a profit on disposal and fully explains how this will be calculated and reflected in all of the financial statements, including the statement of cash flows.	3

Examiner's comments

The second element of this task asked for explanation of how expenditure associated with new baking equipment will be initially recorded in the statement of financial position and how to depreciate the asset. This tested core activity D and was broken down into two marking traits.

Many candidates scored level 3 for the first trait on recognition of the expenditure, showing that candidates were well prepared for this topic. However, for the second trait, other than explaining how depreciation would work, most candidates were not able to identify that there were different components to the asset that would have different depreciation treatments. As a result, many candidates could only achieve a level 2.

The third element of this task asked for explanation of how disposal of the warehouse building would affect both the tax charge for the year and the financial statements for the year ended 31 December 2020. This tested core activity D and was generally poorly answered. Most candidates were able to demonstrate their accounting knowledge, however, very few candidates were able to show how a capital gain would arise and be treated, displaying a lack of ability to apply their understanding when tested together. Candidates should be better prepared for tasks on tax treatments.

Exercise 18

Limiting factor analysis

The principles behind the production schedule

The production schedule has been compiled using a short-term decision-making technique known as limiting factor analysis. It is a decision-making technique that prioritises production based on maximising the contribution obtainable from a single scare resource, in our case packaging labour. The technique uses contribution and not profit as we assume that fixed costs do not change in the short-term and are therefore irrelevant.

However, before we use the technique, we have to make the batches needed in order to fulfil the high priority orders. The schedule show that we need 700 minutes to produce the 9H pencils, 700 minutes to produce the 4H pencils and 1,600 minutes to produce the 8H pencils. This means that we have 5,950 minutes remaining to allocate to non-priority demand.

For each grade of pencil, the contribution per batch was divided by the time needed to package a batch, in order to calculate the contribution generated by a minute of packing labour. As these are specialist pencils, we can assume that the packing time varies across the three grades of pencil due to the differing packaging sizes and types needed by our customers. After we calculated the contribution per minute of packing time, we ranked the three pencil grades in order of highest contribution first. This will be the order that we want to manufacture the pencils, as this will maximise the total contribution and therefore profit earned.

From the schedule we can see that the line labelled, "Packing time allocated after making priority orders (minutes)" allocates the packing time up to the maximum demand for each grade of pencil. The 9H and 4H pencil demand is fully satisfied but 5 batches of 8B will not be completed as there is insufficient packing labour.

Offering overtime premium of G$14 an hour

An overtime premium of G$14 is the same as the standard hourly rate for the finishing department. In effect the packers would be earning double their normal rate. If we offered this premium solely to complete the 5 batches of 8B pencils, needed to fulfil next week's demand, it would be financially beneficial. This is because each minute of packaging labour that can be used making these pencils will generate G$12.48 contribution and this is considerably more than G$14 an hour. However, this only applies to the packaging labour needed to complete the 8B pencils (which is 40 minutes X 5 batches). After this time there is no evidence that overtime will generate any contribution at all and paying a G$14 an hour overtime premium would reduce profit.

Marking guide:

Trait	Level	Descriptor	Marks
Limiting factor		No rewardable material	0
	1	Demonstrates some understanding of the principles of limiting factor analysis but without application of these principles to the information in the schedule. The explanation of the overtime rate is either not given or is incorrect for the context given.	1–3
	2	Demonstrates reasonable understanding of the principles of limiting factor analysis and gives an explanation of how the technique has been applied in the context of the incorrectly embossed pencil grades. Incomplete explanation of the use of the overtime rate and lack of application to the context of the 5 batches of 8B.	4–6
	3	Demonstrates good understanding of the principles of limiting factor analysis plus a comprehensive application of the technique to appendix 1 in order to explain the production schedule. A good explanation of the use of the overtime rate in the context of the 5 batches of 8H pencils.	7–10

Expected values

The expected value of each decision, to investigate or not to investigate, is the sum of the weighted averages of all outcomes, where the weighting is by probability.

To determine whether or not to investigate the barcoding error we need to compare the expected value cost of both options and select the one that gives us the lowest cost. In this case the lowest cost is the option not to investigate as this is G$75,000 compared to G$76,000 (G$73,000 + G$3,000) to investigate.

Limitations of using this information to make the decision

The expected value alone gives no indication of the range of possible outcomes. The expected value is not the most likely result, it is the long run average outcome if the same event was to be repeated over and over. Although the error with barcoding has occurred previously it cannot be considered a recurring event and the costs incurred could be significantly different to this weighted average. This is particularly true as the expected values for both options are so close.

It should also be borne in mind that the probabilities used in the calculation of the expected value for each option are subjective in nature. A subjective probability can be inaccurate, and these are simply estimates compiled based on a previous event. While it is useful to frame the decision like this and is invaluable as a trigger for discussion about the problem we face, they are not accurate.

When using expected values there is an assumption that the decision maker is risk neutral and therefore is not interested in the range of possible outcomes. In this instance, if we were to choose not to investigate there is a 15% chance of barcoding errors costing G$300,000 and this may be totally unacceptable if we take a risk averse view.

This information gives us a decision based upon costs that we can quantify financially. However, there are other factors that we need to consider such as customer dissatisfaction and loss of reputation.

Marking guide:

Trait	Level	Descriptor	Marks
Expected values		No rewardable material	0
	1	Explains some of the limitations of EV but there is limited or no application of these to the situation. Might not explain the concept of EV.	1–3
	2	Explains most of the limitations of EV with some application to the situation. There will be a reasonable explanation of the concept of EV and this will use the table data.	4–6
	3	Explains the limitations of EV with technical accuracy and clearly explains how these apply in this situation. There will be a good explanation of the concept of EV and this will use the table data. The answer will include a clear decision that based on EV the investigation should not go ahead.	7–8

Examiner's comments

The first element of this task asked for an explanation of the principles underlying a production schedule, how it had been used to determine the number of batches of three different types of pencil to make and whether it would be worthwhile paying a G$14 overtime premium. This tested core activity E. To gain a level 3 score, candidates needed to have answered all three parts. Most candidates scored at a level 1 because they only produced a description of the table and not an explanation; an explanation adds value to a description, and this was lacking in many answers. Many candidates also failed to comment at all on the overtime premium.

The third element of this task asked for an explanation of expected value tables and the limitations of using this information to decide whether to investigate mislabelling with the rest of the inventory. This tested core activity E and was generally well answered. Most candidates were able to correctly interpret and explain the expected value tables. The limitations were also quite well explained and as a result many candidates achieved level 3. Candidates that answered this question but were only awarded a level 2 failed to apply any of the limitations of expected value to the case context.

Exercise 19

Decision regarding resin supply

Maximax

A decision maker that uses the maximax criterion is an optimist because they will choose the option which maximises the maximum pay-off available. Because this decision is based on cost, this criterion will be to select the option which gives the lowest total cost for resin, in other words, the minimum of the minimum costs.

Therefore, under this criterion, we would choose Quantity 1 as this gives the lowest possible cost of G$804,800.

Maximin

A decision maker that uses the maximin criterion is a pessimist because they will choose the option which maximises the minimum pay-off available. Again, because this decision is based on cost, this criterion will be to select the option which gives the lowest of the highest costs under each option, in other words, the minimum of the maximum costs.

Therefore, under this criterion, we would choose Quantity 2 because this gives the lowest cost of G$1,080,000.

Minimax regret

A decision maker that uses the minimax regret criterion is often referred to as a 'bad loser' because they are concerned about making the wrong decision. Regret (as shown in the regret table) represents the cost of getting the decision wrong. For example, if production levels end up being high, then the best option would be Quantity 2. If we had chosen Quantity 3, then this will cost G$4,800 more than if we had chosen Quantity 2.

With this decision criterion we want to minimise the maximum regret and would therefore choose Quantity 1. This is because the maximum regret here is an additional cost of G$56,000 which is the lowest of the maximum regrets for the other two options.

Marking guide:

Trait	Level	Descriptor	Marks
Decision criteria		No rewardable material	0
	1	Demonstrates some technical understanding of the decision criteria. Either there has been no attempt to state the decision or the decisions are inaccurate.	1–3
	2	Demonstrates reasonable technical understanding of each of the three decision criteria and mostly selects the correct decision under each criterion.	4–6
	3	Demonstrates good technical understanding of each of the three decision criteria and mostly selects the correct decision under each criterion.	7–9

Other factors to consider

Before deciding to contract with this supplier, we need to assess the quality of the resin that they will supply. There is little point in paying a lower price for the resin if its poorer quality results in either wasted resin or wasted production.

We also need to consider how the resin will be delivered. If it is delivered in one go, there will be implications for us in terms of needing to store the resin. If delivery is throughout the period, we need to be confident that this supplier can deliver the resin when we need it. We do not want to find ourselves in a position that there is significant lead time that could disrupt production schedules.

Marking guide:

Trait	Level	Descriptor	Marks
Other factors		No rewardable material	0
	1	Explains, either briefly or with a lack of clarity, one non-financial factor.	1
	2	Explains at least one non-financial factor, with reasonable clarity and depth.	2–3
	3	Explains clearly and fully two non-financial factors to be considered.	4

Examiner's comments

The second element of this task asked for explanation of three decision criteria that could be used to make a decision about which resin supplier to select. This tested core activity E and was less well answered than might have been expected for an area that is regularly assessed. This was partly due to the failure to recognise that the question was about minimising cost rather than maximising contribution, despite that fact that the task clearly stated this. There was also however a significant number of candidates who tried to answer the question based on risk attitude even although the details given did not include any probabilities. In order for candidates to score at level 3, they needed to clearly demonstrate their understanding of the application of the decision criteria to the information given in the scenario. A significant proportion obviously did not clearly understand the criteria and how they are applied. This was particularly evident for the minimax regret criterion where many stated that the quantity with the lowest regret would be chosen or that the regrets would be added and the lowest of the totals chosen.

The third element of this task asked for explanation of two non-financial factors to be considered before contracting with a new supplier.

Most candidates were able to clearly explain two non-financial factors to be considered and consequently this part of the task scored highly with many candidates achieving a level 3.

Exercise 20

Expected values analysis

The figures in the analysis

Tables 2 and 3 show the expected value of budgeted profit based on reductions in selling price of 5% and 10% respectively. With this analysis, the impact of these selling price reductions on volume is broken down into different possible outcomes with probabilities of occurrence assigned. Looking at Table 2, this shows that if selling prices reduce by 5% there is a 20% probability of no change in sales volumes, a 50% probability of a 7.5% increase in volume and a 30% probability of a 15% increase in volume. Table 3 shows that, where the sales price reduction is 10%, the probability of no change in volume is reduced to 10% (a reduction from Table 2 because presumably because a higher sales price reduction will have more impact on the market), however the probability of the maximum change in sales volume of 30% is also reduced to 10% (presumably because this is such a significant increase in volume). The expected value in the end column of each table is calculated as the sum of budgeted profit at each outcome multiplied by the probability of occurrence of that outcome.

Whether decreasing prices by 5% or 10% gives the best result

Whether decreasing prices by either 5% or 10% is the best course of action depends upon the directors' attitude to risk. A risk seeker would select the option which gave the best result irrespective of the probability of it happening, which would be to reduce selling prices by 10% because this gives the best budgeted profit of G$2,759,000. This is consistent with Ben Thakar's view and also with the what-if analysis. A risk neutral decision maker would ignore risk and select the option with the highest expected value, which is G$2,420,000, and reduce selling prices by 5%. A risk averse decision maker would select the option where the risk is lowest, which is usually determined from calculating standard deviation and coefficient of variation, statistical measures based on the spread of possible of outcomes. Here it is clear that reducing selling prices by 5% has the lowest spread of possible outcomes and therefore is likely to have the lowest risk.

Marking guide:

Trait	Level	Descriptor	Marks
Expected value and attitudes to decision-making		No rewardable material	0
	1	Explains some of the figures in Tables 2 and 3 in the context of the scenario. Explanation of the best result under each attitude is possibly missing or completely inaccurate.	1–3

	2	Explains most of the figures in Tables 2 and 3 in the context of the scenario. Explanation of the best result under each attitude is mostly accurate, but sometimes inaccurate or missing.	4–6
	3	Explains comprehensively the figures in Tables 2 and 3 in the context of the scenario. Accurately explains what would be considered the best result for each attitude.	7–8

Examiner's comments

The second element of this task asked for explanation of expected values based on two different courses of action and how risk attitude would affect the decision about which course of action was most appropriate. This tested core activity E and answers here were mixed. Some candidates tried to apply decision criteria for dealing with uncertainty to the figures despite the fact that the question was clearly about risk attitude. Most candidates could describe how the expected values were calculated and that a risk-neutral decision-maker would base their decision on expected value. Some also knew the approach that would be taken by a risk-taker although many stated.

Exercise 21

Multi-product break-even

Line A

Line A shows the combinations of profit and revenue based on the original budget that will be generated if we sell our pencils in the order of their c/s margin. For the original budget this will be PEXECO, then artist coloured, followed by graphite and finally regular coloured. The line starts on the y axis at negative G$6 million which represents the originally budgeted fixed costs for the month. The line ends at the total amount of revenue and profit as originally budgeted for the month: revenue of approximately G$12.5 million and profit of approximately G$2.2 million.

Based on the original budget the breakeven position based on the assumption of selling in the order of c/s ratio is approximately G$8.8 million. The margin of safety is reasonably high as revenue would need to fall from around G$12.5 million to the breakeven of G$8.8 million before a loss was made. Line A also indicates that in our original budget sales revenue from graphite pencils equates to probably more than half of total revenue (because it's share of the line is probably longer than the other shares combined).

Marking guide:

Trait	Level	Descriptor	Marks
Line A		No rewardable material	0
	1	Demonstrates some understanding of the multi-product break-even chart. The answer makes some attempt to explain Line A and /or identify the break-even point but lacks clarity. Margin of safety unlikely to be commented on.	1
	2	Demonstrates reasonable understanding of the multi-product break-even chart. The answer explains what Line A represents with reference to the scenario and identifies the break-even point, but sometimes lacks clarity. Margin of safety may not be commented on.	2–3
	3	Demonstrates good understanding of the multi-product break-even chart. The answer is comprehensive, clearly explains what Line A represents with reference to the scenario and identifies the break-even point. Margin of safety may not be commented on.	4

How the revised budget changes the analysis

Line B represents the combinations of revenue and profit based on the revised budget, selling our pencils in the following order: S-Pencil, PEXECO, artist coloured, graphite and regular coloured. The order hasn't changed from the original budget other than the addition of the S-Pencil, as the most profitable product, being sold first.

The c/s ratios have changed as a result of the revision to the budget (although the order of profitability hasn't). Compared to the original budget, the c/s margins of graphite and regular coloured have fallen, indicating that the selling prices for these pencil types have been reduced (given that variable costs have not been changed in the revised budget). The PEXECO and artist coloured c/s margins have increased, showing an increase in selling price. These changes in c/s ratio are reflected in different slopes on the line. For example, graphite for line A has a steeper gradient than line B indicating that the c/s margin has fallen.

This has clearly had a knock-on effect on volumes and the mix of pencil sales.

Revenue from graphite pencils appears to be a lesser proportion of sales than the original budget because this product's share of the line is smaller than Line A. This will be partly due to the price reduction but might also indicate lower volumes. Similarly, PEXECO's share of overall revenue has increased (because the length of its portion of the line is longer). This will be the result of the price rise but could also be due to increased volumes.

Line B also shows that fixed costs are approximately G$6.8 million in the revised budget and that total budgeted revenue is greater than originally budgeted. The breakeven position for the revised budget has increased to nearly G$10 million. This increase in breakeven position is because the level of fixed costs has increased: more contribution is needed to make a profit. The changes to the c/s margins will also affect the breakeven, although from the chart it is difficult to establish this effect. The margin of safety is now from approximately G$13.8 million to G$9.9 million (which is a slightly higher differential than the original budget indicating a slight increase in margin of safety).

Marking guide:

Trait	Level	Descriptor	Marks
Line B		No rewardable material	0
	1	Demonstrates some understanding of what Line B represents but little reference is made to compare this to Line A. Explanation is likely to be brief and lack clarity.	1–2
	2	Demonstrates reasonable understanding of what Line B represents and makes some attempt to compare to Line A to establish the impact of the differences in volume, selling price and fixed costs. Explanation may lack clarity.	3–5
	3	Demonstrates clear understanding of what Line B represents and makes a good attempt to compare to line A to establish the impact of the differences in volume, selling price and fixed costs.	6–7

Examiner's comments

The first element of this task asked for an explanation of Line A on a profit volume chart and the information that this gave based on the original budget. It also asked for explanation of how the revised budget, represented by Line B, changed the analysis. This was well answered. Many candidates demonstrated a good understanding of the profit-volume charts and what was shown in relation to the scenario and data provided. Weaker candidates were able to only identify the fixed costs but were unable to clearly demonstrate their understanding of what the breakeven points showed.

Exercise 22

IT app administration supplier decision

How to make the decision and the decision under different risk attitudes

When making a decision such as this there are three approaches that we could adopt: risk neutral, risk seeking and risk averse.

If we have a risk neutral attitude to this decision, we could consider all possible outcomes and choose the provider that would give us the best expected value. We would ignore risk and the coefficient of variation and would choose Provider C which has the lowest expected value of the cost of supply at G$1,624,000.

If we have a risk seeking attitude to this decision, we would choose the option which would give us the best outcome no matter how small the likelihood of it occurring.

We would choose the provider which gives us the lowest overall cost, which is also Provider C (when there are 900,000 users). This provider has the highest coefficient of variation therefore is the riskiest option, which is consistent with it having the largest spread of outcomes: a risk seeking decision maker would ignore this.

If we have a risk averse attitude to this decision, we would choose the provider which given the same level of cost has the lowest level of risk. We would use the coefficient of variation and choose the option with the lowest measure because this represents the amount of risk for each G$1 of additional cost that we would incur. We would therefore choose Provider A.

Marking guide:

Trait	Level	Descriptor	Marks
The decision		No rewardable material	0
	1	Explains how to make the decision using one of the risk attitude approaches and identifies the correct decision for this approach.	1–2
	2	Explains how to make the decision using two of the risk attitude approaches and identifies the correct decision for each of these approaches.	3–4
	3	Explains how to make the decision using all three of the risk attitude approaches and identifies the correct decision for each approach.	5–6

Limitations of the analysis

The decisions identified above are based on assumptions about the number of app users and probability of occurrence. These are all internal estimates based on information that we have available now. However, twelve months in the life of a new product is a relatively long time and therefore it's possible that these estimates are wrong.

There are also issues of using expected value and coefficient of variation approaches to make the decision. Expected value gives no indication of the range of possible outcomes, it is not the most likely result, but the long run average outcome if the same event was to be repeated over and over: therefore, it is of limited use when making a one-off decision. Coefficient of variation assumes a linear relationship between risk and return and that decision makers will be willing to risk more when the return is higher: this is not necessarily practical.

Finally, this analysis ignores other non-financial factors, such as the quality of the service that each provider will supply. We should consider issues such as reliability and the speed of dealing with queries. We might also want to consider credit terms offered as well.

Marking guide:

Trait	Level	Descriptor	Marks
Limitations		No rewardable material	0
(Note this relates to both a critique of the method used and other factors to be considered)	1	Explains at least one of the limitations (the subjectivity of the data, limitations with using EV and/or COV and ignores non-financial factors). The explanation may lack clarity.	1–2
	2	Explains some of the limitations (the subjectivity of the data, limitations with using EV and/or COV and ignores non-financial factors). The explanation may lack some clarity.	3–4
	3	Explains a range of limitations that are well explained.	5–6

Examiner's comments

The first element of this task asked for explanation of how to decide which provider of IT administrative services to use under different attitudes to risk, what the decision would be under each risk attitude and the limitations of this analysis for selecting the provider. This tested core activity E. Given that this is a common type of task in the Operational case exam, it was surprising how few candidates were able to correctly interpret the data that was presented to them. As already noted for variant 2, some candidates tried to apply decision criteria for dealing with uncertainty to the figures despite the fact that the question was clearly about risk attitude, this is disappointing. A distinct lack of understanding of the coefficient of variation (COV) was displayed by most candidates and indeed many candidates ignored it altogether.

Regarding the limitations of the analysis, many candidates did little more than comment on the limitations of expected values, when they could have commented on the subjectivity of the data and non-financial factors as well. This narrow focus limited many to a low level 2 here.

Exercise 23

Improving the receivables days in Feland

As we intend to keep the credit control department, we need to ensure that staff members are trained to execute the duties of the credit control function efficiently and effectively.

The credit control department should have processes in place to enable customers to pay on time. For example, the credit control department must confirm that the customer is fully aware of the credit terms and that processes are in place to guarantee that invoices are accurate and sent to customers on-time. Where applicable, invoice disputes should be resolved, and credit notes raised in a timely manner. Likewise, statements should be accurate and sent to customers as soon as feasible. This will ensure that customers have no excuse to withhold or delay payment.

If customers have exceeded the credit terms, there should be set processes in place to chase the payment. For example, when an amount due is five days late, a reminder letter should be issued. At ten days a second, more strongly worded, letter should follow, at 15 days a telephone call to the customer asking for reasons for the delay, and so on. Usually this process will also include the more severe sanctions of stopping all supply to the customer and ultimately taking court action to recover the monies owed. However, these more extreme actions should be avoided if possible as they rarely result in a successful long-term relationship for the parties involved. It should also be considered that the customers in Feland may be used to exceeding the credit limit by this length of time. Culturally 65 days credit might be the norm and therefore chasing the outstanding debt too enthusiastically may offend customers.

Offering a prompt payment discount to credit customers might encourage at least some of them to pay earlier, which would reduce the receivable days and also the risk of irrecoverable debt. However, we would need to consider the benefits to be gained against the cost of giving away the discount.

More extreme option may be to employ an external debt collection agency to collect specific overdue debt.

As the quality of the service offered by debt collection agencies differ, care must be taken when employing one as this can damage the relationship with the customer irrevocably. This is unlikely to be an option that we take as there is no evidence to suggest that the Feland customers are refusing to pay the debt, only that they are paying late.

Finally, we could take legal action when a customer refuses to pay an overdue amount. Again, this is not likely to be a realistic option.

Marking guide:

Trait	Level	Descriptor	Marks
Receivable days		No rewardable material	0
	1	Explains at least one way to improve receivable days but explanation may lack clarity. Little or no application to the context of the scenario.	1–3
	2	Explains at least one way to improve receivable days although explanation may lack some clarity. Some attempt to link these processes to the facts in the scenario.	4–6
	3	Explains more than one way to improve receivable days using a clear rationale. Reference is made to the scenario.	7–8

Examiner's comments

The third element of this task asked for an explanation of how to improve the receivable days for the Feland customers. This tested core activity F. Answers here were disappointing as many candidates did not answer the task and often contradicted the facts presented in the case. A high proportion of answers suggested that outsourcing the credit control function to a factor would improve receivable days. While this may be true, it could not be awarded any marks as the scenario made clear that the company would be keeping the in-house credit control staff. Likewise, many answers suggested invoice discounting and explained how this would improve the liquidity problem, despite the fact that the scenario did not state that there was a liquidity problem.

Exercise 24

BGF Graphite working Capital Management

<u>Working capital position of BGF Graphite</u>

BGF Graphite's inventory days were, until 2020, consistent with that of the industry as a whole. However, in 2020, inventory days have almost halved to 18 days. Given that graphite is a raw material that does not deteriorate quickly, there is no need to hold such low inventory levels for obsolescence reasons. Therefore, potentially the reduction in inventory days is due in part to BGF Graphite's rapid growth in revenue and its lack of cash. Perhaps BGF Graphite is not able to purchase enough raw material inventory.

Receivable days have grown across the three-year period and in 2020 are higher than the industry average. BGF Graphite has standard credit terms of 30 days and therefore it would appear that it is not as efficient at credit control as it should be.

There has been significant growth in revenue over the same period and therefore it is possible that extended credit terms have been offered to attract new business which will have lengthened receivable days. We might be able to benefit from this.

Payable days have also grown across the three-year period, which could be a symptom of overtrading. Perhaps BGF Graphite has been unable to pay its suppliers as quickly as it would like given its poor cash position.

However, even when it had cash, BGF Graphite was slower to pay its suppliers than the industry average and this could indicate that this business has taken advantage of its suppliers.

Marking guide:

Trait	Level	Descriptor	Marks
Interpretation		No rewardable material	0
	1	Explains briefly, or with a lack of clarity, the supplier's working capital position with reference to each element of working capital days. There is little or no reference to the nature of the supplier or attempt to interpret the figures.	1–2
	2	Explains the supplier's working capital position with reference to each element of working capital days. There is some attempt to link the explanation to the nature of the supplier and to interpret the figures.	3–4
	3	Explains fully the supplier's working capital position with reference to each element of working capital days and to the nature of the supplier.	5–6

Risks of BGF Graphite's working capital position

There are indications that this business is overtrading: significant and quick growth in revenue, depletion of cash, paying suppliers later and a worsening of credit control. The business appears not to have had enough resources to manage the rapid growth and as a consequence cash flow has suffered.

The risk associated with this is that unless BGF Graphite secures finance to support cash flow, it might not be able to continue to trade as it will be unable to pay its liabilities. Clearly this could have serious consequences for our business if we become reliant on this supplier.

There is a risk that BGF Graphite will not be able to supply us with all of the graphite that we need at any one time. Its inventory levels are relatively low which means that the risk of BGF Graphite not being able to meet orders or delaying delivery is quite high.

Marking guide:

Trait	Level	Descriptor	Marks
Risks		No rewardable material	0
	1	Explains at least one risk associated with the supplier's working capital position but overtrading has not been identified. Little or no reference is made to Lottie Graphite and the supplier decision.	1–2
	2	Explains more than one risk associated with the supplier's working capital position but this might not make reference to overtrading. Some reference is made to the supplier decision.	3–4
	3	Explains fully at least two different risks associated with the supplier's working capital position, including the fact that it is potentially overtrading. The explanation identifies how this risk could affect our decision to use them as a supplier.	5

Examiner's comments

The third element of this task asked for an explanation of a potential supplier's working capital position and the risks associated with this that might affect the decision to use them as a supplier. This tested core activity F and was also well answered. Candidates that scored poorly failed to provide an evaluation of the supplier's financial position and simply described the trends. It is not enough to just restate the figures in the question. Stronger candidates explained why the supplier may have different figures (for example, operating JIT or having longer credit periods to generate revenue). Risks were not always clearly identified as risks for Lottie Graphics and were more general. Most candidates spotted the fact that the supplier was overtrading but did not go on to explain how this would affect Lottie Graphics if they used them.

Exercise 25

Receivables management

<u>Profile of the aged receivables report</u>

There are two main changes to the profile of aged receivables. Firstly, whilst the number of large retailer customers has remained the same, the number of small retailer customers has increased considerably during the period. This is because the sales teams successfully secured new customers. Small retailers are often family owned, independent businesses and this means typically that they are more at risk of ceasing to trade than a large retailer business.

Secondly, the proportion of receivables that are overdue has increased considerably over the three-month period. New small retailer customers have been given extended credit terms, although this will not have affected the profile because aged receivables are reported by amounts overdue. However, it would appear that customers are taking longer to pay us which could indicate that our receivables management is not as efficient as it should be (especially as the three large retailer customers also have a greater proportion of the receivables overdue). It could also be that some of the new customers taken on are not as reliable as we would like them to be (perhaps stringent creditworthiness checks were not carried out in order to boost sales).

The potential implications of these changes in profile are:

- Our cash flow could be adversely affected because money from our customers is received later that it should. This increases our investment in working capital and reduces our cash balance.
- The risk for receivables being irrecoverable is increased. Ultimately this could have the effect of reducing profit if receivable balances end up being written off.

Marking guide:

Trait	Level	Descriptor	Marks
Profile		No rewardable material	0
	1	Explains some aspects of how the aged receivables profile has changed but there is little attempt to link this to the changes in customer base. The implications for the business may not be identified.	1–2
	2	Explains how the aged receivables profile has changed and attempts to link this to the changes in customer base. The implications of this for the business may not be identified.	3–4
	3	Explains comprehensively how the aged receivables profile has changed and links this to the changes in customer base. The implications for the business of this change in profile are identified.	5–6

Two suggestions of how to manage the implication

We could factor our S-Pencil receivable balances. Factoring involves a factor advancing us say 75% of the value of invoices as they are raised which means that we would receive a significant proportion of the monies due to us earlier than normal: this would help in managing cash-flow. A factor would also take over responsibility for managing the receivables ledger and because they are experts in credit control this means that it is likely they would recover more of the monies owed to us.

We could even take out a 'without recourse' arrangement which would mean that the factor has responsibility for irrecoverable debts: this would eliminate our risk to irrecoverable debts. However, factoring is expensive, and we would need to consider the cost of this against the benefits to cash flow and reduced risk.

Offering a prompt payment discount might encourage at least some of our customers to pay earlier than they would normally which means that cash comes into the business more quickly, however not all customers will take advantage of it. It might also mean that some customers end up paying before they run into difficulties and the debt becomes irrecoverable, although this is likely to apply in only a small number of cases. As with factoring we would need to consider the benefits to be gained against the cost of giving away the discount (which at a potential 1% or 2% of invoice value could amount to a significant amount).

Marking guide:

Trait	Level	Descriptor	Marks
Measures		No rewardable material	0
	1	Explains at least one suggestion for how to manage the implications of reduced cash flow and irrecoverable debts. The explanation may lack clarity and is unlikely to consider that cost/benefit analysis will be required.	1–2
	2	Explains at least one sensible suggestion for how to manage the implications of reduced cash flow and irrecoverable debts. The explanation may lack some clarity and might not consider that cost/benefit analysis will be required.	3–4
	3	Explains two sensible suggestions for how to manage the implications of reduced cash flow and irrecoverable debts. The explanation considers that cost/benefit analysis will be required.	5–6

Examiner's comments

The second element of this task asked for explanation of how the profile of aged receivables had changed over the last three months, reasons for these changes, the potential implication of these changes and two measures that could be taken to manage these implications. This tested core activity F. Many candidates answered this fairly well, demonstrating good understanding of what the aged receivables report showed. Weaker candidates assumed that the customers were paying late due to extended credit terms which would not be a factor. Many candidates had a reasonable understanding of the implications that this would have for the company and ways in which these impacts could be reduced.